BLOOM'S

HOW TO WRITE ABOUT

Amy Tan

KIM E. BECNEL

Introduction by Harold Bloom

BLOOM'S
LITERARY CRITICISM
An imprint of Infobase Publishing

Bloom's How to Write about Amy Tan

Copyright © 2010 by Infobase Publishing
Introduction © 2010 by Harold Bloom

Bloom's Literary Criticism
An imprint of Infobase Publishing
132 West 31st Street
New York NY 10001

Library of Congress Cataloging-in-Publication Data
Becnel, Kim.
    Bloom's how to write about Amy Tan / by Kim E. Becnel; introduction by Harold
Bloom.
        p. cm.—(Bloom's how to write about literature)
    Includes bibliographical references and index.
    ISBN 978-1-60413-308-0 (hardcover : alk. paper)
1. Tan, Amy—Criticism and interpretation. 2. Criticism—Authorship. 3. Report
writing. I. Bloom, Harold. II. Title. III. Title: How to write about Amy Tan.
    PS3570.A48Z56 2009
    813'.54—dc22   2009000045

Text design by Annie O'Donnell
Cover design by Alicia Post
Composition by Mary Susan Ryan-Flynn
Cover printed by Art Print Company, Taylor, PA
Book printed and bound by Maple Press, York, PA
Date printed: November 2009
Printed in the United States of America

10 9 8 7 6 5 4 3 2 1

This book is printed on acid-free paper.

CONTENTS

SERIES INTRODUCTION

Bloom's How to Write about Literature series is designed to inspire students to write fine essays on great writers and their works. Each volume in the series begins with an introduction by Harold Bloom, meditating on the challenges and rewards of writing about the volume's subject author. The first chapter then provides detailed instructions on how to write a good essay, including how to find a thesis; how to develop an outline; how to write a good introduction, body text, and conclusion; how to cite sources; and more. The second chapter provides a brief overview of the issues involved in writing about the subject author and then a number of suggestions for paper topics, with accompanying strategies for addressing each topic. Succeeding chapters cover the author's major works.

The paper topics suggested within this book are open-ended, and the brief strategies provided are designed to give students a push forward in the writing process rather than a road map to success. The aim of the book is to pose questions, not answer them. Many different kinds of papers could result from each topic. As always, the success of each paper will depend completely on the writer's skill and imagination.

HOW TO WRITE ABOUT AMY TAN: INTRODUCTION

by Harold Bloom

THE CHINESE-AMERICAN immigrant context has to be a determining factor in writing about Amy Tan, since her relatively early position in such fiction is perhaps more important than any intrinsic aesthetic value.

I recommend reading a valid authority such as the psychiatrist Melanie Klein, who makes many fascinating surmises as to the mother-daughter relationship. The rival authority to Klein is Anna Freud, who emphasizes the psychic development of girls in relation to both parents.

Tan's subject, even when she tries to evade it, is the loving strife between mother and daughter. I find Tan's individual talent to be her sense of the overdetermination of all failed later erotic relationships by the unresolved conflicts between parents and children, and particularly mother-daughter conflicts.

A legitimate and fruitful area for investigation is the extent to which Chinese-American family romances deviate from the Western patterns analyzed by Melanie Klein and Anna Freud.

HOW TO WRITE
A GOOD ESSAY

By Laurie A. Sterling and Kim E. Becnel

WHILE THERE are many ways to write about literature, most assignments for high school and college English classes call for analytical papers. In these assignments, you are presenting your interpretation of a text to your reader. Your objective is to interpret the text's meaning in order to enhance your reader's understanding and enjoyment of the work. Without exception, strong papers about the meaning of a literary work are built upon a careful, close reading of the text or texts. Careful, analytical reading should always be the first step in your writing process. This volume provides models of such close, analytical reading, and these should help you develop your own skills as a reader and as a writer.

As the examples throughout this book demonstrate, attentive reading entails thinking about and evaluating the formal (textual) aspects of the author's works: theme, character, form, and language. In addition, when writing about a work, many readers choose to move beyond the text itself to consider the work's cultural context. In these instances, writers might explore the historical circumstances of the time period in which the work was written. Alternatively, they might examine the philosophies and ideas that a work addresses. Even in cases where writers explore a work's cultural context, though, papers must still address the more formal aspects of the work itself. A good interpretative essay that evaluates Charles Dickens's use of the philosophy of utilitarianism in his novel *Hard Times*, for example, cannot adequately address the author's treatment of the philosophy without firmly grounding this discussion in the book itself. In other words, any analytical paper about a text, even one that seeks to evaluate the work's cultural context, must also have a firm handle on the work's themes, characters, and language. You must look for and evaluate these aspects of a work, then, as you read a text and as you prepare to write about it.

WRITING ABOUT THEMES

Literary themes are more than just topics or subjects treated in a work; they are attitudes or points about these topics that often structure other elements in a work. Writing about theme therefore requires that you not just identify a topic that a literary work addresses but also discuss what that work says about that topic. For example, if you were writing about the culture of the American South in William Faulkner's famous story "A Rose for Emily," you would need to discuss what Faulkner says, argues, or implies about that culture and its passing.

When you prepare to write about thematic concerns in a work of literature, you will probably discover that, like most works of literature, your text touches upon other themes in addition to its central theme. These secondary themes also provide rich ground for paper topics. A thematic paper on "A Rose for Emily" might consider gender or race in the story. While neither of these could be said to be the central theme of the story, they are clearly related to the passing of the "old South" and could provide plenty of good material for papers.

As you prepare to write about themes in literature, you might find a number of strategies helpful. After you identify a theme or themes in the story, you should begin by evaluating how other elements of the story—such as character, point of view, imagery, and symbolism—help develop the theme. You might ask yourself what your own responses are to the author's treatment of the subject matter. Do not neglect the obvious, either: What expectations does the title set up? How does the title help develop thematic concerns? Clearly, the title "A Rose for Emily" says something about the narrator's attitude toward the title character, Emily Grierson, and all she represents.

WRITING ABOUT CHARACTER

Generally, characters are essential components of fiction and drama. (This is not always the case, though; Ray Bradbury's "August 2026: There Will Come Soft Rains" is technically a story without characters, at least any human characters.) Often, you can discuss character in poetry, as in T. S. Eliot's "The Love Song of J. Alfred Prufrock" or Robert Browning's "My Last Duchess." Many writers find that analyzing character is one of the most interesting and engaging ways to work with a piece of literature and to shape a paper. After all, characters generally are human, and we all know something about being human and living in the world. While it is always important to remember that these figures are not real people but creations of the writer's imagination, it can be fruitful to begin evaluating them as you might evaluate a real person. Often you can start with your own response to a character. Did you like or dislike the character? Did you sympathize with the character? Why or why not?

Keep in mind, though, that emotional responses like these are just starting places. To truly explore and evaluate literary characters, you need to return to the formal aspects of the text and evaluate how the author has drawn these characters. The 20th-century writer E. M. Forster coined the terms *flat* characters and *round* characters. Flat characters are static, one-dimensional characters that frequently represent a particular concept or idea. In contrast, round characters are fully drawn and much more realistic characters that frequently change and develop over the course of a work. Are the characters you are studying flat or round? What elements of the characters lead you to this conclusion? Why might the author have drawn characters like this? How does their development affect the meaning of the work? Similarly, you should explore the techniques the author uses to develop characters. Do we hear a character's own words, or do we hear only other characters' assessments of him or her? Or, does the author use an omniscient or limited omniscient narrator to allow us access to the workings of the characters' minds? If so, how does that help develop the characterization? Often you can even evaluate the narrator as a character. How trustworthy are the opinions and assessments of the narrator? You should also think about characters' names. Do they mean anything? If you encounter a hero named Sophia or Sophie, you should probably think about her wisdom (or lack thereof), since *sophia* means "wisdom" in Greek. Similarly, since the name Sylvia is derived from the word *sylvan,* meaning "of the wood," you might want to evaluate that character's relationship with nature. Once again, you might look to the title of the work. Does Herman Melville's "Bartleby, the Scrivener" signal anything about Bartleby himself? Is Bartleby adequately defined by his job as scrivener? Is this part of Melville's point? Pursuing questions such as these can help you develop thorough papers about characters from psychological, sociological, or more formalistic perspectives.

WRITING ABOUT FORM AND GENRE

Genre, a word derived from French, means "type" or "class." Literary genres are distinctive classes or categories of literary composition. On the most general level, literary works can be divided into the genres of drama, poetry, fiction, and essays, yet within those genres there are classifications that are also referred to as genres. Tragedy and comedy, for example, are genres of drama. Epic, lyric, and pastoral are genres of poetry. *Form,* on the other hand, generally refers to the shape or structure of a work. There are many clearly defined forms of poetry that follow specific patterns of meter, rhyme, and stanza. Sonnets, for example, are poems that follow a fixed form of 14 lines. Sonnets generally follow one of two basic sonnet forms, each with its own distinct rhyme scheme. Haiku is another example of poetic form, traditionally consisting of three unrhymed lines of five, seven, and five syllables.

While you might think that writing about form or genre might leave little room for argument, many of these forms and genres are very fluid. Remember that literature is evolving and ever changing, and so are its forms. As you study poetry, you may find that poets, especially more modern poets, play with traditional poetic forms, bringing about new effects. Similarly, dramatic tragedy was once quite narrowly defined, but over the centuries playwrights have broadened and challenged traditional definitions, changing the shape of tragedy. When Arthur Miller wrote *Death of a Salesman,* many critics challenged the idea that tragic drama could encompass a common man like Willy Loman.

Evaluating how a work of literature fits into or challenges the boundaries of its form or genre can provide you with fruitful avenues of investigation. You might find it helpful to ask why the work does or does not fit into traditional categories. Why might Miller have thought it fitting to write a tragedy of the common man? Similarly, you might compare the content or theme of a work with its form. How well do they work together? Many of Emily Dickinson's poems, for instance, follow the meter of traditional hymns. While some of her poems seem to express traditional religious doctrines, many seem to challenge or strain against traditional conceptions of God and theology. What is the effect, then, of her use of traditional hymn meter?

WRITING ABOUT LANGUAGE, SYMBOLS, AND IMAGERY

No matter what the genre, writers use words as their most basic tool. Language is the most fundamental building block of literature. It is essential that you pay careful attention to the author's language and word choice as you read, reread, and analyze a text. Imagery is language that appeals to the senses. Most commonly, imagery appeals to our sense of vision, creating a mental picture, but authors also use language that appeals to our other senses. Images can be literal or figurative. Literal images use sensory language to describe an actual thing. In the broadest terms, figurative language uses one thing to speak about something else. For example, if I call my boss a snake, I am not saying that he is literally a reptile. Instead, I am using figurative language to communicate my opinions about him. Since we think of snakes as sneaky, slimy, and sinister, I am using the concrete image of a snake to communicate these abstract opinions and impressions.

The two most common figures of speech are similes and metaphors. Both are comparisons between two apparently dissimilar things. Similes are explicit comparisons using the words *like* or *as*; metaphors are implicit comparisons. To return to the previous example, if I say, "My boss, Bob, was waiting for me when I showed up to work five minutes late today—the snake!" I have constructed a metaphor. Writing about his experiences fighting in World War I, Wilfred Owen begins his poem "Dulce et decorum est," with a string of similes: "Bent double, like old beggars under sacks, / Knock-kneed, coughing like hags, we cursed through sludge." Owen's goal was to undercut clichéd notions that war and dying in battle were glorious. Certainly, comparing soldiers to coughing hags and to beggars underscores his point.

"Fog," a short poem by Carl Sandburg, provides a clear example of a metaphor. Sandburg's poem reads:

> The fog comes
> on little cat feet.
>
> It sits looking
> over harbor and city
> on silent haunches
> and then moves on.

Notice how effectively Sandburg conveys surprising impressions of the fog by comparing two seemingly disparate things—the fog and a cat.

Symbols, by contrast, are things that stand for, or represent, other things. Often they represent something intangible, such as concepts or ideas. In everyday life we use and understand symbols easily. Babies at christenings and brides at weddings wear white to represent purity. Think, too, of a dollar bill. The paper itself has no value in and of itself. Instead, that paper bill is a symbol of something else, the precious metal in a nation's coffers. Symbols in literature work similarly. Authors use symbols to evoke more than a simple, straightforward, literal meaning. Characters, objects, and places can all function as symbols. Famous literary examples of symbols include Moby-Dick, the white whale of Herman Melville's novel, and the scarlet *A* of Nathaniel Hawthorne's *The Scarlet Letter*. As both of these symbols suggest, a literary symbol cannot be adequately defined or explained by any one meaning. Hester Prynne's Puritan community clearly intends her scarlet *A* as a symbol of her adultery, but as the novel progresses, even her own community reads the letter as representing not just *adultery*, but *able, angel*, and a host of other meanings.

Writing about imagery and symbols requires close attention to the author's language. To prepare a paper on symbolism or imagery in a work, identify and trace the images and symbols and then try to draw some conclusions about how they function. Ask yourself how any symbols or images help contribute to the themes or meanings of the work. What connotations do they carry? How do they affect your reception of the work? Do they shed light on characters or settings? A strong paper on imagery or symbolism will thoroughly consider the use of figures in the text and will try to reach some conclusions about how or why the author uses them.

WRITING ABOUT HISTORY AND CONTEXT

As noted above, it is possible to write an analytical paper that also considers the work's context. After all, the text was not created in a vacuum. The author lived and wrote in a specific time period and in a specific cultural context and, like all of us, was shaped by that environment. Learning more about the historical and cultural circumstances that surround the author and the work can help illuminate a text and provide you with productive material for a paper. Remember, though, that when you write analytical papers, you should use the context to illuminate the text. Do not lose sight of your goal—to interpret the meaning of the literary work. Use historical or philosophical research as a tool to develop your textual evaluation.

Thoughtful readers often consider how history and culture affected the author's choice and treatment of his or her subject matter. Investigations into the history and context of a work could examine the work's relation to specific historical events, such as the Salem witch trials in 17th-century Massachusetts or the restoration of Charles II to the English throne in 1660. Bear in mind that historical context is not limited to politics and world events. While knowing about the Vietnam War is certainly helpful in interpreting much of Tim O'Brien's fiction, and some knowledge of the French Revolution clearly illuminates the dynamics of Charles Dickens's *A Tale of Two Cities,* historical context also entails the fabric of daily life. Examining a text in light of gender roles, race relations, class boundaries, or working conditions can give rise to thoughtful and compelling papers. Exploring the conditions of the working class in 19th-century England, for example, can provide a particularly effective avenue for writing about Dickens's *Hard Times.*

You can begin thinking about these issues by asking broad questions at first. What do you know about the time period and about the author? What does the editorial apparatus in your text tell you? These might be starting places. Similarly, when specific historical events or dynamics are particularly important to understanding a work but might be somewhat obscure to modern readers, textbooks usually provide notes to explain historical background. These are a good place to start. With this information, ask yourself how these historical facts and circumstances might have affected the author, the presentation of theme, and the presentation of character. How does knowing more about the work's specific historical context illuminate the work? To take a well-known example, understanding the complex attitudes toward slavery during the time Mark Twain wrote *Adventures of Huckleberry Finn* should help you begin to examine issues of race in the text. Additionally, you might compare these attitudes to those of the time in which the novel was set. How might this comparison affect your interpretation of a work written after the abolition of slavery but set before the Civil War?

WRITING ABOUT PHILOSOPHY AND IDEAS

Philosophical concerns are closely related to both historical context and thematic issues. Like historical investigation, philosophical research can provide a useful tool as you analyze a text. For example, an investigation into the working class in Dickens's England might lead you to a topic on the philosophical doctrine of utilitarianism in *Hard Times*. Many other works explore philosophies and ideas quite explicitly. Mary Shelley's famous novel *Frankenstein,* for example, explores John Locke's tabula rasa theory of human knowledge as she portrays the intellectual and emotional development of Victor Frankenstein's creature. As this example indicates, philosophical issues are somewhat more abstract than investigations of theme or historical context. Some other examples of philosophical issues include human free will, the formation of human identity, the nature of sin, or questions of ethics.

Writing about philosophy and ideas might require some outside research, but usually the notes or other material in your text will provide you with basic information, and often footnotes and bibliographies suggest places you can go to read further about the subject. If you have identified a philosophical theme that runs through a text, you might ask yourself how the author develops this theme. Look at character development and the interactions of characters, for example. Similarly, you might examine whether the narrative voice in a work of fiction addresses the philosophical concerns of the text.

WRITING COMPARISON AND CONTRAST ESSAYS

Finally, you might find that comparing and contrasting the works or techniques of an author provides a useful tool for literary analysis. A comparison and contrast essay might compare two characters or themes in a single work, or it might compare the author's treatment of a theme in two works. It might also contrast methods of character development or analyze an author's differing treatment of a philosophical concern in two works. Writing comparison and contrast essays, though, requires some special consideration. While they generally provide you with plenty of material to use, they also come with a built-in trap: the laundry list. These papers often become mere lists of connections between the works. As this chapter will discuss, a strong thesis must make an assertion that you want to prove or validate. A strong comparison/contrast thesis, then, needs to comment on the significance of the similarities and differences you observe. It is not enough merely to assert that the works contain similarities and differences. You might, for example, assert why the similarities and differences are important and explain how they illuminate the works' treatment of theme. Remember, too, that a thesis should not be a statement of the obvious. A comparison/contrast paper that focuses only on very obvious similarities or differences does little to illuminate the connections between the works. Often, an effective method of shaping a strong thesis and argument is to begin your paper by noting the similarities between the works but then to develop a thesis that asserts how these apparently similar elements are different. If, for example, you observe that Emily Dickinson wrote a number of poems about spiders, you might analyze how she uses spider imagery differently in two poems. Similarly, many scholars have noted that Hawthorne created many "mad scientist" characters, men who are so devoted to their science or their art that they lose perspective on all else. A good thesis comparing two of these characters—Aylmer of "The Birth-mark" and Dr. Rappaccini of "Rappaccini's Daughter," for example—might initially identify both characters as examples of Hawthorne's mad scientist type but then argue that their motivations for scientific experimentation differ. If you strive to analyze the similarities or differences, discuss significances, and move beyond the obvious, your paper should move beyond the laundry list trap.

PREPARING TO WRITE

Armed with a clear sense of your task—illuminating the text—and with an understanding of theme, character, language, history, and philosophy, you are ready to approach the writing process. Remember that good writing is grounded in good reading and that close reading takes time, attention, and more than one reading of your text. Read for comprehension first. As you go back and review the work, mark the text to chart the details of the work as well as your reactions. Highlight important passages, repeated words, and image patterns. "Converse" with the text through marginal notes. Mark turns in the plot, ask questions, and make observations about characters, themes, and language. If you are reading from a book that does not belong to you, keep a record of your reactions in a journal or notebook. If you have read a work of literature carefully, paying attention to both the text and the context of the work, you have a leg up on the writing process. Admittedly, at this point, your ideas are probably very broad and undefined, but you have taken an important first step toward writing a strong paper.

Your next step is to focus, to take a broad, perhaps fuzzy, topic and define it more clearly. Even a topic provided by your instructor will need to be focused appropriately. Remember that good writers make the topic their own. There are a number of strategies—often called "invention"—that you can use to develop your own focus. In one such strategy, called *freewriting*, you spend 10 minutes or so just writing about your topic without referring back to the text or your notes. Write whatever comes to mind; the important thing is that you just keep writing. Often this process allows you to develop fresh ideas or approaches to your subject matter. You could also try *brainstorming*: Write down your topic and then list all the related points or ideas you can think of. Include questions, comments, words, important passages or events, and anything else that comes to mind. Let one idea lead to another. In the related technique of *clustering*, or *mapping*, write your topic on a sheet of paper and write related ideas around it. Then list related subpoints under each of these main ideas. Many people then draw arrows to show connections between points. This technique helps you narrow your topic and can also help you organize your ideas. Similarly, asking journalistic questions—Who? What? Where? When? Why? and How?—can lead to ideas for topic development.

Thesis Statements

Once you have developed a focused topic, you can begin to think about your thesis statement—the main point or purpose of your paper. It is imperative that you craft a strong thesis, otherwise, your paper will likely be little more than random, disorganized observations about the text. Think of your thesis statement as a kind of road map for your paper. It tells your reader where you are going and how you are going to get there.

To craft a good thesis, you must keep a number of things in mind. First, as the title of this subsection indicates, your paper's thesis should be a statement, an assertion about the text that you want to prove or validate. Beginning writers often formulate a question that they attempt to use as a thesis. For example, a writer exploring the theme of romantic relationships in *The Joy Luck Club* might ask, What does the novel say about members of the second generation's ability to establish successful romantic relationships without replicating their mothers' passive behavior? While posing questions like this is a good strategy to use in the invention process to help narrow your topic and find your thesis, it cannot serve as the thesis statement because it does not tell your reader what you want to assert about young women's abilities to establish and maintain relationships in which they and their partners function as equals. You might shape this question into a thesis by instead proposing an answer to that question: While Jing-mei avoids having to negotiate a romantic relationship and its contest of wills by living a single life, her counterparts' romantic entanglements illustrate that second-generation Chinese-American women, having been raised in homes in which men are in control, are in danger of assuming the role of passive partner in their own relationship, as Rose does, or of worrying so much about maintaining equality in the relationship that they create other equally serious problems, as Lena does. Tan's vision is ultimately hopeful, however, as both Rose and Lena, with help from an unlikely source -- their mothers -- begin to understand where they have gone wrong. Further, the portrayal of the healthy, mutually respectful relationship between Waverly and Rich suggests that all of these women have the potential to achieve both personal fulfillment and romantic satisfaction.

Notice that this thesis provides an initial plan or structure for the rest of the paper, and notice, too, that the thesis statement does not necessarily have to fit into one sentence. After discussing the traditional role of women in Chinese marriages, you could turn to a discussion of Rose's relationship, then Lena's, and then Waverly's. Finally, you could explain why Tan's vision of the ability of Chinese-American women to maintain relationships built on equality is hopeful even though both Rose and Lena's relationships have failed.

Second, remember that a good thesis makes an assertion that you need to support. In other words, a good thesis does not state the obvious. If you tried to formulate a thesis about Chinese-American women's ability to function as equal partners in their romantic relationships by simply stating, The younger Joy Luck generation finds it difficult to establish romantic relationship in which power is equally shared between the two parties, you have done nothing but rephrase the obvious. Since much of the novel is devoted to Rose's and Lena's failed relationships, there would be no point in spending three to five pages supporting that assertion. You might try to develop a thesis from that point by asking yourself some further questions: What kinds of relationships do the women in fact seek out? What do they learn from the relationships that have failed or are failing? Do any of them manage to sustain a healthy relationship? If so, what makes it different from the others? Such a line of questioning might lead you to a more viable thesis, like the one in the preceding paragraph. As the comparison with the road map also suggests, your thesis should appear near the beginning of the paper. In relatively short papers (three to six pages) the thesis almost always appears in the first paragraph. Some writers fall into the trap of saving their thesis for the end, trying to provide a surprise or a big moment of revelation, as if to say, "TA-DA! I've just proved that in *The Joy Luck Club* Lindo, Jing-mei, and Rose are able to discover, through soul-searching and reflection that is prompted by feelings of complete despair, a sense of an authentic, autonomous self." Placing a thesis at the end of an essay can seriously mar the essay's effectiveness. If you fail to define your essay's point and purpose clearly at the beginning, your reader will find it difficult to assess the clarity of your argument and understand the points you are making. When your argument comes as a surprise at the end, you force your reader to reread your essay in order to assess its logic and effectiveness.

Finally, you should avoid using the first person ("I") as you present your thesis. Though it is not strictly wrong to write in the first person, it is difficult to do so gracefully. While writing in the first person, beginning writers often fall into the trap of writing self-reflexive prose (writing *about* their paper *in* their paper). Often this leads to the most dreaded of opening lines: "In this paper I am going to discuss . . ." Not only does this self-reflexive voice make for very awkward prose, it frequently allows writers to boldly announce a topic while completely avoiding a thesis statement. An example might be a paper that begins as follows: Tan's *The Joy Luck Club* tells the story of a group of women who undergo traumatic and stressful situations. In this paper, I am going to discuss how they cope in their bleakest moments. The author of this paper has done little more than announce a general topic for the paper (the trauma experienced by the characters in *The Joy Luck Club*). While the last sentence might be a thesis, the writer fails to present an analysis of these struggles. To improve this "thesis," the writer would need to back up a couple of steps. The writer should examine the novel and draw conclusions about the characters' moments of despair before crafting the thesis. After carefully examining key passages in the story, the writer might determine that, for at least some of the characters, the moments of deepest trauma and psychological doubt become their greatest moments of self-discovery. The writer now has something to say and might then craft a thesis such as this: Lindo, Jing-mei, and Rose are able to discover, through soul-searching and reflection that is prompted by feelings of complete despair, a sense of an authentic, autonomous self. This self-discovery enables them to find the strength and courage to move forward through the next phases of their lives in more constructive and purposeful ways.

Outlines

While developing a strong, thoughtful thesis early in your writing process should help focus your paper, outlining provides an essential tool for logically shaping that paper. A good outline helps you see—and develop—the relationships among the points in your argument and assures you that your paper flows logically and coherently. Outlining not only helps place your points in a logical order but also helps you subordinate supporting points, weed out any irrelevant points, and decide if there are any necessary points that are missing from your argument. Most of us are familiar with formal outlines that use numerical and letter designations for each point. However, there are different types of outlines; you may find that an informal outline is a more useful tool for you. What is important, though, is that you spend the time to develop some sort of outline—formal or informal.

Remember that an outline is a tool to help you shape and write a strong paper. If you do not spend sufficient time planning your supporting points and shaping the arrangement of those points, you will most likely construct a vague, unfocused outline that provides little, if any, help with the writing of the paper. Consider the following example:

Thesis: Lindo, Jing-mei, and Rose are able to discover, through soul-searching and reflection that is prompted by feelings of complete despair, a sense of an authentic, autonomous self. This self-discovery enables them to find the strength and courage to move forward through the next phases of their lives in more constructive and purposeful ways.

I. Introduction and thesis

II. Lindo's experience of being forced into an arranged marriage at a young age teaches her to survive by developing distinct public and private identities.
  A. Lindo is preparing to enter into a marriage with a young man whom she finds selfish and greedy.
  B. Lindo experiences an epiphany when she notices the power of the invisible wind.
  C. Consumed by despair, Lindo contemplates suicide.

III. Jing-mei's childhood experiences of being harassed by her mother, who is trying to turn her into a child prodigy, prompts Jing-mei to define herself against her mother's expectations

in order to retain control of her burgeoning
identity.
   A. Jing-mei's mother tests her every night
      to see what she is best at.
   B. Jing-mei fails all the tests and constantly
      disappoints her mother.

IV. Waverly's decision to give up chess.
   A. Waverly and her mother get into a fight
      and engage in a battle of wills.
   B. Waverly gives up playing chess.
   C. When she resumes, her mother no longer
      supports her in the same way, and Waverly
      no longer has the confidence to succeed.

V. Rose is only able to move forward with her
   life when she begins to reconnect with her own
   desires and opinions.
   A. Rose has lost her identity by allowing
      -- in fact, insisting -- that Ted make
      all the decisions in their lives.
   B. When Ted leaves Rose, she retreats to her
      bed and sleeps for three days.
   C. When she awakens, Rose rediscovers her
      own wishes and desires.
   D. Jing-mei decides to define herself in
      complete opposition to her mother's
      wishes.

VI. Conclusion
   A. Although Lindo, Jing-mei, and Rose all
      experience self-discovery in their
      bleakest moments, their identity formation
      operates in different ways depending on
      their circumstances.

This outline has a number of flaws. First, the thesis makes no mention
of Waverly and her decision to quit playing chess, yet the writer includes

this as a major topic in the outline. While Waverly's chess career and her relationship with her mother are interesting aspects of the novel, if they do not relate to the thesis, they should not appear in the outline or in the essay for that matter. Second, the writer includes "Jing-mei decides to define herself in opposition to her mother's wishes" under section V: "Rose is only able to move forward with her life when she begins to reconnect with her own desires and opinions." While Jing-mei's method of self-definition makes a good contrast with Rose's, the point about Jing-mei belongs in the section devoted to her character, section III. Third, the points in section II seem out of order. Letter C should come before letter B as it makes more sense to discuss Lindo's despair before her resulting epiphany. A fourth problem is the inclusion of a section A in section VI. An outline should not include an A without a B, a 1 without a 2, and so forth. The final problem with this outline is the overall lack of detail. None of the sections provide much information about the content of the argument, and it seems likely that the writer has not given sufficient thought to the content of the paper.

A better start to this outline might be the following:

Thesis: Lindo, Jing-mei, and Rose are able to discover, through soul-searching and reflection that is prompted by feelings of complete despair, a sense of an authentic, autonomous self. This self-discovery enables them to find the strength and courage to move forward through the next phases of their lives in more constructive and purposeful ways.

   I. Introduction and thesis

  II. Lindo's experience of being forced into an arranged marriage at a young age teaches her to survive by developing distinct public and private identities.
     A. Lindo is preparing to enter into a marriage with a young man whom she finds selfish and greedy.
     B. Consumed by despair, Lindo contemplates suicide.

   C. Lindo experiences an epiphany when she notices the power of the invisible wind; she begins to understand that she can keep her own thoughts inside herself where they can be unseen yet powerful like the wind.

III. Jing-mei's childhood experiences of being harassed by her mother, who is trying to turn her into a child prodigy, prompts Jing-mei to define herself against her mother's expectations in order to retain control of her burgeoning identity.

   A. Jing-mei's mother tests her every night to see what she is best at.

   B. Jing-mei fails all the tests and constantly disappoints her mother.

   C. Jing-mei reaches a moment of despair in which she feels that her mother is trying to take complete control of her identity; in rebellion, she decides to define herself in opposition to her mother's wishes.

IV. Rose, who reaches her crisis point when her husband leaves her and she finds herself suddenly responsible for making her own decisions, is only able to move forward with her life when she begins to reconnect with her own desires and opinions.

   A. Rose has lost her identity by allowing -- in fact, insisting -- that Ted make all the decisions in their lives.

   B. When Ted leaves Rose, she finds herself unmoored; Rose retreats to her bed and sleeps for three days.

   C. When she awakens, Rose feels like a blank slate and, from this new space, she begins

to rediscover her desires and gives herself
permission to simply act on them.

V. Conclusion
   A. Although Lindo, Jing-mei, and Rose all
      experience self-discovery in their bleakest
      moments, their identity formation operates
      in different ways depending on their
      circumstances.
   B. Tan suggests that it is the threat of
      the complete dissolution of the self
      that motivates each of these three women
      to crystallize her identity and work to
      nurture and protect it.
   C. This focus on the resiliency and
      adaptability of the human spirit is one way
      that Tan introduces hope into a narrative
      suffused with loss and tragedy.

This new outline would prove much more helpful when it came time to write the paper.

An outline like this could be shaped into an even more useful tool if the writer fleshed out the argument by providing specific examples from the text to support the main points. Once you have listed your main points and your supporting ideas, develop this raw material by listing related supporting ideas and material under each of those main headings. From there, arrange the material in subsections and order the material logically.

For example, you might begin with one of the theses cited above: While Jing-mei avoids having to negotiate a romantic relationship and its contest of wills by living a single life, her counterparts' romantic entanglements illustrate that second-generation Chinese-American women, having been raised in homes in which men are in control, are in danger of assuming the role of passive partner in their own relationship, as Rose does, or of worrying so much about maintaining equality in the relationship that they create other equally serious problems, as Lena does. Tan's vision is ultimately hopeful, however, as both Rose and Lena, with help from a most unlikely source -- their mothers -- begin to understand where they have gone wrong. Further, the portrayal of the healthy, mutually respectful relationship between Waverly and Rich suggests that all of these women have the potential to achieve both personal fulfillment and romantic satisfaction. As noted above, this thesis already gives you the beginning of an organization: You might begin your outline with topic headings along these lines: (1) Rose's unsuccessful relationship with Ted replicates the pattern of male dominance; (2) Lena and Harold try to purposefully create a relationship in which they are equals, but these overly analytic maneuvers doom their marriage; and (3) Waverly's relationship with Rich seems like a healthy, mutually respectful one, and as such, it demonstrates that it is possible to break away from patterns one learns in childhood without overcompensating and creating new problems. An informal outline might look like this:

Thesis: While Jing-mei avoids having to negotiate a romantic relationship and its contest of wills by living a single life, her counterparts' romantic entanglements illustrate that second-generation Chinese-American women, having been raised in homes in which men are in control, are in danger of assuming the role of passive partner in their own relationship, as Rose does, or of worrying so much about maintaining equality in the relationship that they create other equally serious problems, as Lena does. Tan's vision is ultimately hopeful, however, as both Rose and Lena, with help from a most unlikely source -- their mothers -- begin to understand where they have gone wrong. Further, the portrayal of the healthy, mutually respectful relationship between Waverly and Rich suggests that all of these women have the potential to achieve both personal fulfillment and romantic satisfaction.

1. Introduction and thesis

2. Rose's relationship with Ted replicates the traditional pattern of male dominance, and, in large part because of this, it is ultimately unsuccessful.
   - Rose allowed and encouraged Ted to make all decisions concerning their life together.
     - She describes their courtship this way: "I was victim to his hero" (119).
     - Rose ended every discussion with Ted by saying "Ted, you decide," until Ted finally learned to stop asking and simply make the decisions himself.
   - The relationship fell apart when Ted lost confidence and decided he needed Rose to be more of an equal partner.
     - Ted loses a malpractice suit and, with it, the confidence that the decisions he makes for himself and Rose are always the right ones.
     - Ted unsuccessfully tries to get Rose to give input, arguing that by avoiding the decision-making process, Rose is not only avoiding power or control but also responsibility and blame, and thus Ted has to take everything on himself.
   - Rose is forced to take responsibility for her life and to figure out what she really wants.
   - Rose's mother encourages her process of self-discovery, advising her not to save her marriage but to stand up for herself.

3. Lena and Harold try to purposefully create a relationship in which they are equals, but

these overly analytic maneuvers doom their marriage.

- Lena and Harold keep all of their finances strictly separate in the belief that this will help them to prevent one spouse from being dependent on or indebted to the other.
  - Lena and Harold keep separate bank accounts out of which they pay their own expenses and their prorated share of the couple's joint expenses.
  - Lena and Harold do not own equal stakes in their home; they have a prenuptial agreement that states that Lena's share of the community property is what she put into it, and no more.
- This strategy does not really establish equality, since Harold is Lena's boss.
  - Harold determines how much money he makes and how much money Lena, as his employee, makes.
  - Harold controls Lena's position at the company and chooses not to promote her so as not to appear biased to the other employees.
- The constant accounting prevents Lena and Harold from becoming true partners in large part by replacing the emotional and psychological components of marital decisions with strict logic and columns of dollars and cents.
- Lena would prefer a relationship in which emotion and devotion mattered more than money.
  - Early in the relationship, Lena wants to tell Harold that she does not want

to be so precise in their accounting, that she is "really into giving freely" (157).

- Lena longs for the "feeling of surrendering everything to [Harold], with abandon, without caring what [she] got in return" (157).
- Lena's concerns about maintaining equality in the relationship keep her from expressing her extreme dissatisfaction with the arrangement that she and Harold have agreed on.
- Lena's mother helps her to see her unhappiness.

4. Waverly's relationship with Rich seems like a healthy, mutually respectful one, and as such, it demonstrates that it is possible to break away from patterns one learns in childhood without overcompensating and creating new problems.
   - Rich does not seek to control or change Waverly.
     - According to Waverly, Rich's love did not depend on her acquiescing to his desires; his "love was unequivocal. Nothing could change it. He expected nothing from me" (175).
     - Not only did Rick not expect Waverly to change to suit his expectations and desires, he himself is willing to change in response to her.
   - Because Waverly and Rich are not preoccupied with protecting their status and power in the relationship, Waverly is able to make herself vulnerable to Rich, exposing her

weaknesses as well as her strengths, which brings them closer together.

5. Conclusion

- Waverly's relationship with Rich demonstrates that empowering, mutually respectful relationships are possible for women who grew up influenced by traditional Chinese culture.
- In the end, despite their broken marriages, even Rose and Lena show signs of moving toward the self-actualization that will enable them to construct healthy relationships in the future.
- Lena's and Rose's mothers help them by telling stories of their own pasts, and this in turn brings the mothers closer to their own personal fulfillment and contentment.
- Tan ultimately presents a hopeful vision that suggests that self-examination, communication, and perseverance can combine to help women leave behind traditions and family patterns that oppress them and work toward a healthier paradigm for themselves and their future relationships and families.

You would set about writing a formal outline with a similar process, though in the final stages you would label the headings differently. A formal outline for a paper that argues the thesis about *The Joy Luck Club* cited above—that many of the women achieve self-discovery in the midst of despair—might look like this:

Thesis: Lindo, Jing-mei, and Rose are able to discover, through soul-searching and reflection that is prompted by feelings of complete despair, a sense of an authentic, autonomous self. This self-discovery enables them to find the strength and courage to move forward through the next phases of their lives in more constructive and purposeful ways.

   I. Introduction and thesis

  II. Lindo's experience of being forced into an arranged marriage at a young age teaches her to survive by developing distinct public and private identities.
   A. Lindo is preparing to enter into a marriage with a young man whom she finds selfish and greedy.
   B. Consumed by despair, Lindo contemplates suicide.
   C. Lindo experiences an epiphany when she notices the power of the invisible wind; she begins to understand that she can keep her own thoughts inside where they can be unseen yet powerful like the wind.
      1. Lindo notices the curtains swaying in the breeze and the effects of the weather outside, and she realizes "it was the first time [she] could see the power of the wind. [She] couldn't see the wind itself, but [she] could see it carried the water that filled the rivers and shaped the countryside. It caused men to yelp and dance" (58).
      2. Lindo examines her character and discovers that she is "strong" and "pure" and that she has "genuine thoughts inside [her] that no one could ever take away from [her]. [She] was like the wind" (58).

III. Jing-mei's childhood experiences of being harassed by her mother, who was trying to turn her into a child prodigy, prompts Jing-mei to define herself against her mother's expectations in order to retain control of her burgeoning identity.

    A. Jing-mei's mother tests her every night to see what she is best at.

    B. Jing-mei fails all the tests and constantly disappoints her mother.

    C. Jing-mei reaches a moment of despair in which she feels that her mother is trying to take control of her identity; in rebellion, she decides to define herself in opposition to her mother's wishes.

        1. Jing-mei decides to be as ordinary and unexceptional as possible.

        2. In this way, she maintains control of her identity but only to a limited degree since she chooses to define herself in relation to her mother's desires.

IV. Rose, who reaches her crisis point when her husband leaves her and she finds herself suddenly responsible for making her own decisions, is only begins to move forward with her life when she beings to reconnect with her own desires and opinions.

    A. Rose has lost her identity by allowing -- in fact, insisting -- that Ted make all the decisions in their lives.

    B. When Ted leaves Rose, she finds herself unmoored; Rose retreats to her bed and sleeps for three days.

    C. When she awakens, Rose feels like a blank slate, and from this new space, she begins to rediscover her desires and gives herself permission to simply act on them.

1. Rose thinks to herself: "for the first time in months, after being in limbo all that time, everything stopped. All the questions: gone. There were no choices. [She] had an empty feeling -- and [she] felt free, wild" (194).

2. Rose tells Ted to come over after work, confessing, "I didn't know why I said that, but I felt right saying it" (195). Rose continues to let her instincts and desires come to the forefront and acts on them, telling Ted that she wants the house and that he "can't just pull [her] out of [his] life and throw [her] away" (196).

V. Conclusion

A. Although Lindo, Jing-mei, and Rose all experience self-discovery in their bleakest moments, their identity formation operates in different ways depending on their circumstances.

1. Lindo develops a split between her public and private selves in order to coexist with the forces controlling her life.

2. Jing-mei defines herself in opposition to the force controlling her life -- her mother -- which gives her only partial control of her identity as so much of it developed in relation to her mother's desires instead of her own.

3. As for Rose, she suddenly finds herself in control of her life and learns that she must discover her authentic self, her wishes and desires, so that she can exert that control in a purposeful and fulfilling manner.

B. Tan suggests that it is the threat of the complete dissolution of the self that motivates each of these three women to crystallize her identity and work to nurture and protect it.

C. This focus on the resiliency and adaptability of the human spirit is one way that Tan introduces hope into a narrative suffused with loss and tragedy.

As in the previous example outline, the thesis provided the seeds of a structure, and the writer was careful to arrange the supporting points in a logical manner, showing the relationships among the ideas in the paper.

Body Paragraphs

Once your outline is complete, you can begin drafting your paper. Paragraphs, units of related sentences, are the building blocks of a good paper, and as you draft you should keep in mind both the function and the qualities of good paragraphs. Paragraphs help you chart and control the shape and content of your essay, and they help the reader see your organization and your logic. You should begin a new paragraph whenever you move from one major point to another. In longer, more complex essays you might use a group of related paragraphs to support major points. Remember that in addition to being adequately developed, a good paragraph is both unified and coherent.

Unified Paragraphs:

Each paragraph must be centered around one idea or point, and a unified paragraph carefully focuses on and develops this central idea without including extraneous ideas or tangents. For beginning writers, the best way to ensure that you are constructing unified paragraphs is to include a topic sentence in each paragraph. This topic sentence should convey the main point of the paragraph, and every sentence in the paragraph should relate to that topic sentence. Any sentence that strays from the central topic does not belong in the paragraph and needs to be revised or deleted. Consider the following paragraph about Rose's relationship with Ted. Notice how the paragraph veers away from the main point.

> Of all the women of the second generation, Rose most clearly follows in her mother's footsteps. In her doomed relationship with Ted, Rose replicates the traditional Chinese pattern in which the husband is the clear head of the household and is responsible for making the decisions in regard to the family; it is only after Ted leaves Rose that she begins to take control of her life. Rose describes the early years of her courtship with soon-to-be-ex-husband Ted in the following way: "I was victim to his hero. I was always in danger and he was always rescuing me" (119). Soon, Ted was making all of the decisions in the relationship; every conversation ended with Rose's capitulation: "Ted, you decide," until at last the conversations themselves stopped, and Ted simply made all the decisions. While this arrangement worked for a while, it did not last. After Ted lost a malpractice suit and had his confidence shaken, he began to seek Rose's counsel more and more. Accustomed, culturally, to the idea of marriage as a mutual partnership, Ted had no qualms about asking for Rose's help when he needed it; indeed, he seems to have expected that when he faltered, she would step up and take a more decisive role in their relationship. When she refused to help, imploring Ted to just decide, "Ted would say in his impatient voice, 'No, you decide. You can't have it both ways, none of the responsibility, none of the blame'" (120). Ted became very dissatisfied with Rose, and as a result, he began to lash out at her in anger. While Ted had the opportunity to work on the problems he and Rose were having, he opted instead to engage in behavior that caused the marriage to disintegrate further.

Although the paragraph begins solidly, and the very first sentence provides the central idea of the paragraph, the author goes on a tangent in the paragraph's last two sentences. While the comments on Ted's anger may be true, they take the focus of the paragraph away from Rose and her part in the relationship and, consequently, these sentences should be deleted and replaced with sentences that discuss the personal progress that Rose makes as a result of the failure of her marriage.

Coherent Paragraphs:

In addition to shaping unified paragraphs, you must also craft coherent paragraphs, paragraphs that develop their points logically with sentences that flow smoothly into one another. Coherence depends on the order of your sentences, but it is not strictly the order of the sentences that is important to paragraph coherence. You also need to craft your prose to help the reader see the relationship among the sentences.

Consider the following paragraph about Rose's relationship with Ted and her response to its failure. Notice how the writer uses the same ideas as the paragraph above yet fails to help the reader see the relationships among the points.

Of all the women of the second generation, Rose most clearly follows in her mother's footsteps; in her doomed relationship with Ted, Rose replicates the traditional Chinese pattern in which the husband is the clear head of the household and is responsible for making the decisions in regard to the family; it is only after Ted leaves Rose that she begins to take control of her life. Rose reflects: "I was victim to his hero. I was always in danger and he was always rescuing me" (119). Ted was making all of the decisions in the relationship, with Rose contributing only: "Ted, you decide." At last, the conversations themselves stopped, and Ted simply made all the decisions. While this arrangement worked for a while, it did not last. After Ted lost a malpractice suit and had his confidence shaken, he began to seek Rose's counsel more and more. Ted had no qualms about asking for Rose's help when he needed it; he seems to

> have expected that when he faltered she would step up
> and take a more decisive role in their relationship. When
> she refused to help, "Ted would say in his impatient
> voice, 'No, you decide. You can't have it both ways,
> none of the responsibility, none of the blame'" (120).
> Ted was seeking a partner in Rose, and she was unable
> to change the pattern of their relationship to function
> in this way. It is the breakup with Ted that results in
> her realization that the time has come for her to take
> stock of her life and begin to chart her own course.
> Rose gets much needed support and encouragement from her
> mother, who does not tell her to save her marriage, as
> Rose expects, but simply to stand up for herself and make
> her own decisions.

This paragraph demonstrates that unity alone does not guarantee paragraph effectiveness. The argument is hard to follow because the author fails both to show connections between the sentences and to indicate how they work to support the overall point.

A number of techniques are available to aid paragraph coherence. Careful use of transitional words and phrases is essential. You can use transitional flags to introduce an example or an illustration (*for example, for instance*), to amplify a point or add another phase of the same idea (*additionally, furthermore, next, similarly, finally, then*), to indicate a conclusion or result (*therefore, as a result, thus, in other words*), to signal a contrast or a qualification (*on the other hand, nevertheless, despite this, on the contrary, still, however, conversely*), to signal a comparison (*likewise, in comparison, similarly*), and to indicate a movement in time (*afterward, earlier, eventually, finally, later, subsequently, until*).

In addition to transitional flags, careful use of pronouns aids coherence and flow. If you were writing about *The Wizard of Oz*, you would not want to keep repeating the phrase *the witch* or the name *Dorothy*. Careful substitution of the pronoun *she* in these instances can aid coherence. A word of warning, though: When you substitute pronouns for proper names, always be sure that your pronoun reference is clear. In a paragraph that discusses both Dorothy and the witch, substituting *she* could lead to confusion. Make sure that it is clear to whom the pronoun refers. Generally, the pronoun refers to the last proper noun you have used.

While repeating the same name over and over again can lead to awkward, boring prose, it is possible to use repetition to help your paragraph's coherence. Careful repetition of important words or phrases can lend coherence to your paragraph by reminding readers of your key points. Admittedly, it takes some practice to use this technique effectively. You may find that reading your prose aloud can help you develop an ear for effective use of repetition.

To see how helpful transitional aids are, compare the paragraph below to the preceding paragraph about the way that Rose's marriage and divorce affect her identity. Notice how the author works with the same ideas and quotations but shapes them into a much more coherent paragraph whose point is clearer and easier to follow.

Of all the women of the second generation, Rose most clearly follows in her mother's footsteps. In her doomed relationship with Ted, Rose replicates the traditional Chinese pattern in which the husband is the clear head of the household and is responsible for making the decisions in regard to the family; it is only after Ted leaves Rose that she begins to take control of her life. Rose describes the early years of her courtship with soon-to-be-ex-husband Ted in the following way: "I was victim to his hero. I was always in danger and he was always rescuing me" (119). Soon, Ted was making all of the decisions in the relationship; every conversation ended with Rose's capitulation: "Ted, you decide," until at last the conversations themselves stopped, and Ted simply made all the decisions. While this arrangement worked for a while, it did not last. After Ted lost a malpractice suit and had his confidence shaken, he began to seek Rose's counsel more and more. Accustomed, culturally, to the idea of marriage as a mutual partnership, Ted had no qualms about asking for Rose's help when he needed it; indeed, he seems to have expected that when he faltered, she would step up and take a more decisive role in their relationship. When she refused to help, imploring Ted to just decide, "Ted would say in his impatient voice, 'No, you decide. You can't have it both ways, none of the responsibility, none of the blame'" (120). Obviously, Ted was seeking a partner in Rose, and she was unable to change the pattern of their relationship to function in this way. Ironically, it is the breakup with Ted that results in her realization that the time has come for her to take stock of her life and begin to chart her own course. In this process, Rose gets much needed support and encouragement from her mother, who does not tell her to save her marriage, as Rose expects, but simply to stand up for herself and make her own decisions.

Similarly, the following paragraph from a paper on trauma and self-discovery in Tan's *The Joy Luck Club* demonstrates both unity and coherence. In it, the author argues that Lindo's despair over her impending marriage enables her to construct both a public and a private identity and so allows her to retain her personal thoughts and opinions while outwardly going along with what custom and tradition dictated:

Lindo is forced at the young age of twelve to live with her future husband's family. After several years there, Lindo's mother-in-law decides that it is time for Lindo and her son Tyan to get married. Lindo is alone, afraid, and not in love with the selfish, greedy boy she is soon to marry. On her wedding day, she feels such despair that she considers suicide. It is only when she contemplates losing herself entirely, either through forced marriage or suicide, that Lindo comes to understand that she possesses an authentic, inviolable selfhood. Looking out of the window, she has an epiphany. Lindo asks herself, "What is true about a person?" and wonders if she could "change in the same way the river changes color but still be the same person." Then, Lindo notices the curtains swaying in the breeze and the effects of the weather outside, and she realizes "it was the first time [she] could see the power of the wind. [She] couldn't see the wind itself, but [she] could see it carried the water that filled the rivers and shaped the countryside. It caused men to yelp and dance" (58). Lindo examines her character and discovers that she is "strong" and "pure" and that she has "genuine thoughts inside [her] that no one could ever take away from [her]. [She] was like the wind" (58). This realization helped Lindo to see that, essentially, she could maintain separate and distinct public and private selves; she could behave outwardly as she was expected to while still retaining her own secret thoughts and ideas. Like the wind could make the curtains move, she could go through with her marriage and behave as a dutiful wife and daughter-in-law, but just as the wind remained invisible and unknowable, so her true self could still exist and remain unobserved and hence unmolested. Armed with this knowledge, Lindo is able to go through with her marriage and yet also to eventually devise a way out of it that will not harm her family's reputation.

Introductions

Introductions present particular challenges for writers. Generally, your introduction should do two things: capture your reader's attention and explain the main point of your essay. In other words, while your introduction should contain your thesis, it needs to do a bit more work than that. You are likely to find that starting that first paragraph is one of the most difficult parts of the paper. It is hard to face that blank page or screen, and as a result, many beginning writers, in desperation to start somewhere, start with overly broad, general statements. While it is often a good strategy to start with more general subject matter and narrow your focus, do not begin with broad sweeping statements such as Human suffering has always existed. Such sentences are nothing but empty filler. They begin to fill the blank page, but they do nothing to advance your argument. Instead, you should try to gain your readers' interest. Some writers like to begin with a pertinent quotation or with a relevant question. Or, you might begin with an introduction of the topic you will discuss. If you are going to be writing about the good that can come out of deep psychological crises as demonstrated in *The Joy Luck Club*, you might hook your reader by laying out the extraordinary amount of suffering and trauma experienced by the characters. Another common trap to avoid is depending on your title to introduce the author and the text you are writing about. Always include the work's author and title in your opening paragraph.

Compare the effectiveness of the following introductions.

1. Many people on this earth, especially women, suffer through tragedies and traumas so severe that they can lose all sense of themselves and harbor little hope of recovery. Recovery though, and even success, are certainly possible. For at least some women, moments of deepest crisis become moments of significant and life-changing psychological discoveries. Lindo, Jing-mei, and Rose are able to discover, through soul-searching and reflection that is prompted by feelings of complete despair, a sense of an authentic, autonomous self. This self-discovery enables them to find the strength and courage to move forward through the next phases of their lives in more constructive and purposeful ways.

2. The women of Amy Tan's *The Joy Luck Club* are nothing if not survivors. Together, they have suffered countless personal indignities and family tragedies. The first generation of women suffered through traumatic events such as arranged marriages, the suicide of mothers, the physical and psychological effects of war, and a difficult relocation to a new and very different country. As for the second generation, they must deal with parents who are still scarred from past trauma, and they are forced to constantly negotiate between their family's expectations, values, and language, and the significantly different expectations, values, and language of the American culture they encounter as soon as they step out of their parents' homes. Without exception, the women of *The Joy Luck Club* experience moments of psychological trauma. For at least some of them, the moments of deepest crisis become moments of significant and life-changing psychological discoveries. Lindo, Jing-mei, and Rose

are able to discover, through soul-searching and
reflection that is prompted by feelings of complete
despair, a sense of an authentic, autonomous self.
This self-discovery enables them to find the strength
and courage to move forward through the next phases
of their lives in more constructive and purposeful
ways.

The first introduction begins with a vague, overly broad sentence; cites unclear, undeveloped examples; and then moves abruptly to the thesis. Notice, too, how a reader deprived of the paper's title does not know the title of the story that the paper will analyze. The second introduction works with the same material and thesis but provides more detail and is consequently much more interesting. It begins by discussing biophilia and the human need for connection to nature. The paragraph ends with the thesis, which includes both the author and the title of the work to be discussed.

The paragraph below provides another example of an opening strategy. It begins by introducing the author and the text it will analyze, and then it moves on to provide some necessary background information before introducing its thesis.

Through the stories told by the Chinese characters of Amy
Tan's *The Joy Luck Club*, we are introduced to a culture
very unlike 21st-century American culture. When the women
of *The Joy Luck Club* immigrated to the United States in
the mid-20th century, they, naturally, brought with them
cultural constructs, including the notion of the clearly
subordinate role of women in society and in the family
unit. According to Kazuko Ono, "in pre-Communist Chinese
society, a woman was not considered a human being, but a
thing, a piece of private property -- indeed, something
on the order of a domestic animal" (179). As second-
generation immigrants, the four girls featured in *The
Joy Luck Club*, Jing-mei, Waverly, Lena, and Rose, grow up
with a great deal of exposure to American culture and
its emphasis on individual and equal rights for men and
women, but their nuclear families are still very much
influenced by Chinese tradition in which the will of

the individual, particularly the female individual, is sublimated for the good of the group and in which the father figure is responsible for deciding what is, in fact, good for the group when the group in question is the family unit. Out of the clash between the competing Eastern and Western ideologies of romance and family, the women of the younger generation find themselves pulled in opposite directions and ultimately left to find their own way, having to decide among clinging to their parents' Chinese ways, rebelling entirely and embracing a thoroughly American philosophy, or blazing a new trail altogether. While Jing-mei avoids having to negotiate a romantic relationship and its inherent contest of wills by remaining single, her counterparts' romantic entanglements illustrate that second-generation Chinese-American women, having been raised in homes in which men are in complete control, are in danger of assuming the role of passive partner in their own relationships, as Rose does, or of worrying so much about maintaining equality in the relationship that they create other equally serious problems, as Lena does. Tan's vision is ultimately hopeful, however, as both Rose and Lena, with help from a most unlikely source -- their mothers -- begin to understand where they have gone wrong. Further, the portrayal of the healthy, mutually respectful relationship between Waverly and Rich suggests that all of these women have the potential to achieve both personal fulfillment and romantic satisfaction.

Conclusions

Conclusions present another series of challenges for writers. No doubt you have heard the old adage about writing papers: "Tell us what you are going to say, say it, and then tell us what you've said." While this formula does not necessarily result in bad papers, it does not often result in good ones either. It will almost certainly result in boring papers (especially boring conclusions). If you have done a good job establishing your points in the body of the paper, the reader already knows and understands your argument. There is no need to merely reiterate. Do not just summarize your main points in your conclusion. Such a boring and mechanical conclusion does nothing to advance your argument or interest your reader. Consider the following conclusion to the paper about trauma and self-discovery in Tan's *The Joy Luck Club*.

> In conclusion, Jing-mei, Lindo, and Rose all experience self-discovery in their bleakest moments, but the process is different for each of them because of their different circumstances. Lindo's self-discovery happens when she develops a split between her public and private selves in order to survive in a situation in which other forces are in control of her life. A young Jing-mei decides to define herself in opposition to the force controlling her life, her mother, and although this method of identity formation still affords her mother a great deal of power, at least Jing-mei is able to maintain a modicum of control over her developing identity. When Rose is abandoned by her husband, Ted, and suddenly finds herself in control of her life, she learns that she must discover her authentic self, her wishes and desires, so that she can exert that control in a purposeful and fulfilling manner.

Besides starting with a mechanical transitional device, this conclusion does little more than summarize the main points of the outline (and it does not even touch on all of them). It is incomplete and uninteresting.

Instead, your conclusion should add something to your paper. A good tactic is to build upon the points you have been arguing. Asking "why?" often helps you draw further conclusions. You might also speculate on other directions in which to take your topic by tying it into larger issues. You might do this by envisioning your paper as just one section of a larger paper. For example, in a paper on trauma and self-discovery in *The Joy Luck Club* you might touch on the similar experiences of characters that you did not focus on in the essay or you might spend some time commenting on the differences in the discovery processes that each woman went through. Alternatively, you might compare the characters discussed in the essay to those who do not seem changed for the better by their traumatic experiences and speculate on the reasons for the different responses to adversity. In the following conclusion, the author

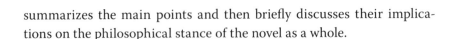

summarizes the main points and then briefly discusses their implications on the philosophical stance of the novel as a whole.

> Although Lindo, Jing-mei, and Rose all experience self-discovery in their bleakest moments, the process is different for each of them because of their different circumstances. Lindo's self-discovery happens when she develops a split between her public and private selves in order to survive in a situation in which other forces are in control of her life. A young Jing-mei decides to define herself in opposition to the force controlling her life, her mother, and although this method of identity formation still affords her mother a great deal of power, at least Jing-mei is able to maintain a modicum of control over her developing identity. When Rose is abandoned by her husband, Ted, and suddenly finds herself in control of her life, she learns that she must discover her authentic self, her wishes and desires, so that she can exert that control in a purposeful and fulfilling manner. Thus, in this novel Tan gives us not one but three examples of women who are able to construct or maintain a sense of self in the face of difficult circumstances. In fact, she suggests that it is the threat of the complete dissolution of the self that motivates each woman to crystallize her identity and work to nurture and protect it. Tan implies here that these women would likely not have achieved self-discovery had they not been severely challenged. This focus on the resiliency and adaptability of the human spirit and the benefits that can come from the most unlikely places is one way that Tan introduces hope into a narrative suffused with loss and tragedy.

Similarly, in the following conclusion to a paper on female empowerment and equality in relationships in *The Joy Luck Club*, the author uses the conclusion to discuss the significance of the mothers' decisions to help their daughters in their quests for selfhood, especially by sharing their stories and memories with them.

Waverly's relationship with Rich demonstrates that empowering, mutually respectful relationships are indeed possible for women who grew up influenced by traditional Chinese culture. By novel's end, despite their broken marriages, Rose and Lena, too, show signs of moving toward the self-actualization that will enable them to construct healthy relationships in the future. Remarkably, the two women are both helped by their mothers, An-mei and Ying-ying, who decide to not only encourage and support their daughters in their quests for self-fulfillment but to share the stories of their own struggles and regrets with them in hopes of steering them in a different direction. This decision adds a new dimension to the struggle for female empowerment; as Marina Heung writes, "For An-mei and Ying-ying self-articulation remedies early teachings in silence and self-denial" (35). In essence, these women's determination to help their daughters ultimately enables them to reclaim their own identities by telling their stories. Thus, through the second generation's struggles and the original Joy Luck women's determination that their daughters be both empowered and fulfilled, Tan ultimately presents quite a hopeful vision that suggests that self-examination, communication, and perseverance can combine to help women leave behind traditions and family patterns that oppress them and work toward a healthier paradigm for themselves and their future relationships and families.

Citations and Formatting
Using Primary Sources:

As the examples included in this chapter indicate, strong papers on literary texts incorporate quotations from the text in order to support their points. It is not enough for you to assert your interpretation without providing support or evidence from the text. Without well chosen quotations to support your argument you are, in effect, saying to the reader, "Take my word for it." It is important to use quotations thoughtfully and selectively. Remember that the paper presents *your* argument, so choose quotations that support *your* assertions. Do not let the author's voice overwhelm your own. With that caution in mind, there are some guidelines you should follow to ensure that you use quotations clearly and effectively.

Integrate Quotations:

Quotations should always be integrated into your own prose. Do not just drop them into your paper without introduction or comment. Otherwise, it is unlikely that your reader will see their function. You can integrate textual support easily and clearly with identifying tags, short phrases that identify the speaker. For example:

> Rose describes her relationship to Ted as "victim to his hero."

While this tag appears before the quotation, you can also use tags after or in the middle of the quoted text, as the following examples demonstrate:

> "Ted, you decide," says Rose.

> "I'm not really this way about money, the way we've been doing it," Lena wants to tell Harold. "I'm really into giving freely."

You can also use a colon to formally introduce a quotation:

> Rose describes the early years of her courtship with soon-to-be-ex-husband Ted in the following way: "I was victim to his hero. I was always in danger and he was always rescuing me."

When you quote brief sections of poems (three lines or fewer), use slash marks to indicate the line breaks in the poem:

> As the poem ends, Dickinson speaks of the power of the imagination: "The revery alone will do, / If bees are few."

Longer quotations (more than four lines of prose or three lines of poetry) should be set off from the rest of your paper in a block quotation. Double-space before you begin the passage, indent it 10 spaces from your left-hand margin, and double-space the passage itself. Because the indentation signals the inclusion of a quotation, do not use quotation marks around the cited passage. Use a colon to introduce the passage:

Waverly describes the intense vulnerability she feels with Rich:

> with him I was completely naked, and when I was feeling the most vulnerable -- when the wrong word would have sent me flying out the door forever -- he always said exactly the right thing at the right moment. He didn't allow me to cover myself up. He would grab my hands, look me straight in the eye and tell me something new about why he loved me.

By neither allowing one person to control the relationship nor instituting harmful measures to ensure constant equality, Waverly and Rich are bound to experience some conflicts in their future; however, there is a good chance that they can work through them by expressing themselves in the context of the meaningful, mutually respectful relationship they have established.

The whole of Dickinson's poem speaks of the imagination:

> To make a prairie it takes a clover and
>   one bee,
> One clover, and a bee,
> And revery.
> The revery alone will do,
> If bees are few.

Clearly, she argues for the creative power of the mind.

It is also important to interpret quotations after you introduce them and explain how they help advance your point. You cannot assume that your reader will interpret the quotations the same way that you do.

Quote Accurately:

Always quote accurately. Anything within quotations marks must be the author's exact words. There are, however, some rules to follow if you need to modify the quotation to fit into your prose.

1. Use brackets to indicate any material that might have been added to the author's exact wording. For example, if you need to add any words to the quotation or alter it grammatically to allow it to fit into your prose, indicate your changes in brackets:

   > Lena only gets upset about her job when she thinks about "how much [she] gets paid, how [hard] she works, [and] how fair Harold is to everybody except [her]."

2. Conversely, if you choose to omit any words from the quotation, use ellipses (three spaced periods) to indicate missing words or phrases:

   > Harold said that he "valued [his and Lena's] relationship too much . . . to contaminate it with money."

3. If you delete a sentence or more, use the ellipses after a period:

   > As Lindo prepared to be married, she looked out the window in despair, and for the first time, she "could see the power of the wind. . . . It caused men to yelp and dance."

4. If you omit a line or more of poetry, or more than one paragraph of prose, use a single line of spaced periods to indicate the omission:

   > To make a prairie it takes a clover and one bee,
   > . . . .
   > And revery.
   > The revery alone will do,
   > If bees are few.

Punctuate Properly:

Punctuation of quotations often causes more trouble than it should. Once again, you just need to keep these simple rules in mind.

1. Periods and commas should be placed inside quotation marks, even if they are not part of the original quotation:

   ```
   Rose tells Ted to come over after work, confessing,
   "I didn't know why I said that, but I felt right
   saying it."
   ```

   The only exception to this rule is when the quotation is followed by a parenthetical reference. In this case, the period or comma goes after the citation (more on these later in this chapter):

   ```
   Rose tells Ted to come over after work, confessing,
   "I didn't know why I said that, but I felt right
   saying it" (195).
   ```

2. Other marks of punctuation—colons, semicolons, question marks, and exclamation points—go outside the quotation marks unless they are part of the original quotation:

   ```
   What does Lindo mean when she says that she
   "made the Huangs think it was their idea to get
   rid of [her], that they would be the ones to say
   the marriage contract was not valid"?
   ```

   ```
   The women who fished Ying-ying out of the water
   yelled to the people she had left behind in the
   boat: "Have you lost a little girl, a girl who
   fell in the water?"
   ```

Documenting Primary Sources:

Unless you are instructed otherwise, you should provide sufficient information for your reader to locate material you quote. Generally, literature papers follow the rules set forth by the Modern Language Association (MLA). These can be found in the *MLA Handbook for Writers of Research*

Papers (sixth edition). You should be able to find this book in the reference section of your library. Additionally, its rules for citing both primary and secondary sources are widely available from reputable online sources. One of these is the Online Writing Lab (OWL) at Purdue University. OWL's guide to MLA style is available at http://owl.english.purdue.edu/owl/resource/557/01/. The Modern Language Association also offers answers to frequently asked questions about MLA style on this helpful Web page: http://www.mla.org/style_faq. Generally, when you are citing from literary works in papers, you should keep a few guidelines in mind.

Parenthetical Citations:
MLA asks for parenthetical references in your text after quotations. When you are working with prose (short stories, novels, or essays) include page numbers in the parentheses:

```
Rose tells Ted to come over after work, confessing, "I
didn't know why I said that, but I felt right saying it"
(195).
```

When you are quoting poetry, include line numbers:

```
Dickinson's speaker tells of the arrival of a fly: "There
interposed a Fly -- / With Blue -- uncertain stumbling
Buzz -- / Between the light -- and Me -- " (12-14).
```

Works Cited Page:
These parenthetical citations are linked to a separate works cited page at the end of the paper. The works cited page lists works alphabetically by the authors' last name. An entry for the above reference to Tan's *The Joy Luck Club* would read:

```
Tan, Amy. The Joy Luck Club. New York: Penguin, 1989.
```

The *MLA Handbook* includes a full listing of sample entries, as do many of the online explanations of MLA style.

Documenting Secondary Sources:
To ensure that your paper is built entirely upon your own ideas and analysis, instructors often ask that you write interpretative papers

without any outside research. If, on the other hand, your paper requires research, you must document any secondary sources you use. You need to document direct quotations, summaries or paraphrases of others' ideas, and factual information that is not common knowledge. Follow the guidelines above for quoting primary sources when you use direct quotations from secondary sources. Keep in mind that MLA style also includes specific guidelines for citing electronic sources. OWL's Web site provides a good summary: http://owl.english.purdue.edu/owl/resource/557/09/.

Parenthetical Citations:

As with the documentation of primary sources, described above, MLA guidelines require in-text parenthetical references to your secondary sources. Unlike the research papers you might write for a history class, literary research papers following MLA style do not use footnotes as a means of documenting sources. Instead, after a quotation, you should cite the author's last name and the page number:

> "[I]n pre-Communist Chinese society, a woman was not considered a human being, but a thing, a piece of private property -- indeed, something on the order of a domestic animal" (Ono 179).

If you include the name of the author in your prose, then you would include only the page number in your citation. For example:

> According to Kazuko Ono, "in pre-Communist Chinese society, a woman was not considered a human being, but a thing, a piece of private property -- indeed, something on the order of a domestic animal" (179).

If you are including more than one work by the same author, the parenthetical citation should include a shortened yet identifiable version of the title in order to indicate which of the author's works you cite. For example:

> Tan writes: "This turns out to be joyous news for Huang Taitai, for she liked nothing better than to reclaim all her gold and jewelry" (*Joy Luck* 63).

Similarly, and just as important, if you summarize or paraphrase the particular ideas of your source, you must provide documentation:

> An-mei and Ying-ying overcome childhood lessons in sacrifice and silence when they tell their stories to their daughters (Heung 35).

Works Cited Page:

Like the primary sources discussed above, the parenthetical references to secondary sources are keyed to a separate works cited page at the end of your paper. Here is an example of a works cited page that uses the examples cited above. Note that when two or more works by the same author are listed, you should use three hyphens followed by a period in the subsequent entries. You can find a complete list of sample entries in the *MLA Handbook* or from a reputable online summary of MLA style.

WORKS CITED

Heung, Marina. "Daughter-Text/Mother-Text: Matrileneage in Amy Tan's *Joy Luck Club.*" *Amy Tan.* Modern Critical Views Series. New York: Chelsea House, 2000. 25–41.

Kazuko, Ono. *Chinese Women in a Century of Revolution, 1850–1950.* Ed. Joseph Fogel. Stanford, CA: Stanford UP, 1989.

Tan, Amy. *The Joy Luck Club.* New York: Penguin, 1989.

———. *The Kitchen God's Wife.* New York: Putnam's, 1991.

Plagiarism:

Failure to document carefully and thoroughly can leave you open to charges of stealing the ideas of others, which is known as plagiarism, and this is a very serious matter. Remember that it is important to include quotation marks when you use language from your source, even if you use just one or two words. For example, if you wrote, in traditional Chinese culture, women held a similar status to pieces of private property, you would be guilty of plagiarism, since you used Kazuko Ono's distinct language without acknowledging him as the source. Instead, you should write something like: in traditional Chinese culture, women held a similar status to "piece[s] of private property" (Ono 181). In this case, you have properly credited Ono.

Similarly, neither summarizing the ideas of an author nor changing or omitting just a few words means that you can omit a citation. E. D. Huntley's *Amy Tan: A Critical Companion* is the source of the following passage about mother/daughter relationships in *The Joy Luck Club*.

> Unfortunately, [the] American daughters do not recognize a symbiotic relationship between mothers and daughters; these second-generation Americans see only that their mothers appear to be trying to live through their children. . . . Because they have been schooled in the tradition of individuality, the daughters resist their mothers' attempts to define their lives or to participate vicariously in their accomplishments.

Below are two examples of plagiarized passages:

> Having been raised in an American culture that emphasizes the individual, the second-generation American daughters resent their mother's intense engagement in the details of their lives; this behavior is natural on the part of the mothers who perceive their daughters' identities to be connected to their own.

> The American daughters resent what they perceive as their mothers' interference in their lives because they have been schooled in the tradition of individuality and do not view their relationships with their mothers as symbiotic (63).

While the first passage does not use Huntley's exact language, since the interpretation it offers is Huntley's distinct idea, this constitutes plagiarism. The second passage has changed some wording from the original and included a citation, but some of the phrasing is Huntley's. The first passage could be fixed with a parenthetical citation. Because some of the wording in the second remains the same, though, it would require the use of quotation marks in addition to a parenthetical citation. The passage below represents an honestly and adequately documented use of the original passage:

> According to E. D. Huntley, the American daughters, "schooled in the tradition of individuality," resent what

they perceive as their mothers' interference in their lives; for the mothers, this behavior is not interfering or "partipat[ing] vicariously" in their daughters' lives, it is simply the natural outgrowth of a "symbiotic relationship" (63).

This passage acknowledges that the interpretation is derived from Huntley while appropriately using quotations to indicate his precise language.

While it is not necessary to document well-known facts, often referred to as "common knowledge," any ideas or language that you take from someone else must be properly documented. Common knowledge generally includes the birth and death dates of authors or other well-documented facts of their lives. An often-cited guideline is that if you can find the information in three sources, it is common knowledge. Despite this guideline, it is, admittedly, often difficult to know if the facts you uncover are common knowledge or not. When in doubt, document your source.

Sample Essay

Allen Tran
Ms. Wade
English II
February 15, 2010

LOOKING FOR LOVE IN *THE JOY LUCK CLUB*

Through the stories told by the Chinese characters of Amy Tan's *The Joy Luck Club,* we are introduced to a culture very unlike 21st-century American culture. When the women of the Joy Luck Club immigrated to the United States in the mid-20th century, they, naturally, brought with them cultural constructs, including the notion of the clearly subordinate role of women in society and in the family unit. According to Kazuko Ono, "in pre-Communist Chinese society, a woman was not considered a human being, but a thing, a piece of private property -- indeed, something on the order of a domestic animal" (179). As second-generation immigrants, the four girls featured in *The Joy Luck Club*, Jing-mei, Waverly, Lena, and Rose, grow up with a great deal of exposure to American culture and its emphasis on individual and equal rights for men and women, but their nuclear families are still very much influenced by Chinese tradition in which the will of the individual, particularly the female individual, is sublimated for the good of the group and in which the father figure is responsible for deciding what is, in fact, good for the group when the group in question is the family unit. Out of the clash between the competing Eastern and Western ideologies of romance and family, the women of the younger generation find themselves pulled in opposite directions and ultimately left to find their own way, having to decide among clinging to their parents' Chinese ways, rebelling entirely and embracing a thoroughly American philosophy, or blazing a new trail altogether. While Jing-mei avoids having to negotiate a romantic relationship and its inherent contest of wills by remaining single, her counterparts' romantic entanglements illustrate that second-generation Chinese-American women, having been raised in homes in which men are in control, are in danger of assuming the role of passive partner in their own relationships, as Rose does, or of worrying so much about maintaining equality in the relationship that they create other equally serious problems, as Lena does. Tan's vision is ultimately hopeful, however, as both Rose and Lena, with help from a most unlikely source -- their mothers -- begin to understand where they have gone wrong. Further, the portrayal of the healthy, mutually respectful relationship between Waverly and Rich suggests that all of these women have the potential to achieve both personal fulfillment and romantic satisfaction.

Of all the women of the second generation, Rose most clearly follows in her mother's footsteps; in her doomed relationship with Ted, Rose replicates the traditional Chinese pattern in which the husband is the clear head of the household and is responsible for making the decisions regarding the family. Rose describes the early years of her courtship with soon-to-be-ex-husband Ted in the following way: "I was victim to his hero. I was always in danger and he was always rescuing me" (119). Soon, Ted was making all of the decisions in the relationship; every conversation ended with Rose's capitulation, "Ted, you decide," until at last the conversations themselves stopped, and Ted simply made all the decisions. While this arrangement worked for a while, it did not last. After Ted lost a malpractice suit and had his confidence shaken, he began to seek Rose's counsel more and more. Accustomed, culturally, to the idea of marriage as a mutual partnership, Ted had no qualms about asking for Rose's help when he needed it; indeed, he seems to have expected that when he faltered she would step up and take a more decisive role in their relationship. When she refused to help, imploring Ted to just decide, "Ted would say in his impatient voice, 'No, you decide. You can't have it both ways, none of the responsibility, none of the blame'" (120). Obviously, Ted was seeking a partner in Rose, and she was unable to change the pattern of their relationship to function in this way. Ironically, it is the breakup with Ted that results in her realization that the time has come for her to take stock of her life and begin to chart her own course. In this process, Rose gets much needed support and encouragement from her mother, who does not tell her to save her marriage, as Rose expects, but simply to stand up for herself and make her own decisions.

The incongruent mixture of Chinese and American values, epitomized by Rose and Ted's unhappy marriage, is not the only unsuccessful coupling strategy in the novel. Lena and Harold's relationship is diametrically opposed -- philosophically -- to the traditional Chinese pattern. The two are nearly obsessed with establishing and maintaining equality in the relationship, a goal they strive to achieve primarily through keeping their finances entirely separate in the belief that neither should ever feel obligated or indebted to the other.

However, because Harold owns the company at which Lena works, he controls Lena's position -- and chooses not to promote her so as not to appear biased to the other employees -- and sets her salary as well as his own. Since Harold's salary is so much larger than Lena's, the two have decided in a prenuptial agreement that their contributions to the mortgage payments on their home and that, in the case of divorce, the amount of community property each owns, should be based on a percentage of their income. Thus, Harold owns a larger share of the couple's home, and because of this, he and Lena agree that Harold should also have the final say in decisions about the house, including the manner in which it should be decorated. Harold's larger income also allows him to make other decisions including the destinations of most of the couple's vacations. In this arrangement -- into which Lena and Harold have entered with the explicit goal of protecting themselves -- money and earning power have come to determine the value of each person's will or desire; thus, even if the financial situation were more equitable, the couple would still fail to engage in the essentially unaccountable give-and-take that makes a marriage a true union. While the couple's arrangement provides Lena with a degree of self-determination and independence that few, if any, women could have dreamt of in traditional Chinese society, the purely capitalistic foundations of their interactions never afford them the opportunity to grow emotionally as a couple. Lena's qualms about the situation -- early on she thinks about telling Harold, "No! I'm not really this way about money, the way we've been doing it. I'm really into giving freely" (157) -- and the rush of love she feels when she remembers "the first time [she and Harold] made love, this feeling of surrendering everything to him, with abandon, without caring what I got in return" indicate her desire for a different kind of relationship, but her fear of inequality or indebtedness in the relationship prevents her from aggressively pursuing it. Lena's mother recognizes the "emptiness of Lena's life," and imagining her life through her mother's eyes helps Lena to acknowledge her unhappiness (Heung 35).

Lest we think all of these young women are doomed to failed relationships, Tan presents us with a promising one in Waverly. Clearly, Rich does not expect to be in constant control in the relationship as Ted does in the early days with Rose, and Rich's love is not dependent on Waverly's submission. As Waverly puts it: "His love was unequivocal. Nothing could change it. He expected nothing from me; my mere existence was enough. And at the same time, he said that he had changed -- for the better -- because of me . . ." (175). Not only does Rich never demand that Waverly change; he is willing to allow her to inspire changes in him. Perhaps because of this lack of demands and conditions, Waverly, unlike Lena who is always worried about establishing and maintaining equal footing in her relationship, is able to let her guard down and allow Rich to get to know her at her best and at her worst. She reveals: "with him I was completely naked, and when I was feeling the most vulnerable . . . he always said exactly the right thing at the right moment. He didn't allow me to cover myself up. He would grab my hands, look me straight in the eye and tell me something new about why he loved me" (175). By neither allowing one person to control the relationship nor instituting harmful measures to ensure constant equality, Waverly and Rich are bound to experience some conflicts in their future; however, there is a good chance that they can work through them by expressing themselves in the context of the meaningful, mutually respectful relationship they have established.

Waverly's relationship with Rich demonstrates that empowering, mutually respectful relationships are indeed possible for women who grew up influenced by traditional Chinese culture and can perhaps serve as a model for her peers. By novel's end, despite their broken marriages, Rose and Lena, too, show signs of moving toward the self-actualization that will enable them to construct healthy relationships in the future. Remarkably, the two women are both helped by their mothers, An-mei and Ying-ying, who decide to not only encourage and support their daughters in their quests for self-fulfillment but to share the stories of their own struggles and regrets with them in hopes of steering them in a different direction. This decision adds a new dimension to the struggle for female empowerment; as Marina Heung writes, "For An-mei and Ying-ying self-articulation remedies early teachings in silence and self-denial" (35). In essence, these women's determination to help their daughters ultimately enables them to reclaim their own identities by telling their stories. Thus, through the second generation's struggles and the original Joy Luck women's determination that their daughters be both empowered and fulfilled, Tan ultimately presents a hopeful vision that suggests that self-examination, communication, and perseverance can combine to help women leave behind traditions and family patterns that oppress them and work toward a healthier paradigm for themselves and their future relationships and families.

WORKS CITED

Heung, Marina. "Daughter-Text/Mother-Text: Matrileneage in Amy Tan's *Joy Luck Club*." *Amy Tan*. Modern Critical Views Series. New York: Chelsea House, 2000. 25–41.

Kazuko, Ono. *Chinese Women in a Century of Revolution, 1850–1950*. Ed. Joseph Fogel. Stanford, CA: Stanford UP, 1989.

Tan, Amy. *The Joy Luck Club*. New York: Penguin, 1989.

HOW TO WRITE ABOUT
AMY TAN

A S ONE of America's premier contemporary authors, Amy Tan provides students of literature with a dynamic, fresh, and still-growing body of work, much of which has yet to be analyzed in a rigorously critical fashion. While the number of possible interpretations of a piece of good literature theoretically approaches infinity, it is not difficult to feel as if "everything has already been said" when faced with the prospect of writing an essay on a classically canonical text such as *Hamlet.* One of the benefits of writing on a relatively new author such as Amy Tan—whose first novel appeared a little more than 20 years ago—is the exhilaration of reaching new interpretations of her works and characters without having to elbow your way through generations of critics who were there before you. In fact, it is quite possible that your reading of a particular facet of one of Tan's works might very well represent the very first time that anyone has ever looked at that work in precisely that way.

Just as with any author, though, writing about Tan's novels comes with a set of special challenges and considerations. That there may not be a huge body of criticism on Tan's works yet does not mean that you should be careless when approaching her work. Some of the biggest challenges when writing about Tan have to do with the fact that she is a living author. Often, when we read and write about authors from the past, we tend to forget that the books they produced were not immediately considered classics, that they were written originally for a literary marketplace by a person hoping to make a living through her writing. Shakespeare, for instance, no doubt poured his soul into his plays and hoped that they would endure beyond his lifetime, but he was also trying to please the London play-going public and put food on the table. With an author such as Amy Tan, we are much more aware of the "business" side of her writing because we are witness to its initial appearance in bookstores and are targeted by publicity and advertising for it. When her most recent book, *Saving Fish from Drowning*, appeared, we could watch as it climbed up the best-seller lists. Because several of the titles featured on the lists strike us as being a lot more entertaining than literary, we might be tempted to dismiss Tan's works merely as "good reads" but not worthy of serious critical study. Hopefully, what you have already read of Tan's work has convinced you of how wrong such an assumption would be. If not, then perhaps the range of essay topics suggested in this book will demonstrate how new, popular works can also be complex and meaningful.

A second pitfall to watch out for when analyzing the work of a living writer is the author's commentary on his or her own publications. Even when writing about long-dead authors, we have to take into consideration what the authors said about their creations; with living writers, this can be especially challenging simply because there has been no "final word" yet. In an interview next week, Amy Tan might make statements about *The Joy Luck Club* that seemingly undercut the interpretive essay you have just written on that novel. Sometimes this can make students hesitant to put forth a strongly opinionated thesis about the work of a contemporary writer, but it should not. While learning what an author thinks about her own works can be fascinating and can give us new viewpoints from which to approach the writing, the author's opinions in no way trump those of her readers, even when the author's opinions themselves are codified in print, as with Amy Tan's reflections on her writing process and output in *The Opposite of Fate: A Book of Musings*. One of the defining characteristics of good literature is that it carries and supports a vast multitude of interpretations, far more than the few interpretations that the author consciously strove for while creating it. Amy Tan can tell you what *The Joy Luck Club* means to her, but she can never tell you what it means to you. Nor can she even tell you with certainty all the meanings with which she encodes the story. As a great writer, Tan is blessed with a fecund and imaginative unconscious that expresses itself in ways that she cannot always see, much less control. So you should never feel constrained by the musings of a writer on her own works; as you compose your essay, you are the literary critic, and your job is to make sense of the text you have in front of you.

One particular facet of Tan's novels that requires careful consideration is the close interweaving between her fiction and her biography. The plots of many of her works closely mirror aspects of her own and her family member's lives. In *The Opposite of Fate*, she admits, "I'd never be able to borrow from a stranger's life to create my stories. What's *my* reason for writing the story in the first place, if not to masochistically examine my own life's confusion, my own hopes and unanswered prayers?" (109). Tan also has shared the story of how her mother, while proud of the success of *The Joy Luck Club*, did not feel like it did justice to her own life story and so admonished Amy to tell the story "right" the next time. That admonition led Tan to produce *The Kitchen God's Wife*, a powerful novel that reads so much like a biography of her mother that Daisy Tan reportedly became confused as to why the characters' names did not match the names of the people she knew from the real-life stories. If a piece of fiction comes so close to nonfiction as to confuse some of the principal characters, then readers at a further remove are certain to have difficulty trying to decide where to draw the line between creativity and reporting. The danger in confusing a work of fiction for fact is that, as readers, we tend to accept what is happening in the book as inarguably true, thus limiting our critical engagement with the characters and the structure of the plot. Regardless of how much detail Tan has borrowed from her own life or from family stories, the fact remains that the novels she has created are just that, creations. Though perhaps based on real people, her characters are controlled by her. As the author, she chooses which actions to emphasize and which to exclude, what the dialogue sounds like, and what the characters think. Ultimately, these are products of her imagination and can certainly be treated just as a fictional character can be.

Having stories based so closely on reality can open up new ways for us to look at Tan's work. For instance, finding out what you can about Daisy Tan's actual experiences and then comparing them to Winnie's experiences in *The Kitchen God's Wife* provides you with a set of contrasts that give you insight into what Amy Tan wanted to accomplish in her novel. Asking the questions "why did she change what she did?" and "why did she leave out what she did?" brings into sharp focus the difference between the biography and the constructed artistic work in ways that will most likely give you more than enough material for a good essay. This same strategy can be used to overcome the aforementioned challenge of dealing with a living writer's ongoing pronouncements on her own creations. When you read or hear that Amy Tan has said one thing about *The Bonesetter's Daughter* when you have interpreted it to mean something entirely different, think about why that is. Ask how the text supports both your and Tan's readings and how the contrast between the two might open up yet another, completely new interpretation between them. Rather than being intimidated by a living author, rejoice in the virtual conversation that the two of you can now have.

TOPICS AND STRATEGIES

The sample topics provided below are designed to provide some ideas for how you might approach writing an essay about a work of Tan's. Many of the samples will give you the titles of some possible works to focus on. Keep in mind the length of your essay when you are deciding on which works, and how many of them, you want to consider. You will want to make sure that you have adequate space to give thorough treatment to each work you address in your essay. You are certainly free to select works not mentioned in the sample topics as well. Bear in mind, too, that if you choose multiple texts, it is good to have a rationale for grouping those texts in your essay. Ideally, you do not want the determining factor simply to be which texts you already happened to have read. Instead, you might choose stories that were written at a certain period in history or stories that explore similar themes, for example.

Themes

One of the most common methods of approaching a piece of literature is to consider its themes, or major concerns. When we ask ourselves what a piece is really "about," or what it wants to say, we are trying to discern its themes. Of course, it is not enough to identify the topics with which a work is concerned. We must then investigate the text to discover what unique message the writer is conveying about a particular theme. Like many writers, Tan revisits the same, or similar, themes in several of her works. For instance, one of the subjects she seems to explore consistently in her novels is the relationship between mothers and daughters. It would not be enough, however, merely to note this pattern in an essay; instead, you want to examine closely what the works are saying about mother/daughter relationships. You might argue, for example, that according to *The Kitchen God's Wife* the close connection desired by most mothers and daughters is achieved at the cost of sharing one another's deepest and darkest secrets. Or you might argue that, across several of Tan's works, the message clearly emerges that, as important as the mother/daughter relationship may be, it is not strong enough ultimately to reach across generational and cultural divides, leaving each generation of daughters to fend for itself and forge its own paths.

Sample Topics:

1. **Mothers and daughters:** Tan's works are rife with mother/ daughter relationships, many of them strained. Her novels most often revolve around a mother and daughter trying to understand one another, with varying degrees of success. What do Tan's characters finally discover about this complex family relationship?

   Nearly any of Tan's works could be used in an essay on this topic. Tan's first novel, *The Joy Luck Club,* might be particularly useful simply because it presents so many variations on the theme, uncovering the dynamics between several pairs of mothers and daughters over more than two generations. *The Joy Luck Club* also provides an interesting twist in that Jing-mei takes her mother's place in the club, giving her the opportunity to experience being her mother in a sense. Both *The Kitchen God's Wife* and *The Bonesetter's Daughter* pick up some of the very same threads begun in *The Joy Luck Club* and spin them out in much greater detail, focusing specifically on the ways that daughters come to change their perceptions of their mothers as they learn more and more of their life stories. With any of these works, take careful note of how the relationships evolve. Pay close attention to how the mothers and daughters perceive one another at the beginning of the book and then compare that to how they perceive one another by book's end. What has changed? Why? Will these changes endure beyond the end of the story? What insights into mother/daughter dynamics does this provide?

2. **Quest for identity:** Most of Tan's works incorporate the immigrant experience, usually Chinese immigrants and their children in the United States. As if that alone did not offer enough challenges to one's identity, the narratives are usually begun by members of the younger generation who are trying desperately to define themselves in ways very distinct from their parents. What do Tan's novels have to say about identity, how it is formed, and how important it is to one's well-being?

Practically any of Tan's works would be an excellent choice for writing about this theme; however, some of her novels take a particularly interesting approach to wrestling with the complexities of identity. *Saving Fish from Drowning,* for instance, is narrated by Bibi Chen, a ghost. Though dead for the entirety of the book, Bibi seemingly learns new things about herself and even, perhaps, grows as a person after being given a front-row seat to the other characters' lives. One of Amy Tan's children's books, *The Moon Lady,* deals almost exclusively with little Ying-ying's quest for identity. From the harsh lessons she receives about what behaviors are appropriate for little girls to the fishing family's easy identification of her as a member of an upper-class family, Ying-ying's adventures teach her who she is, or at least who her culture expects her to be. Finally, not only does Tan explore identity issues through her fictive creations, but in *The Opposite of Fate* she explicitly tackles issues of authorial identity as well. Irrespective of which work or works you choose to work on, consider how identity is formed and shaped. Is identity something, according to Tan's novels, that is given to us by others—our society, parents, and friends? Or is identity a self-forged phenomenon, something created by the accretion of individual choices we make? How does learning about their mother's identities affect the identities of the daughters in these stories? How much does being Chinese, or being Chinese-American, determine the characters' identities?

3. **Romantic love:** Romantic love would most likely not be one of the first things most readers would associate with Tan's work.

However, romantic relationships and entanglements drive a great deal of the plot in most of her works. What do her novels have to say about the desirability of romantic attachment?

Behind the mother/daughter dynamics, *The Joy Luck Club* is concerned with romantic love. In fact, the novel focuses over and over again on the relationships between the daughters and their spouses and lovers. Most of these relationships seem to be doomed, a theme that appears again and again in Tan's writing. As brutal a novel as it is, *The Kitchen God's Wife* could be interpreted as a novel about love. Winnie suffers mightily at the hands of Wen Fu, her first husband, but finds happiness and rescue at last in the form of Jimmy Louie, her second husband. The characters' trip to China in *The Bonesetter's Daughter*—along with the important discoveries and plot points that follow—is driven primarily by Kwan's scheming to salvage Simon and Olivia's marriage (and, in her mind, to reunite Nelly and Yiban, the doomed lovers of a previous lifetime). Approached objectively, it would seem that the failed and ugly relationships far outweigh the positive, affirming ones in Tan's body of work. Why is this? Are the examples of good love enough to redeem all of the reminders of frustrated or disappointed love? What makes the successful pairings better than the unsuccessful ones? Are these couplings, both happy and not so, the result of the characters' actions or are they fate? Does Tan seem to be saying at times that romantic happiness can only come after one has paid the price of romantic despair?

Character

If you are having difficulty devising a topic or method of critical approach to a piece of literature, it can be helpful to begin with an examination of its characters. List all of the characters and their traits, noting whether or not they develop during the course of the story or novel. Record what you know about the characters' relationships with one another as well. Then, you might look for any patterns—is there something interesting to be said about Tan's portrayal of immigrants? Or men? Or perhaps you might choose to focus on a particular character who changes in an interesting way, analyzing his or her development and the reasons for and results of this evolution. Or there might be a particular relationship or group of relationships you can analyze and evaluate—romantic pairings or parent/child relations, for example.

Sample Topics:

1. **First-generation immigrant characters:** One thing common to all of Tan's works is the inclusion of immigrant characters who meet with varying degrees of success at settling into life in the United States. What do these characters have in common, and how do they differ? What is Tan trying to convey through her novels about the immigrant experience?

   This is one theme for which, quite literally, any of Tan's works would be appropriate, though the children's books do not provide as much material to work with and might need to be combined with one of the longer works. To write an essay on one or more of these characters, it is important to demarcate as precisely as possible how the immigrant experience has affected them. Why did they leave their native country? And why did they end up in the United States? Are they happy with their lives in the United States or do they dream of returning home one day? In the United States, do they cling to traditions from their original country or do they embrace American culture wholeheartedly? Using evidence gathered from the text and your imagination, think about how they would be different people had they not left their homelands. With that in mind, are they better people for having immigrated to the United States? Somehow worse? Or, simply different?

2. **Second-generation characters:** Paired with the ubiquity of first-generation immigrant characters are their children, the second-generation Americans. How are the various second-generation characters alike? How much does their status as the children of immigrants affect their core identity? How does Tan seem to feel about this status, one that she shares with these characters?

   Again, any of Tan's novels, or even her collection of essays, *The Opposite of Fate*, would prove fertile ground for an essay on this subject. Even if you choose to write on a single character, it will be useful during your research phase to study more than one character at first. Look carefully at several of the second-generation immigrant characters. What experiences and circumstances do they all have in common? What traits? Are the similar traits a necessary result of their similar experiences and circumstances? What ranges of reactions do these characters display in dealing with their first-generation immigrant families? Are they proud of their families' heritages, or would they prefer to be fully assimilated into American culture? Are their feelings on this topic static, or do they change as the characters age and learn more about their parents' histories? What seems to be the essential characteristic of the second-generation characters? Does Tan seem to suggest that this characteristic is ultimately a blessing or a curse?

3. **Male characters:** While the main characters of Tan's novels are inevitably women, her fictional universe is populated by a great many male characters, many of whom tend to stand in the way of the female characters. Tan has even been accused of creating male characters who are either vicious or flat. Is this true? Do Tan's male characters have anything to teach us?

Tan's stories contain their fair share of villainous men. Wen Fu of *The Kitchen God's Wife* is perhaps the epitome of the monstrous male characters that Tan is capable of portraying. Chang, the coffin maker of *The Bonesetter's Daughter*, is similarly despicable, like Wen Fu willing to destroy others for the slightest gains for himself. However, these characters are often set against other much more respectable male characters in the same work. For instance, Jimmy Louie becomes Winnie's salvation from Wen Fu, while Kai Jing provides a counterpoint to Chang. Further complicating matters, the "good" men, like Jimmy Louie and Kai Jing, tend to die early and often violently, long before they have had a chance to evolve as characters in the same way that the female characters do. The question then becomes: Does Tan create any fully realized three-dimensional male characters? Or are they all unspeakable villains, typecast heroes, or flat background characters? If so, what implications does this have for Tan's worldview? Why not focus on developing more fully formed male characters? If you find in your own research male characters who seem, to your estimation, to be fully formed, why do readers tend not to pick up on the complexities of these particular individuals?

History and Context

Tan's works often cross international lines and reach back to historical time periods that are not always familiar to a 21st-century Western audience. Most of *The Kitchen God's Wife*, for instance, takes place in China during the Sino-Japanese War, World War II, and the Chinese Revolution, which itself consisted of the final few years of the decades-long Chinese Civil War. These events do not merely provide a scenic backdrop for the story, they drive much of the action and determine and influence many of the characters' behaviors. One of Tan's only works not to focus primarily on China, *Saving Fish from Drowning*, still takes readers to a foreign land, in this case Myanmar, and introduces them to strong political undercurrents that many of us might not be familiar with. Even those works, or parts of a work, set in the United States tend to be filled with nuances of culture, particular the culture of the Chinese-American immigrants, that many readers will find unfamiliar. Attaining some background knowledge of Chinese history or Chinese traditions and acknowledging the context of these works can prove extremely valuable to your understanding of them and can also help you to arrive at an interesting idea for your essay. You will want to learn not only what major historical events were happening in the given time period, but you will also want to investigate what people believed. What ideas were important? Which were being challenged or revised? Once you have learned this, you can return to Tan's works with a sharper gaze in order to determine what her prose is saying about the society in which her characters live and grow.

Sample Topics:

1. **The Chinese Revolution:** Not coincidentally, many of Tan's Chinese immigrant characters left China for the United States in 1949, the year when it became evident the Communists were going to win the long Chinese Civil War. What role did the triumph of the Communists in China and the Chinese Revolution in general play in the lives of these characters? How would all of these characters' lives—and their children's lives—have changed had the Kuomintang been victorious instead?

Perhaps more than any of her other novels, Tan's *The Kitchen God's Wife* requires some knowledge of the Chinese Revolution—as well as other important historical events in China, such as the Sino-Japanese War—to appreciate it fully. Examine how the fortunes of the various sides influence the course of Winnie's life in China, for instance. How might Wen Fu have been a different person had he been fighting for the victorious side instead? How did the privations of war, particularly as supporters of the Kuomintang, irrevocably change the lives of Winnie and her first children? Scrutinize what happens to Winnie's father because of his entanglements with both the Communists and the Kuomintang. Would he ultimately have sacrificed to save Winnie had he not been ruined by the war? And, lest we carry too much Western bias to the story, consider that it is through the help of the Communists, in the form of Peanut and her revolutionary friends, that Winnie ultimately finds a support network that aids her in escaping from Wen Fu. In order to understand more fully the ways that the revolution shaped China and the Chinese at this time, do some background research. Begin with a source such as Paul Bailey's *China in the Twentieth Century* or John E. Schrecker's *The Chinese Revolution in Historical Perspective.* Your reading will prepare you to work on most of Tan's works, from better understanding why Kwan and Olivia's father fled China the way he did in *The Hundred Secret Senses* to appreciating most of the histories of the older generation of *The Joy Luck Club* to perhaps tracing the ways that the wars in China affected Daisy Tan and shaped her into the mother who had such a big influence on her daughter as an author, as is partially revealed in *The Opposite of Fate.*

2. **Chinese-American immigrant experience:** Although Tan sets most of her books primarily in the United States—usually in San Francisco, in particular—her characters inhabit a space that is more Chinese-American than strictly American. The heavily ethnic enclaves Tan's families inhabit, as well as the Chinese associations they consciously strive to maintain, make their experience in the United States unlike the generic American experience, if such a thing can be imagined. How do these

characters' particularly hybrid lifestyles affect their experience of America and its values?

Considering the peculiar experiences of Chinese immigrants and their American-born progeny is an appropriate approach to take with any of Tan's adult novels and will probably require you to do some background reading to get started. A couple of good places to begin your research would be *Becoming Asian-American: Second-Generation Chinese and Korean American Identities* by Nazli Kabria or *Chinese Americans and Their Immigrant Parents: Conflict, Identity, and Values* by May Tung. Armed with a deeper understanding of the challenges facing these immigrant families, return to Tan's fiction. Are her depictions of Chinese-American life realistic according to your research? What particular challenges and features of immigrant life has she chosen to emphasize? And which features does she not acknowledge? Can an understanding of immigrant culture help you to understand the motivations that drive the characters? What does Tan seem to say about assimilation versus retaining one's original culture?

Philosophy and Ideas

Another way to approach a piece of literature is to think about what social ideas or philosophies it comments on or engages in some way. Many of Tan's works concern characters who are grappling with the idea of what it means to be American, for example. Tan's characters often wonder, does being born in the United States automatically confer Americanness on someone, or does one have to embody certain traits and beliefs? Even more complicated questions arise in Tan's novels having to do with ideas of free will and fate, topics wrestled with since the beginning of organized thought by philosophers and thinkers of every culture. For the characters in these novels, though, such concepts are more than mere intellectual abstractions; they have everything to do with these individuals' everyday lives. Like most writers, Tan often works more at exploring these ideas than at trying to provide some definitive answer. These philosophical ideas are ones that we all must confront from time to time, and approaching them through the context of a well-wrought piece of fiction often feels like a more organic and accessible way to begin our own discussions on these topics than tackling tomes of hard-core philosophy.

Sample Topics:

1. **Cultural identity/Americanness:** Tan's work often deals with people straddling two, or sometimes more, cultures, usually Chinese and American. In the clash between these two very different cultures, characters are often left flailing, trying to grasp a solid cultural identity for themselves or, in some cases, trying desperately to escape one culture in favor of another. What do these characters and situations tell us about what it means to belong to a particular culture? What defines an American as an American? And can one adopt Americanness, or Chineseness, at will?

   All of Tan's novels and essays deal heavily with this question. For the most part, characters of the second generation try to define themselves as American, particularly during their younger years when their parents' habits and customs—so foreign and strange when contrasted to their American playmates' parents—embarrass them socially. In these cases, the characters are able to observe the larger culture of the United States at will, trying to discern exactly what it is that makes their family so different and what they can do to fit in better with their American-born peers than with their Chinese-born parents. *The Hundred Secret Senses* enacts this concept by having an American-born girl suddenly find herself living, still in the United States, with a newly discovered, smothering Chinese sister who brings with her the oddest and most embarrassing behaviors. The contrast takes another turn later in the novel when Olivia travels to China with Simon and Kwan and finds herself suddenly the odd one. This paradigm is taken to an extreme in *Saving Fish from Drowning,* in which the tour group becomes cut off from all things Western, an American bubble in the middle of Myanmar. Cultural contrasts are thrown into sharp relief, and, at times, the Americans themselves seem to have trouble figuring out exactly what makes them American. How do these questions of cultural identity play out in Tan's body of work? Does she ever seem to have an answer to the underlying question of what makes one an American? Does the question itself seem to become more or less important over the course of her novels?

2. **Fate versus free will:** Fate is a word, and an idea, that pops up obsessively in Amy Tan's writing, even appearing in the title of her collection of autobiographical essays, *The Opposite of Fate.* Generally, the Chinese characters in her novels tend to believe strongly in the forces of fate, while the second-generation American characters hold tight to notions of free will. How does this ideological divide tend to be resolved in Tan's works?

Approach this topic by rereading the novel you are working on with this issue of fate and free will firmly in mind. What parts of the novel suggest that our lives are governed by fate or destiny? Are there other aspects of the story that indicate that free will plays a role as well? In what specific instances do the characters seem to be forced along preordained paths, and in what instances do they seem to make independent, spontaneous decisions? Can you spot a pattern or make a generalization about what seems to control the direction of these characters' lives? Does one character's belief system tend to become a self-fulfilling prophecy? For instance, does Kwan's insistence on fated reincarnation in *The Hundred Secret Senses* mean that she ends up seeing patterns in her and Olivia's lives that she forces to match her stories about Nunumu and Nelly Banner? Does she then take actions that further reinforce the supposed similarities until it begins to seem like the parallels have been fated rather than generated by her own actions?

3. **Evil:** While, on the whole, Tan's novels end on positive, affirming notes, the characters often have to survive incredible cruelty and misery in order to reach their happy endings. What do Tan's works have to say about the existence of evil in the world?

Nearly all of Tan's novels are partly informed by a dark vision. Though the novel tends to make light of them, *Saving Fish from Drowning* brushes against the dangers of a repressive regime in Myanmar. In *The Hundred Secret Senses,* characters are forced to perform cannibalistic acts for the general's amusement, while Chang, in *The Bonesetter's Daughter,* appears to have little conscience when it comes to getting what he wants. However, *The Kitchen God's Wife* reigns supreme among Tan's oeuvre for exploring the darkness of the human heart. In it, readers are exposed to systematic and organized evil in the rape of Nanking and an individualized portrait of evil in the character of Wen Fu. What do you make of Tan's portrayal of evil in these works? Is it true evil or merely ignorance? Can a person like Wen Fu ever be redeemed, or is he something less than human? Does Tan seem to suggest that much of the goodness in the world results from the reaction of good people to evil, meaning that, in some ways, evil is a necessary part of human existence? Does good win out over evil in the end, according to Tan's view?

Form and Genre

Thinking about the building blocks that Tan used to create her texts can be very instructive. Analyzing the form and genre of a piece can help you to arrive at a strong claim in your essay and provide you with the evidence to support it. You might consider, for example, where Tan got her ideas; is the novel you are writing about based on biographical details from her own life or her mother's life? If so, you will want to think about how learning these details can help you to arrive at a better understanding of the work's themes and meanings. You will want to study also how the novel is put together. Are the events presented in strictly chronological order? Does it shift between the present and past? If there are multiple levels of stories, which seems to be the most important? What function do the secondary stories fulfill in relationship to the master narrative? Is the order in which the various narratives are told important? You will also want to consider the actual telling of the story. Who is the narrator? What do we know about him or her? How does the narrator affect our interpretation of the events he or she presents to us? When we think about form and genre, it is helpful to keep in mind that the author is a careful artist who makes deliberate decisions about what stories to tell and precisely how to tell them; thus, you are justified in your effort to figure out how these decisions contribute to the meaning of a work, and your analysis of the story or novel's inspiration, structure, and/or narration can help you to arrive at an interpretation to present in your essay.

Sample Topics:

1. **Narration:** Questions of narrative choices and consequences abound in Amy Tan's work. Rarely opting for a straightforward,

single narratorial scheme, much of the deeper meaning of Tan's work can be accessed by examining the way that the story is told as much as by examining the story itself.

Explore Tan's repertoire of narrative technique and think about the implications of her choices. In *The Joy Luck Club,* each of the women tells her story, giving us at least eight different narrators for this single work. In *The Kitchen God's Wife, The Hundred Secret Senses,* and *The Bonesetter's Daughter,* the main narrative, which takes place sometime in the past, is framed by an outer narrative, told by a different narrator, set in the present. Often these embedded narratives are further complicated by the inclusion of even more deeply nested narrations within narrations. In her children's books, Tan employs older narrators who tell stories of the past to their younger listeners. In *Saving Fish from Drowning,* we are presented with an omniscient first-person narrator, omniscient because she is a ghost. And in *The Opposite of Fate,* Tan herself—or, more precisely, a constructed persona called Amy Tan—speaks directly to the reader. What do these narrative choices ultimately mean for the works? What is the effect, for instance, of having multiple narrators in a single novel? What does that allow Tan to accomplish that a single narrator could not? How would these novels differ if alternate narrative choices had been made? How would *Saving Fish from Drowning* play out, for instance, if one of the living characters were to take over the duties of narrating? Looking at this vast array of narrative options and the way that Tan wields them, what can you say about Tan's beliefs about how stories are told?

2. **Biographical connections:** Like all writers, Tan takes her initial inspiration for her fiction from her own life. To a greater degree than some other writers, however, she sticks closely to the events and family stories that have inspired her, sometimes making it difficult to draw the line between memoir and fiction. What effect does her generous reliance on biographical and autobiographical detail ultimately have on the way that we read her works?

In writing an essay on this topic, the place to begin is Tan's collection of essays, *The Opposite of Fate*. In this work of non-fiction, she willingly reveals a number of details—from her life—and from the lives of her mother and grandmother—that served as the basis for her fiction. After reading *The Opposite of Fate*, turn to one of the novels—particularly *The Joy Luck Club, The Kitchen God's Wife*, or *The Bonesetter's Daughter*—and read it, keeping close track of what details from the novel are clearly taken from real-life events. Which details did Tan choose to include? To leave out? What names, places, and events did she alter? And which did she add from her own imagination? The stories from her and her family's lives are compelling in and of themselves; why, then, did Tan choose to fictionalize them rather than writing them as nonfiction? What does fiction allow her to do that nonfiction would not? How is your reading of the novel affected by your knowledge of the actual inspiration?

3. **Organization:** Rarely does Tan adhere to a strictly chronological telling of a story for more than a chapter at a time. What effect does this sort of structure, the constant moving back and forth between past and present, have on her novels?

Though never fragmented, Tan's novels are never quite linear either. *The Joy Luck Club* moves between the past and the present of both the mothers and the daughters, geographically shifting from China to the United States, from the distant past to the present moment. Several of the other novels are framed by present-time narration but cut away for the bulk of the novel to events from the past, related by narrators other than the original speaker. Even these embedded narrations are broken up frequently by interpolations of present events. The result of these strategies is often the paralleling of two separate narratives, each with its own cast of distinct characters and setting. Why do you think Tan chooses to structure her novels like this? What would be the effect of a more linear tale as opposed to the constantly shifting focus? What connections does Tan seem to be making by shuttling the narrative between the past and the present?

Symbols, Imagery, and Language

Works of literature are filled with symbols and images that can lead us to significant discoveries about the themes and meanings of the piece. When reading, we should pay close attention to images that recur throughout a piece and to images that seem to be especially significant because of the attention the author devotes to them or their location near an important scene or character. Once you have identified potentially meaningful images and symbols, you will want to close read the passages that include them. First, ask yourself what traditional associations these images or symbols carry, and then look closely at the particular way they function in the literary work you are studying. Is the author enhancing an image's traditional associations or perhaps transforming them in some way? Once you have some ideas about the meaning of a particular image, think about ways to connect these insights to the central ideas of the work. How does what you have discovered about a symbol or image help you to interpret the story or novel? You can look at symbols and images within a single work or locate similar images in multiple works if you wish to consider Tan's work as a whole instead of focusing on a single text. In addition to symbols and imagery, you will want to pay close attention to the author's language as you read. It is helpful to keep in mind that the English language contains many ways to say the same thing. Thinking about why the author chose exactly the words that she did and not other options available will often lead to meaningful discoveries about a work's theme that can help you to construct or support a claim in your essay.

Sample Topics:

1. **Chinese characters and English speech:** Having so many first-generation and second-generation Chinese-American characters in her works, Tan has to deal with the problems of language barriers and communication. What are the implications of the ways she confronts these issues in her works?

   As a writer, Tan has to deal with certain challenges that arise from her own creations. For instance, quite a few of her works feature first-generation immigrants whose command of the English language is shaky at best. At the same time, Tan wants to have these characters narrate a large portion of the story being told. If she is sensitive to her readers' needs, however, it is unlikely that she will include several hundred pages of narrative in broken English. How does she deal with this challenge in her novels? What does it mean, for instance, that Ruth of *The Bone-setter's Daughter* grows up mortified by her mother's inability even to pronounce her name correctly in English yet ends up not being able to read the manuscript in which LuLing has written her life story? Does the fact that she ultimately has to hire a translator have an impact on the relationship between mother and daughter? How does it affect the story in *The Hundred Secret Senses* that Olivia does speak Chinese—learning it from Kwan as a child—so that Kwan is able to switch between clumsy English and more elegant Chinese narration? And what of situations like the St. Clair household in *The Joy Luck Club*, where Ying-ying, because she never learned to speak English intelligibly, is at the will of her husband's capricious translations?

2. **Funerals:** One scene that recurs throughout Tan's works is that of funerals. In and of itself, a funeral is a highly symbolic event, full of pomp and ceremony intended to send off the deceased in a prescribed manner and to bring meaningful closure to the survivors. Why does Tan revisit this scene so often, and what can you intuit about her feelings about death and mourning from her portrayal of funerals in her fiction?

Whether the sedate funeral of China Mary that Rose and her mother attend in *The Joy Luck Club*, the wake for her murdered friend at which Tan had a psychic experience as she describes it in *The Opposite of Fate*, the long-delayed, rural Chinese funeral for Big Ma in *The Hundred Secret Senses*, or the fabulous and ornate send-off for Bibi in *Saving Fish from Drowning*, final farewells always make an appearance in Tan's works. Because this is a symbolic act that not everyone agrees on—some people think funerals are necessary rites, some hate them and refuse to attend—this is a particularly telling moment to examine in these novels. What is Tan attempting to accomplish with these scenes? Are they marked by grief or by celebration? Are they private affairs or public? Is there a sense of solemnity in the way she orchestrates these scenes, or are they more lighthearted? What might Tan be trying to convey about the meaning of death and grief in the way that she describes these funeral scenes in her works?

Compare and Contrast Essays

Setting two elements side by side in order to determine their similarities and differences can be illuminating to your thinking and writing. You might choose two elements that seem similar to you and spend some time focusing on their distinguishing characteristics, or you might select two elements that seem very different and examine them closely for underlying similarities. You can choose elements within a single work, elements in two or more works by the same author, or even elements in works by different authors. You will want, of course, not only to identify differences and similarities but to choose the most meaningful ones and interpret them for your reader. This way, your essay will not amount to a list of interesting details but will instead use significant similarities and differences to make a point about the work(s) you are analyzing.

Sample Topics:

1. **Amy Tan's novels compared to the works of Louise Erdrich or Maxine Hong Kingston:** How do Amy Tan's novels compare to the work of two other contemporary American female authors who write on similar subjects?

   Tan, Erdrich, and Kingston are authors with very different styles and artistic concerns; however, they are contemporary authors, all three American, all three women, and all three writing about often marginalized ethnic groups that lie outside mainstream America. Therefore, comparing and contrasting the works of these three authors is potentially rich and especially so on issues that would matter to all three, such as the assimilation of groups into the mainstream, the importance of cultural heritage, and generational differences among culturally unique groups. Any of these authors' works are suitable for comparison, though Erdrich's *Love Medicine* and

Kingston's *The Woman Warrior* are most often compared to Tan's works. Whichever works you choose to look at, pay close attention to those issues that appear in all the authors' fiction. Why are these issues important to these authors? How does each of them portray the issue differently? What accounts for these differences? And what messages about these issues comes through when studying all three authors' works together?

2. **Amy Tan's old and new Chinas:** One contrast that appears repeatedly in Tan's novels is that between the China of yesteryear and the nation today. Several of her characters are born and raised in China, leave for the United States for many years, and then return—though only for a visit—to China after several decades of absence. How does Tan portray the differences in the China of memory versus the China of direct, present experience in these works?

Characters are constantly crossing the Pacific in Amy Tan's works. The primary pattern is that the older generation is born in China, spends its formative years there, and then leaves for the United States, usually as a result of the Communist takeover in 1949. After many decades in the new land, they, usually the women, visit China, almost always with their grown American daughters in tow. Invariably, things have changed during their long absence, but, strikingly, many things are remarkably unchanged for so many of the characters, as if they really have managed to go home again. The pattern has a number of variations, of course. In *The Joy Luck Club*, Jingmei goes in place of her dead mother. In *The Hundred Secret Senses*, Kwan never returns from China. In *Saving Fish from Drowning*, Bibi returns to China as a ghost and only on her way to Myanmar with the tour group. Across the course of her fictional universe, what elements of both old and new China does Tan choose to highlight consistently? What are the characters' reactions to returning to China after such a long absence? Is there a sense that the cultural connection to one's place of birth is unbreakable and eternal? Or do things change so much that these characters are forced to take refuge in their memories? How does going to China affect the younger generations that were not born there? Do they have a connection to their parents' homelands or not?

Bibliography

Bailey, Paul. *China in the Twentieth Century.* Malen, MA: Wiley-Blackwell, 2001.

Bloom, Harold, ed. *Amy Tan.* Modern Critical Views. Philadelphia: Chelsea House, 2000.

Huntley, E. D. *Amy Tan: A Critical Companion.* Critical Companions to Popular Contemporary Writers. Westport, CT: Greenwood, 1998.

Kabria, Nazli. *Becoming Asian-American: Second-Generation Chinese and Korean American Identities.* Baltimore: Johns Hopkins UP, 2002.

Morton, W. Scott. *China: Its History and Culture.* 3rd ed. New York: McGraw-Hill, 1995.

Roberts, J. A. G. *A Concise History of China.* Cambridge, MA: Harvard UP, 1999.

Schrecker, John E. *The Chinese Revolution in Historical Perspective.* 2nd ed. Westport, CT: Praeger, 2004.

Shields, Charles J. *Amy Tan.* Women of Achievement. Philadelphia: Chelsea House, 2002.

Tan, Amy. *The Bonesetter's Daughter.* New York: Penguin, 1991.

———. *The Chinese Siamese Cat.* New York: Macmillan, 1994

———. *The Hundred Secret Senses.* New York: Putnam's, 1995.

———. *The Joy Luck Club.* New York: Penguin, 2006.

———. *The Kitchen God's Wife.* New York: Putnam's, 1991.

———. *The Moon Lady.* New York: Macmillan, 1992.

———. *The Opposite of Fate: A Book of Musings.* New York: Putnam's, 2003.

———. *Saving Fish from Drowning.* New York: Putnam's, 2005.

Tung, May Paomay. *Chinese Americans and Their Immigrant Parents: Conflict, Identity, and Values.* Binghamton, NY: Haworth Clinical Practice, 2000.

THE JOY LUCK CLUB

READING TO WRITE

A MY TAN's first novel, *The Joy Luck Club* (1989), quickly earned her both a large fan base and much critical praise. It became a sort of cultural phenomenon, translated into many languages, including Chinese, taught in classrooms across the country, and made into a popular movie, which Tan coproduced and for which she cowrote the screenplay. The novel centers on four Chinese immigrants and their American-born daughters. The women have formed a Joy Luck Club, which meets every week for the purpose of sharing and validating the women's experiences and giving the members of the group a sense of community. Suyuan Woo founded this San Francisco group based on a similar gathering she had begun back in wartime China. In the following passage Suyuan justifies the existence of the original Joy Luck Club, an endeavor that some criticized for indulging in joy while so much trauma and pain surrounded them:

> It's not that we had no heart or eyes for pain. We were all afraid. We all had our miseries. But to despair was to wish back for something already lost. Or to prolong what was already unbearable. How much can you wish for a favorite warm coat that hangs in the closet of a house that burned down with your mother and father inside of it? How long can you see in your mind arms and legs hanging from telephone wires and starving dogs running down the streets with half-chewed hands dangling from their jaws? What was worse, we asked among ourselves, to sit and wait for our own deaths with proper somber faces? Or to choose our own happiness? (25)

Acknowledging the public outcry against a social gathering focusing on luck and joy during such a chaotic and brutal time and the assumptions by some community members that the women of the Joy Luck Club must either be emotionally unbalanced or somehow insulated from the pain and loss surrounding them, Suyuan explains just how erroneous these conclusions were. The Joy Luck members were in no way ignorant of the pain occurring around them; they suffered their own fears and "miseries," just like everyone else. Suyuan suggests that it was the very intensity of their suffering that made it imperative for the women to somehow cut themselves off from the pain they had experienced in order to survive.

Suyuan conveys the severity of the situation by introducing a loss many readers will instantly connect with and then illustrating how small that loss actually is compared with the traumas that she and others like her faced. When Suyuan speaks about wishing for a favorite coat that was lost in a fire, we feel a sympathetic response for the loss of something special; however, when she continues to describe the coat as the one that "hangs in the closet of a house that burned down with your mother and father inside of it," she takes us into a world in which our powers of empathy fail us, a world in which the losses are not simply of a special garment or even a childhood home but of an entire family. She then makes even this loss seem almost inconsequential by following it with an especially graphic and horrific description of "starving dogs running down the streets with half-chewed hands dangling from their jaws," a scene emblematic of the breakdown of the very fabric of society. Suyuan introduces this scene with the phrase "How long can you see in your mind," revealing that she is recounting not simply a scene that she once witnessed firsthand but one that has obviously replayed itself continuously in her mind. The progression of the images in this scene—from comfort in the form of a warm coat to the loss of home and family by fire to gruesome dismemberment and a reversal of the hierarchy of human and animal—suggests a world rapidly descending into chaos. Suyuan's response, however, rather than progressive, is direct, sudden, final, and rational. There is a limit, Suyuan suggests, to how much suffering and trial the mind can take. As long as we are masters of our own minds, she implies, we ultimately have the choice of how to confront even the most horrendous of circumstances.

The Joy Luck women feel that they have two choices, to try to stay connected to the violence and trauma that surrounds them as their critics would have them do, which would mean, in Suyuan's words, that the women would simply "sit and wait for [their] own deaths with proper somber faces." Alternatively, they could "choose [their] own happiness," cutting themselves off, at least for a period each week, from reality and redefining their world as one of hope and happiness.

An examination of this passage provides us with a glimpse into Suyuan's world and the processes by which she copes with trauma, and it can inspire us to ask further questions that might ultimately lead to an essay topic or thesis. You might, for instance, examine the rest of the novel for the ramifications of shielding or cutting oneself off from individual losses. The mind might only be able to experience horrible things for so long, but for how long can it look away? Alternatively, you might examine the way that other characters handle trauma, or you might compare the origins and function of the Joy Luck Club of China to Suyuan's new version in the United States. Whatever line of inquiry you decide to pursue, you will want to identify several relevant passages and bring deliberate attention to Tan's carefully crafted language in order to arrive at an insightful claim to make in your essay.

TOPICS AND STRATEGIES

The following topic suggestions are designed to help spark your thinking and to help you along in the planning process of your essay. Avoid approaching them as test questions in which you move from beginning to end, carefully answering all of the subsections. Instead, pick and choose the parts of the topics that seem interesting and relevant. Combine topics, if you wish, or use a subject or element mentioned briefly in a topic suggestion to come up with a new topic of your own. Whatever subject you end up selecting, remember that the key to a successful essay is thorough planning. You must spend time rereading the text, doing research, and taking notes. The more attention you pay to this stage of the writing process, the easier writing the actual essay will be and the better the quality of the argument and evidence presented in the essay.

Themes

The Joy Luck Club offers a complicated and richly nuanced examination of two broad themes: the intersection of ethnicity, cultural heritage, and identity and also the relationships between mothers and daughters, which are themselves profoundly affected by cultural differences. There is too much to be said about either of these topics in one essay. If you choose to tackle either of them, the key to success will be to narrow your focus to something more manageable. If you choose to write about ethnicity, cultural heritage, and identity, for example, you might choose to concentrate on how the Joy Luck mothers acclimated to life in the United States or analyze to what extent their Chinese background and ethnicity shapes the lives of the American-born daughters. If you write about mother/daughter relationships, you might wish to narrow your focus to one of the specific parent/child pairs, or you might wish to write about how the mothers as a group regard their daughters or vice versa.

Sample Topics:

1. **Ethnicity, cultural heritage, and identity:** According to the novel, the Joy Luck mothers wanted their children to have "American circumstances" with "Chinese character." They wanted their children to think and behave in a traditionally Chinese manner while enjoying all of the opportunities and freedoms available to them as Americans. The mothers, however, feel that their daughters have turned out to be much more American than they had hoped, leading them to fear that their daughters are losing something of great importance: their Chinese heritage and their connection to their pasts, including their own mothers' stories. What is the novel ultimately trying to say about the nexus of ethnicity, cultural heritage, and identity?

   According to Chinese belief, "Your mother is in your bones" (Huntley 63). In other words, there is a fundamental interconnectedness among generations. As An-mei puts it: "I was born to my mother and I was born a girl. All of us are like stairs, one step after another, going up and down, but all going the same way" (215). Critic E. D. Huntley writes that, "Unfortunately, [the] American daughters do not recognize a symbiotic relationship between mothers and daughters; these second-generation Americans see only that their mothers appear to be trying to live through their children" (63). Additionally, the daughters resist following the goals and paths that their families dream up for them. Huntley continues: "Because they have been schooled in the tradition of individuality, the daughters resist their mothers' attempts to define their lives or to participate vicariously in their accomplishments" (63).

Go back to the novel with these thoughts in mind. Do you think the mothers' expectations that their daughters have "Chinese character" and "American circumstances" are realistic or even possible? Why or why not? Do you think the daughters have little or no Chinese in them as some of the mothers lament, or is there a Chinese foundation somewhere inside them, as Suyuan insisted, that will some day rise to the surface? What, according to the novel, are the most important factors of identity formation? Is cultural background, ethnicity, or current environment the most powerful factor?

2. **Mother/daughter relationships:** One of the most poignant aspects of *The Joy Luck Club* is the nature of the tense and complicated relationships between the mothers and their daughters. They all seem to be good, decent people who feel genuine affection for each other, but somehow misunderstandings, hurt feelings, and disappointments characterize their relationships. Write an essay in which you analyze the mother/daughter relationships of *The Joy Luck Club,* explaining their difficulties and tensions and evaluating whether any of the pairs seem to be on the path to a more constructive kind of interaction.

For this essay, you might look at all of the mother/daughter pairs, or you might restrict your study to one or two of them. No matter what specific approach you adopt, you will want to pay particular attention to the discrepancies between what the women want their relationships to be and what they, in fact, are. How can you explain the way these relationships are continually thwarted despite the best intentions of the women? Are there any ways that these relationships could be structured or managed so that they would work better, or are they fundamentally flawed?

3. **Community:** Suyuan begins the first Joy Luck Club in China during the Sino-Japanese War. She tells many stories to Jing-mei about this original club, including the way that the members

feasted together on the meager food that was available, played mah jong for luck, and told happy, funny stories late into the night. After arriving in San Francisco in 1949, Suyuan begins another Joy Luck Club, this one lasting for decades, at least until the 1980s when the novel is set. Obviously, the women benefit from this interaction. What exactly are these benefits? What need does this group fill in these women's lives?

Think about both clubs, the original one in China and the new one in San Francisco. How are the two incarnations of the club similar and different? How does the San Francisco club evolve during its long existence? Why do you think it continues to exist? What role does it play in the families' lives? Examine the differences in the circumstances of the mothers, when they were young, and the daughters. Is it possible that the existence of the Joy Luck Club in one generation makes its existence in the next generation unnecessary?

What did the daughters think about the Joy Luck Club as they were growing up? What do they think of it now as adults? None of the daughters are eager to become a member of such a club. Do they have different needs from their mothers, or are they simply having these needs fulfilled in a different way?

4. **Trauma:** We learn through the course of the novel of the major traumatic events in the lives of Suyuan, Lindo, Ying-ying, and An-mei. Many of these involve in some way the loss of a child. Suyuan is forced to abandon her twin baby girls as she retreats from Kweilin. Lindo loses a 16-year-old son to a car accident, while An-mei loses her four-year-old son, Bing, to a drowning accident. Ying-ying aborts her first child after her husband leaves her for another woman. How do these women handle these traumatic events, and how do these events shape them?

Think about the traumas endured by these women. How does each woman process and deal with everything she has endured? Does any woman's method seem to be preferable to the others'? Have they told their husbands and their daughters about these tragedies? Have they told one another? What are

the consequences of these decisions about sharing or with-
holding these formative experiences? You might also consider
whether the loss of a child functions as a metaphor in this
novel. What might the lost child stand for?

5. **Masculinity:** Because all of the eight main characters of *The
Joy Luck Club* are female, we have a strong tendency to think
about what the novel has to tell us about femininity and the role
of women in society. While that is an invaluable line of inquiry,
it is also worthwhile to ask how the novel constructs masculinity. According to *The Joy Luck Club*, what does it mean to be a
man?

Jot down all of the male characters in the novel and what you
know about them. What patterns can you discern? What do
you know about Joy Luck fathers? What were their relationships
like with their wives? With their daughters? What about the
daughters' romantic partners: What sort of masculinity do they
embody? Is it a model similar to their fathers? How rooted in
culture and time does masculinity seem to be? How is what it
means to be a man in 1930s China different from what it means
to be man in the United States in the 1990s? What is similar and
what is different, and what does this tell us about the way that
Tan perceives the role of men in modern society?

Character

The Joy Luck Club is populated by eight complicated and fascinating
women, any of whom would provide enough material for a thorough character analysis. Instead of focusing on just one of the characters, however,
you could choose a mother/daughter pair, comparing and contrasting
two of the mothers or two of the daughters, or consider all four daughters or all four mothers as a group. In any case, after you have recorded
all of the information you know about your character(s) and analyzed her
dialogue, inner thoughts, and relationships with other characters, you
will want to spend some time thinking about the reason that Amy Tan
included a character exactly like this in the novel. How does your character help to develop the overall themes and meanings of the entire work?

Sample Topics:

1. **Jing-mei Woo:** Jing-mei's voice opens the novel as she tells us about her mother's recent death and her father's request that she take her mother's place as the fourth member of the Joy Luck Club meeting. Jing-mei also closes the novel with the description of her trip to China to meet her sisters, the babies that her mother had been forced to abandon when leaving Kweilin all those years ago. While the other women each tell two stories, Jing-mei's voice speaks to us four times, once in each section of the novel. Why do you think Jing-mei's narrative takes up such a disproportionately large percentage of the novel's space? Would you say she functions as the "main character" or the most important protagonist in this novel? Why or why not?

   Begin by recording everything you know about Jing-mei. What kind of a person is she? What was her childhood like? What is she like as an adult? What do you think her mother means at the New Year's dinner when, after Jing-mei tries to pick the worst crab so that her mother can have a good one, Suyuan says to her "Everybody else want best quality. You thinking different" (208). Does Jing-mei think differently from everyone else, especially from the other daughters? Think about what she has in common with them and how she is different. Then, trace the connections among Jing-mei and the other members of the Joy Luck Club and their daughters and think about the way that Jing-mei's story and particularly the recent loss of her mother intersects with and influences the lives of all of these other women. Finally, also consider why Tan chose to begin and end the novel with the voice of one of the daughters instead of the mothers. What does this choice, and her choice of Jing-mei in particular, tell us about the overarching themes and meanings of the novel?

2. **Suyuan Woo:** When the novel opens, we learn that Jing-mei's mother, Suyuan, has just died. As such, Suyuan is the only main character in the novel who does not get to speak in her own voice. Analyze and evaluate the role that Suyuan, in memory and in her palpable absence, plays in the novel.

What do you know about Suyuan? What was her life like in China, and what was it like after she immigrated to America? What were her innermost hopes and fears? How important was Suyuan to the other characters? Once you have answered these questions, consider how we learn these things about Suyuan. Who seems to have known her best? Do you feel that we as readers come to know her as well as we do the other characters? Why or why not? Another way to think about Suyuan is to consider how her death affects the other characters. What events and journeys does it set, or help to set, into motion?

3. **Lindo, An-mei, or Ying-ying:** Analyze and evaluate one or more of the Joy Luck Club mothers.

Whether you are writing about one woman or all three, you will want to ask the following questions about each: What was her childhood like? What were the circumstances of her immigration to America? What has her life in America been like? Is her American life what she thought it would be? What are her regrets?

4. **Rose, Waverly, or Lena:** Analyze and evaluate the character of one or more of the daughters: Rose, Waverly, or Lena.

You will undoubtedly want to ask yourself similar questions no matter which daughter(s) you choose to concentrate on. You will want to know what her childhood was like, including what her parents expected of her and how much Chinese culture they expected her to absorb and retain. You will want to examine her narrative for clues as to what she considers the most formative events in her life and also examine her mother's personal history for information about the family she grew up in and to glean any insight the mothers have into their daughters' characters. You will want to ascertain as well how self-aware the character is of her own strengths and limitations.

History and Context

Especially in the case of a novel like Tan's *The Joy Luck Club*, a little historical research is an absolute necessity. A good portion of the novel takes place in 1940s China during a time of intense social upheaval. Many Westerners have little familiarity with Chinese history, and our studies of this period in particular tend to focus on the European theater of World War II. Based on Tan's text, you know that China was in crisis in the mid-20th century. Some background reading will help you to better understand the precise cultural and political climate in China at this time and to place Tan's characters Suyuan, Ying-ying, An-mei, and Lindo's experiences into context. Why was Japan invading China? How was China responding? What factions were at war within China at this time? What was the prevailing ideology and what new cultural movement was threatening that ideology? What was China's relationship with the rest of the world like at this time? You will also want to do some background reading on Chinese culture, beliefs, and traditions, paying particular attention to the closely related topics of the role of women in Chinese culture and its marriage traditions and laws. All of this context will help you to better understand the motivations of the Joy Luck Club mothers and give you a sense of the framework through which they see the world.

Sample Topics:

1. **Warfare in China:** Between 1928 and 1949, the Chinese people were faced with a civil war waged between the Kuomintang (Chinese Nationalist [NP]) and the Chinese Communist Party (CCP) as well as an invasion by the Japanese, culminating in the Sino-Japanese War. Ultimately, the Chinese prevailed over the Japanese, and the CCP over the NP. The Chinese people not only experienced the violence and related horrors of war, but they also saw their countrymen fighting one another as their country struggled to define itself. How did living in this tumultuous period of Chinese history affect the Joy Luck women?

   Begin by doing some historical research. You might start with chapters 6 and 7 of J. A. G. Roberts's *A Concise History of China*. What were the causes of the war with Japan and the civil war? What was life like for Chinese people during this time period? What does *The Joy Luck Club* tell you about its members' wartime experiences? How did these experiences change their relationship with their native land? Consider also the ways that Tan has chosen to present the war. According to your research, are her depictions realistic or has she altered the Chinese experience of the war in some way? Why did she choose either to be faithful in her rendering or to manipulate it in some way?

2. **Role of women:** Born in early 20th-century China, An-mei, Ying-ying, Suyuan, and Lindo grew up in a culture in which "the position of women—as daughters, wives, and mothers . . . is markedly provisional, with their status and expendability fluctuating according to their families' economic circumstances, their ability to bear male heirs, and the proclivities of authority figures in their lives" (Heug 29). Their daughters, on the other hand, grew up in the United States during the 1960s and 1970s, a society becoming increasingly invested during that time in demonstrating the value of women and insisting on their independence and equality to men. How did the different social and cultural environments—particularly in regard to women's social roles—in which the mothers and daughters grew up help to shape their identities and influence their relationships with one another?

Do some reading on the role of women in Chinese society. You might start with W. Scott Morton's *China: Its History and Culture.* You will also want to spend time reading about women's roles in the latter half of the 20th century in the United States and the various waves of the feminist movement that coursed through the United States in these decades. Based on the cultural understanding of women's roles in the environment in which they were raised, how do you think the Joy Luck mothers and daughters understand themselves and their relationships to their families? Do you think the daughters accept American beliefs completely, or are they influenced by their mothers' understanding of femininity and womanhood? How do they reconcile these two competing ideas?

3. **Marriage in mid-20th-century China:** Much of China's belief system is rooted in Confucianism, which emphasizes among other things the subservience of women to men. Although these "foundational beliefs came under attack by some Chinese thinkers of the early twentieth century, real change for women, including the outlawing of prostitution, child marriages, the sale of brides, and concubinage" did not occur until the Maoist years, beginning in 1949 (Morton 271–72). Thus, the society the Joy Luck Club mothers fled from was one that still firmly embraced many of the Confucian ideas of the inferior nature of women. Write an essay in which you examine the romantic lives and marriages of Lindo, An-mei, Suyuan, and Ying-ying and discuss what the novel as a whole has to say about the role of women in marriage and the effect on women occupying that role in mid-20th-century China.

First, do some background reading on the traditional role of women in Chinese society, particularly in terms of marriage. Did romantic love play any part? How did it factor into marriage? What were the laws regarding marriage, divorce, and property ownership? How were marriages arranged? What was the goal of marriage? What was a woman's duty in marriage? What rights or protections did marriage give her? How was marriage in 1930s China similar to and different from marriage in the United States in the 1940s? Once you have some background knowledge, return to the novel and examine the romantic lives of Ying-ying, An-mei, Suyuan, and Lindo. How did they come to marry the men they married? What did they perceive to be their options in life in regard to marriage and economic independence? What role did they play in their marriages and domestic environments? Did moving to the United States change the way they saw themselves and their role as women?

Philosophy and Ideas

The Joy Luck Club is, in large part, the story of a group of women who grew up in a society that espouses a strong belief in supernatural forces and their power over the living. These individuals then relocate to the United States, the land that perhaps more than any other celebrates the supremacy of the individual. Opportunities for essays that focus on philosophy and ideas abound. You might, for instance, write about how these women manage to take control of their destinies within the framework of their stifling Chinese culture. Or you might elect to write about how they integrate themselves into American society to build successful lives and the extreme level of cultural and personal negotiation that this process entails.

Sample Topics:

1. **Chinese beliefs and customs and individual agency:** Analyze and evaluate what the novel has to say about the intersection of Chinese beliefs in supernatural forces and an individual's free will.

Begin with some research into traditional Chinese beliefs in regard to the supernatural. You might start with "Feng Shui, Astrology, and the Five Elements: Traditional Chinese Belief in Amy Tan's *The Joy Luck Club*" by Patricia Hamilton. How did Chinese belief in the supernatural affect individuals' everyday lives? How did these beliefs affect women, in particular, and their sense of control over their lives?

Return to the novel, rereading the sections set in China, and ask yourself how the Joy Luck mothers were able to take control of their destinies in a society that devalued the individual's, especially women's, personal desires. Examine An-mei's mother, for instance, who used the belief that spirits come back to collect debts at the New Year to her advantage, orchestrating the timing of her suicide to give An-mei and her brother some measure of protection. Look also at Lindo's story and examine the way that she used her husband's family's belief in the supernatural to orchestrate a way out of her arranged marriage. In each case the young woman manipulates the belief system of those around her in order to improve her own situation or the situation of those dearest to her. Did these women believe in the superstitions they were using to their own benefit? What were the risks they were assuming, practically, psychologically, and spiritually? What might this tell us about the position of women in Chinese culture as well as their relationship to traditional beliefs?

You might also want to think about the even more complicated question of what happens to these beliefs when the women immigrate to the United States? Do they impart them to their children? What happens to these beliefs when Christianity is introduced? Would you say that an individual has more or less control over his or her destiny in the traditional Chinese framework or in the Christian tradition?

2. **Assimilation:** What does *The Joy Luck Club* have to say about the nature of assimilation?

You will want to begin by asking yourself how An-mei, Suyuan, Ying-ying, and Lindo have changed since moving to the United States. What parts of themselves did they need to transform in order to function successfully in their new society? Did they make these transformations intentionally, or did they simply happen automatically or gradually over time? You will also want to ask how the women feel about the compromises and adaptations they have made in order to get along in their new home. Certainly, the Joy Luck mothers have managed to achieve some level of success in the United States, but think about whether you would say that An-mei, Suyuan, Ying-ying, and Lindo have assimilated into American culture. What exactly does it mean to be assimilated? What does one gain by being so; what does one sacrifice? Do you think the women had assimilation as their goal? If not, how would you describe the way they wanted to integrate themselves into their new land, and do you think they were successful?

Form and Genre

You can, of course, examine the form and genre of any piece of literature, but *The Joy Luck Club* is an especially fruitful text for such investigations. For one thing, the text is narrated by seven different women, all of whom have different narrative styles. For another, the novel avoids the typical linear narrative we are used to, as Tan gives us a series of stories divided into sections with no clear unifying plot or climactic event or moment. Focusing on these fundamental choices made by the author as she was constructing the novel—by asking yourself, for instance, why she chose to have all of the women tell their stories instead of using a single narrator and why she opted for a fragmentary effect rather than interweaving the stories into a more coherent narrative—can bring to light significant aspects of the work you may not have otherwise noticed and lead to interesting insights into the novel's meanings.

Sample Topics:

1. **Narration:** According to E. D. Huntley, the Joy Luck mothers use "talk story" to communicate with their daughters. Critic Linda Ching Sledge defines talk story as "a conservative, communal folk art by and for the common people, performed in the various dialects of diverse ethnic enclaves and never intended for the ears of non-Chinese." Sledge explains that as it helped to "redefine an embattled immigrant culture by providing its members immediate, ceremonial access to ancient lore, talk story retained the structures of Chinese oral wisdom (parables, proverbs, formulaic description, heroic biography, casuistical dialogue) long after other old-century traditions had died" (qtd. in Huntley 32). What is the significance of this type of narration to the meanings of the stories these mothers tell and to the overarching themes of the novel?

   Do some background reading on talk story. Reread the novel, paying close attention this time to the narrative style of each protagonist. What generalizations can you make about the daughters' narratives? The mothers'? To whom does each woman seem to be speaking? Would you agree with Huntley that the form of the mothers' stories just as much as the content of those stories is an attempt to remain connected and to connect their daughters to the China they left behind?

2. **Structure:** Analyze and evaluate the structure and organization of *The Joy Luck Club*, a novel with only a loose connection among its various narratives. What is Tan communicating by making the structural choices she does?

   Literary critic Ben Xu, in an essay entitled "Memory and the Ethnic Self: Reading Amy Tan's *The Joy Luck Club*," observes that the stories share no recognizable pattern or fully integrated narrative structure. The character relations are suggested but never fully interwoven or acted out as a coherent drama. Our attention is constantly called to the characteristics of fiction that are missing from the book. It is neither a novel nor a group of short stories. It consists of isolated acts and events, which remain scattered and disbanded. It has neither a major plot around which to drape the separate stories, nor a unitary exciting climax which guides the book to a final outcome (13–14).

These conclusions are not surprising, given that Tan wrote the book as a collection of short stories. Readers, scholars, and reviewers, however, have insisted on calling it a novel. Why do you think this is? Does the text work as a novel? What holds it together? What makes it a strong work of literature? How might the form chosen by Tan be connected to or reflective of the themes of the piece as a whole? To answer these questions, you will want to chart out for yourself all the various parts of the book and how they are related to each other. Locate the critical moments in each person's story. You will also want to spend some time thinking about how *The Joy Luck Club* would be different if it were presented as a traditional novel complete with a linear narrative, a clear climax, and a single protagonist as well as how it would be different if it were considered a short story collection.

Language, Symbols, and Imagery

Tan's novel is rife with symbolism. You might choose to do an essay on a symbol that appears in one set of stories, such as the modern, sleek, and very slanted end table that decorates the guest room in Lena and Harold's renovated barn. An examination of the origins of that piece of furniture, its aesthetic and functional characteristics, and the responses it draws from the various characters can give you a glimpse into the dynamics of Lena and Harold's relationship as well as, perhaps, its fate. Alternatively, you might focus on a type of symbol that makes an appearance in more than one instance, the gift of jewelry from mother to daughter, for example: You might consider Suyuan's gift of the jade pendant to Jing-mei and the necklace of pearls and the sapphire ring given to a young An-mei. You would ask yourself in this case what prompts the gifting in each of these occasions as well as what the gift represents to both daughter and mother. You might expand your inquiry to include other gifts such as Suyuan's gift of the piano to Jing-mei on her 30th birthday, or you might decide to look also at the gifts given from daughter to mother to deepen your investigation into the symbolic exchanges between the two generations. No matter what symbol or set of symbols you choose to concentrate on, remember not to stop at simply figuring out what the symbol represents. You do not want simply to conclude that the end table represents Lena and Harold's relationship. You want to use your analysis of the symbol to help explore one of the novel's major themes or characters. You might, for instance, conclude that Tan's use of the end table suggests that Harold's modern, edgy take on the world may be pleasing on the surface—Lena can never quite articulate what is wrong with his seemingly logical and progressive vision of the world, including the way they divide up their income to ensure their equality—but it is ultimately exposed as impractical and unsustainable.

1. **Swan feather:** In the introduction to the first section of the novel, Tan tells the story of a Chinese woman who buys a swan from a merchant who tells her it was a duck that tried to be a goose by stretching its neck out. The woman brings the swan with her to the United States, where she believes she will have a daughter and then, one day, give her the swan "a creature that became more than what was hoped for" (17). When the woman arrives in America, the swan is taken from her, and all she can hold on to is a single feather. The woman decides to pass on the feather to her daughter, but she never attains the perfect English she believes is necessary to pass this treasure on to her daughter. Why do you think Tan chose to begin *The Joy Luck Club* with this story? What might the swan and the feather represent in the overarching pattern of the novel?

Think about what similarities there might be between the experiences of the Joy Luck women and the woman in the swan story. The woman is unable to hold on to the swan, which to her represents possibility and hope. Are the Joy Luck club women able to keep their hopes and dreams intact when they arrive in America, or do they have to abandon or adjust them once they are faced with the reality of life in San Francisco? How do the women feel about their own broken English, especially when compared with their daughters' English? Finally, do they feel that their daughters understand and appreciate the precious things that they have to pass on to them? Will they keep waiting, like the woman in the story, for the right time to share with their progeny what is important to them, or do they ultimately seize the moment, whether perfect or not?

2. **End table:** What does the end table symbolize? What statement does it make about Lena and Harold's relationship? What do Ying-ying's reaction to the table and Lena's response to that reaction tell us about each of them and their relationship to each other?

   Locate the passages in the text that describe the end table and analyze them carefully. Where does the table come from? What words are used to describe it? How do Harold, Lena, and Ying-ying feel about it? How is the end table related to the rest of the house? What is the significance of the fact that the vase of flowers that Lena sets on the table to decorate the room for her mother crashes to the floor? What are Lena and Harold saying to each other when the crash occurs?

3. **Pearl necklace/jewelry:** An-mei is stunned by the gift of a pearl necklace from Wu Tsing's second and most powerful wife. Her mother stomps on it, breaking one of the beads, which turns out to be glass, saying to An-mei, "I will not let her buy you for such a cheap price" (231). An-mei's mother then removes the crushed bead and knots the strand back together, making An-mei wear it for a week until she learns her lesson. At the end of the week, she gives An-mei a "heavy ring of watery blue sapphire, with a star in its center so pure that [she] never ceased to look at that ring without wonder" (232). What do the string of pearls and the sapphire ring represent?

   How does An-mei's mother know that the pearls are fake? What can she see that An-mei's young eyes cannot? In what spirit was the gift of the necklace made? How about the ring? What kind of person is Second Wife? What kind of person is An-mei's mother? What lesson has An-mei learned through this experience? You might think about other gifts of jewelry from mother to daughter in the novel as well, such as Suyuan's gift of the jade pendant, her "life's importance," to Jing-mei at the New Year's dinner. What does this piece of jewelry and this gesture represent? Is it similar to An-mei's mother's gift of the sapphire ring?

4. **Piano:** What does the piano represent for Jing-mei and her mother? What commentary does their treatment of it make on the nature of their relationship?

Reread the portions of the novel having to do with Jing-mei's piano lessons and her disastrous piano recital in "Two Kinds," paying particular attention to the fight she and her mother have after the recital. Jing-mei says to her mother: "You want me to be someone I'm not! . . . I'll never be the kind of daughter you want me to be! . . . I wish I wasn't your daughter. I wish you weren't my mother" (142). After this, Suyuan never makes Jing-mei practice piano again. She does, however, offer to give Jing-mei the piano for her 30th birthday. Jing-mei "saw the offer as a sign of forgiveness, a tremendous burden removed" (143). Why did Suyuan want Jing-mei to master the piano in the first place? What did her daughter's playing mean to her? What did the piano lessons and the recital mean for Jing-mei? What did Jing-mei's awful performance at the recital mean to each of them? Do you think that Jing-mei was right, that the offer of the piano as a birthday gift was meant as a sign of forgiveness? For what exactly does Jing-mei feel the need for forgiveness? For the spiteful words she said to her mother years ago, or for something more?

5. **Chinese/English language:** According to scholar Victoria Chen, "Speaking a language is inherently political" (86). What does this mean? How is language connected to power and privilege in *The Joy Luck Club*?

Chen continues: "Language and identity are always positioned within a hierarchical power structure in which the Chinese American immigrants' form of life has never been granted a status equal to that of their European counterparts in the history of this country" (86). How is language connected to power in the novel? Think in particular about Ying-ying: Her daughter must translate for her or else her husband simply forms his own interpretation of what she must be intending to say.

Why do the mothers want their children all to speak perfect English? How do they feel about their own command of the English language? How are the daughters' positions in American culture determined in part by their mastery of the English language? Do any of the daughters speak Chinese? Do the mothers want their daughters to speak Chinese as well as English? Why or why not?

Compare and Contrast Essays

Comparing two elements of a particular work or two separate works to each other can enable you to notice features of the work that might not have seemed significant when examined alone but that take on significance or additional dimensions when viewed in this new context. Take Waverly and Jing-mei and their careers, for example. Both seem like successful career women supporting themselves doing work they enjoy. When you pit them against each other, however, you can see that, comparatively speaking, Waverly is a much greater success in the working world than Jing-mei. We learn that Waverly's firm has deemed copywriting work done by Jing-mei as so inadequate they will not pay her fee. You might use this observation as a springboard to discuss how success is defined in the novel. Does it have to do with money, prestige, power? You might also observe that despite the disparity in levels of success, both young women seem to feel that they have somehow disappointed their mothers. If only one of them felt this way, you might deem the reaction an idiosyncrasy, but having observed this pattern, you can begin to investigate the causes. Could this perception of filial failure have more to do with the nature of their mothers' expectations, perhaps, than the actual level of success or happiness the daughters have personally achieved?

Sample Topics:

1. **Waverly and Jing-mei:** Waverly and Jing-mei have been rivals since they were children, in part because of their mothers' desire to pit them against each other. While Waverly was a chess prod-

igy, Suyuan tried to prod Jing-mei into discovering where her genius lay. Despite the fact that Waverly seems to have always enjoyed success, while Jing-mei has often struggled and failed, the two share a sense that they have disappointed their mothers. Write an essay in which you compare and contrast these characters, using them to draw some conclusions about what it was like to be a second-generation Asian American in the later half of the 20th century.

Make a list of similarities and differences in Jing-mei's and Waverly's circumstances, upbringings, and personalities. From what do the commonalities stem? What about the differences? Which of the characters is shown in a more positive light in the novel? Does either ultimately seem happier than the other? Because their lives have always been somehow intertwined, consider how either of them might appear more or less successful if the other were not there as a comparison. Are they, in fact, defined largely in contrast to each other?

2. **Old and new China:** Compare and contrast the China of 1949 when Ying-ying, Suyuan, An-mei, and Lindo left it and the China they visit in the later part of the 20th century. How does Tan characterize the evolution?

Reread the stories set in 1930s and 1940s China. Based on Tan's plots and characterization, how would you describe the land? The people? The customs? What would you describe as negative and what as positive? Now examine the scenes set in modern-day China, focusing especially on the final chapter in which Jing-mei and her father travel to China to meet Jing-mei's two half sisters. What is this new China like? What does it have in common with the old? What would you describe as positive and negative about Tan's presentation of 1980s China?

3. *The Joy Luck Club* **and** *The Woman Warrior* **or** *Love Medicine:* *The Joy Luck Club* is most often compared to Maxine Hong Kingston's *The Woman Warrior* and Louise Erdrich's

Love Medicine, each of which presents the story of a marginalized culture with a series of interconnected stories. Compare and contrast *The Joy Luck Club* with either *The Woman Warrior* or *Love Medicine,* using your analysis to draw conclusions about both texts.

Read the two texts that you have decided to compare and contrast. How is each of them structured and organized? What point of view is used to tell the stories? How are the stories connected to one another? Why do you think each author opted to construct the work in this way instead of creating a more cohesive, linear narrative? What effect does this type of presentation achieve in each case? Why do you think that these women writing about marginalized populations would make similar choices about the presentation of the story they wish to tell in fragments?

Bibliography and Online Resources for *The Joy Luck Club*

Bloom, Harold, ed. *Amy Tan.* Modern Critical Views. Philadelphia: Chelsea House, 2000.

Hamilton, Patricia. "Feng Shui, Astrology, and the Five Elements: Traditional Chinese Belief in Amy Tan's *The Joy Luck Club.*" *MELUS* 24 (1999). Accessed on 08 Apr. 2008. <http://findarticles.com/p/articles/mi_m2278/is_2_24/ai_59211511>.

Huntley, E. D. *Amy Tan: A Critical Companion.* Critical Companions to Popular Contemporary Writers. Westport, CT: Greenwood, 1998.

Morton, W. Scott. *China: Its History and Culture.* 3rd ed. New York: McGraw-Hill, 1995.

Roberts, J. A. G. *A Concise History of China.* Cambridge, MA: Harvard UP, 1999.

Tan, Amy. *The Joy Luck Club.* New York: Penguin, 2006.

Zenobia, Mistri. "Discovering the Ethnic Name and the Genealogical Tie in Amy Tan's *The Joy Luck Club.*" *Studies in Short Fiction* (1998). Accessed on 08 Apr. 2008. <http://findarticles.com/p/articles/mi_m2455/is_3_35/ai_83585386>.

THE KITCHEN
GOD'S WIFE

READING TO WRITE

A MY TAN's second novel, *The Kitchen God's Wife*, draws so extensively
from her mother's life story that it blurs the line between fiction and
biography. Amy's mother, Daisy, got so frustrated at having to explain to
people that none of the mothers in *The Joy Luck Club* was actually her that
she encouraged her daughter to tell her true story in Tan's next book. So
Amy Tan began to learn the details of her mother's life. Previously, Daisy
told Amy that she had not been affected by the war in China. Amy was
shocked then to learn that, by this, Daisy had simply meant that she had not
been killed. Biographer Charles J. Shields writes, "The contrast between her
mother's view of what was important in life—surviving the near-breakdown
of civilization—versus Amy's own, upper-middle class American outlook,
opened the door to a new book" (75). Like her debut novel, *The Joy Luck
Club*, *The Kitchen God's Wife* became a best seller and earned Tan critical
praise. Also, like *The Joy Luck Club*, this second novel has much to say about
gender roles, specifically the role of women in Chinese culture.

Examine what exactly the novel says about women's status in mid-
20th-century China by studying the conversation that ensues when
Winnie's family brings her to her father to obtain his permission for her
to marry Wen Fu. Winnie's father recalls a conversation they had about
a certain painting that she liked to study when she was a little girl. Winnie's father reminds her:

> You said the painting was very confusing. You could not tell if the lady
> playing the lute was singing a happy or a sad song. You could not tell if the

woman carrying a heavy load was beginning her journey or ending it. And this woman on the balcony, you said one moment she looked as though she was waiting with hope, the next moment watching with fear. (144)

Winnie becomes frustrated that she cannot know these women's stories. She studies the painting, trying to discover how the women portrayed in it are feeling, whether at this moment in their lives they are experiencing joy, sadness, a sense of accomplishment, hope, or fear. Winnie is "confused" about the painting because she can interpret it several different ways; the women seem to signify something different depending on how she looks at the painting. They are blank slates that hold whatever meaning the viewer ascribes to them. The artist has painted the women in such a way that they do not express anything that would give the viewer more information about their inner states. One cannot help but wonder: Is this simply the manner in which all Chinese paintings portray their human subjects? Is it because the artist, presumably male, did not care about the inner lives of these subjects? Or does the painting represent what Chinese women really looked like?

Consider the remainder of the conversation between Winnie and her father. Winnie's father remarks that he liked the courage she displayed when giving her opinion as a child and asks her what she thinks of this same painting now. Winnie begins to offer opinions on its composition and color. Her father responds: "From now on . . . you must consider what your husband's opinions are. Yours do not matter so much anymore. Do you understand?" (145). In the way that Winnie responds to her father's question, we can tell that she has already become a bit more like the women in the painting than she was as a child. She does not reveal how the painting affects her personally as she had previously done; instead, she tries to speak about its merits as a work of art. Yet even this response draws a correction from her father, who warns her that it is her husband's opinions that count now. After studying this exchange, it is perhaps easier to believe that the women in the painting appear emotionless because this is how they have been trained to appear.

Through Winnie's response as a child to this painting and their later conversation about it, as well as through Winnie's later experiences with Wen Fu, we can see clearly how women were deterred from expressing themselves in any meaningful way, even through their voices or facial expressions. In some ways, the more women were like the ones portrayed in the painting, going through the motions in the most unobtrusive manner possible, the easier their lives were. Though patriarchal Chinese society could stop women's opinions from counting, and could even stop women from expressing these opinions, it could not stop the inner workings of women's minds and hearts. The stories of their lives, their desires and suffering, were still there, only hidden under the surface. In writing this novel, *The Kitchen God's Wife*, Amy Tan gives voice to her mother's story—the young girl who is courageous enough to wonder aloud about the lives of the women in that painting retains enough of that courage as an adult to allow her daughter to put her life story into writing to be shared by the public.

If this line of thinking interests you, you might decide to pursue these kinds of questions in your essay. Look for passages that illustrate how women are discouraged from expressing themselves. How do men effectively silence women, and how do women cope with this state of affairs? Are they able to express themselves to one another? What happens when they do? You might also decide to trace the evolution of Winnie's voice. How does she change when she marries Wen Fu? Does she come to believe her opinions and feelings are worthless? If so, then how does she find the courage to leave Wen Fu? What does it mean to her to tell her daughter the story of her life? Is it significant that these revelations are forced out of her rather than freely given?

Locate the passages that seem to contain answers to these questions and analyze them carefully. Ask yourself why Tan phrased things in exactly the way she did and what the effect would have been had she said things another way. Especially as you are considering voice and self-expression, you should also consider what things are left unsaid and think about the reasons for the omission. Once you have analyzed all of the relevant passages, you will need to synthesize your observations and analysis into a coherent argument or interpretation of the text that will become the basis for your essay.

TOPICS AND STRATEGIES

Amy Tan's *The Kitchen God's Wife* is a long, complex, and sophisticated novel, and, as such, there are countless successful and insightful essays that can be written about it. Not surprisingly, then, the topics below are not exhaustive. They are designed to show you possible directions you might wish to go with your essay. Do not feel compelled to select one of the listed topics; let these suggestions inspire you to develop a topic of your own. If you decide to use one of the suggested topics, do not restrict yourself to answering the sub-questions when developing and expanding on the topic you have chosen. Use these only as a guide to help you in your prewriting and planning process as you work toward arriving at your thesis or the main point you want your essay to support. Once you arrive at your thesis, cull the best supportive points from your prewriting and planning and develop them further to create the body of your essay.

Themes

When you set out to explore the themes of a literary piece, you are essentially asking yourself to determine the fundamental concerns of the work. What is *The Kitchen God's Wife* really about? What are the issues that it encourages readers to think deeply about? There are many themes that you could choose to write about in connection with *The Kitchen God's Wife*, but perhaps the most central include mother/daughter relationships, the changing role of women in modern society, and the way that individuals respond to and deal with traumatic events in their lives. No matter which of these topics you choose, you will want to ask yourself exactly what the novel is trying to say about it. It is not enough to state, for example, that the novel is about the tense, but loving, relationship between Winnie and Pearl. Instead, you might posit that the novel illustrates that while mother/daughter relationships are often characterized by keeping secrets in an effort by both mother and daughter to protect each other, the key to developing a close and supportive relationship is confiding in each other and trusting in the strength and resiliency of the other person. Alternatively, you might conclude that *The Kitchen God's Wife* illustrates the additional strains placed on mother/daughter relationships when the mother is an immigrant and the daughter American-born, and you could discuss the long-term consequences of this cultural conflict. There is no right or wrong thesis to arrive at. The key is to analyze significant passages, using them to arrive at your conclusions about what the work has to say concerning, for example, mother/daughter relationships. If your conclusions are reached through rigorous analysis of relevant passages, then you will have a convincing essay.

Sample Topics:

1. **Mother/daughter relationship between Winnie and Pearl:**
The Kitchen God's Wife hinges on the tension-filled but loving
relationship between Winnie and Pearl. How does this relationship evolve through the course of the novel? What is Tan saying
about the nature of mother/daughter relationships, particularly
ones that involve first- and second-generation immigrants?

Begin by establishing what you know about these two women
and their relationship with each other. What were their child-
hoods like? What was Winnie's relationship with her own
mother like, and how do you think this might have affected the
relationship she ultimately cultivates with her own daughter?
What was Winnie's childhood like? What conflicting cultural
expectations did she encounter? How do the women behave
toward one another after Pearl grows up and establishes her
own family? Why do you think they keep the most important
secrets of their lives from each other? Think about what happens to their relationship once they reveal these secrets to one
another. How does their relationship reconfigure itself after
they have both shared their stories?

2. **The role of women:** How is Winnie's perception of her own
role, that of daughters, and of women in general, shown through
her evolving relationship with the Kitchen God and his wife?

Return to the end of chapter two of *The Kitchen God's Wife*,
and review the story of the Kitchen God as told by Winnie as
she gives Pearl the altar with a figure of the god inside it that
has been left to her by Grand Auntie Du. Pay particular attention to the following passage:

> Sometimes he is in a bad mood. Sometimes he says, I don't like
> this family, give them bad luck. Then you're in trouble, nothing
> you can do about it. Why should I want that kind of person to
> judge me, a man who cheated his wife? His wife was the good
> one, not him. (55)

What kind of person was the Kitchen God before he became a god? What kind of a god is he? Why does Winnie decide to keep the Kitchen God herself and choose another lucky god for Pearl's inherited altar? Later in the novel, Winnie is inspired by a sermon on forgiveness and reflects on her inability to forgive Wen Fu for all the suffering he caused her, invoking the story of the Kitchen God and his wife:

> When Jesus was born, he was already the son of God. I was the daughter of someone who ran away, a big disgrace. And when Jesus suffered, everyone worshipped him. Nobody worshipped me for living with Wen Fu. I was like that wife of the Kitchen God. Nobody worshipped her either. He got all the excuses. He got all the credit. She was forgotten. (255)

What can this passage tell us about Winnie's perception of herself and her understanding of what gender roles were and ought to be in the China she left? Finally, scrutinize the novel's conclusion in which Winnie buys a goddess figure that, by some mistake of the manufacturer, bears no name:

> So I bought that mistake. I fixed it. I used my gold paints and wrote her name on the bottom. And Helen bought good incense, not the cheap brand, but the best. I could see this lady statue in her new house, the red temple altar with two candlesticks lighting up her face from both sides. She would live there, but no one would call her Mrs. Kitchen God. Why would she want to be called that, now that she and her husband are divorced. . . . Look at her hair, how black it is, no worries. Although maybe she used to worry. I heard she once had many hardships in her life. So maybe her hair is dyed. But her smile is genuine, wise and innocent at the same time. And her hand, see how she just raised it? That means she is about to speak, or maybe she is telling you to speak. She is ready to listen. (414)

What has Winnie done here? Why do you think she chose an unnamed statue that she could make into the Kitchen God and rename "Lady Sorrowfree" instead of simply choosing a different lucky god for Pearl's altar?

3. **Trauma:** In China, Winnie left behind a life replete with trauma, including continual physical abuse and sexual violence in her marriage as well as the physical and psychological effects of war and of losing her children. Her daughter, Pearl, has been diagnosed with multiple sclerosis, a potentially debilitating disease. How does each woman cope with the trauma in her life? What does the novel ultimately have to say about the nature of trauma and healing?

Begin by rereading the novel, paying careful attention to the ways in which Winnie and Pearl deal with the traumatic events in their lives. What coping techniques do they use? Which seem to work best? You will also want to pay attention to the behavior of the people closest to Winnie and Pearl who are privy to their suffering, such as Phil, Helen, and Pearl's old friend Mary. How do they handle these issues in their loved ones' lives? Are they helpful, supportive forces? Finally, you will also want to think about why Winnie and Pearl keep their suffering from each other. What does this say about their relationship? How does their relationship change when they reveal their secrets to one another?

Character

When you are writing an essay about a character, you will, of course, want to pay close attention to that character's actions and dialogue. You will also want to analyze how you are receiving information about this character. Who is presenting the information? Is the narrator reliable? What are his or her motives? Think about how the story of Wen Fu's life would sound different if, for example, if it were told not by Winnie but by Wen Fu's mother. When a character is telling his or her own story, you still cannot assume that you are getting a factual, unbiased account. You must consider the narrator's reason for telling the story and the audience for the story as well. Think, for example, about how Winnie's story might be different if Helen had not forced her to tell it and how it would be different if she were telling it to a stranger rather than to her daughter, Pearl. We get to know characters through stories, and these stories are always shaped and constructed by the people who tell them. Often this means that even when a narrator is telling you all about someone else, she is revealing a great deal about herself in the manner in which she molds the tale.

Sample Topics:

1. **Winnie:** Analyze and evaluate the character of Jiang-Wei, or Winnie Louie as she comes to be called in America. Jimmy Louie, her husband, thinks of her as both fragile and yet extremely strong. Is this an accurate description of Winnie? Why or why not?

   Begin by recording what you know of the circumstances of Winnie's life. What is her childhood like, and how does she come to be married to Wen Fu? What is her early married life like, and how does her relationship with Wen Fu affect her character? What are the other major influential factors in Winnie's life? How is she different when she relocates to America and is reunited with Jimmy? How does Winnie deal with her traumatic past? Is she able to make peace with it? How so?

   Additionally, you might wish to do some research into Amy Tan's biography to learn how much of Winnie's character's story is based on actual events in the life of her mother, Daisy. How do these factual connections affect the way you perceive the story in general and Winnie's character in particular?

2. **Pearl:** Analyze and evaluate Pearl's character. Write an essay in which you argue whether or not Pearl is fundamentally changed by exchanging secrets with her mother and, if you think that she is changed, articulate precisely how she has changed and why.

   Begin by recording what you know about Pearl. What was her childhood like? How was she treated by her parents? How did she feel about her Chinese heritage? What has her adult life been like? Think about her marriage and the way that she is raising her daughters. Consider also her relationship with her mother and the feelings that she expresses about her obligations to her family. Then, begin to think about whether Pearl experiences some kind of change in the course of the novel. Is she different after hearing her mother's story and sharing her own? What exactly changes about her and what do you think accounts for these changes?

3. **Hulan/Helen:** How does the novel present Helen overall? Is she basically a good person and a good friend, or does her desire for control make her treat others unfairly?

Begin by considering your initial impressions of Pearl's Aunt Helen. What kind of a person does she seem to be? What are her motivations for forcing Winnie and Pearl to confide in each other? Do you think that this is a fair and/or good thing to do? Next, write down what you discover about Hulan/Helen from Winnie's story. Write down what you know about her childhood, her first marriage, her life during the war, and her second marriage. How are your initial impressions of Helen affected by this new knowledge? Does she become a more or less sympathetic character? Now, study the final scenes of the novel in which Helen appears. What does she confide to Pearl, and how does Pearl feel about Helen's manipulative behavior?

4. **Wen Fu:** While ambiguity might shroud some of the characters, Wen Fu is most certainly the villain of *The Kitchen God's Wife*. Does the novel present him as a one-dimensional character who basically represents evil and injustice, or is Wen Fu more complicated than that? What clues does the novel give us as to his motivations?

Reread the novel, focusing on the descriptions of Wen Fu. What are Winnie's early memories of him? How did he behave in the early days of their marriage? After the car accident in which he was severely injured and partially blinded, his behavior seemed to change for the worse. Why do you think this is? What do you think motivates Wen Fu's atrocious treatment of Winnie and their children? Why do you think he is allowed to perpetuate this kind of behavior with no consequences? Does Wen Fu possess any redeeming qualities?

5. **Winnie's father:** Analyze and evaluate the character of Winnie's father.

What kind of person is Winnie's father? What do you know about his relationship with Winnie's mother? What kind of a father has he been to Winnie? Why do you think he allows her to marry Wen Fu? Reread chapter 19 in which Winnie and Wen Fu return to Winnie's father's house to find it in ruins. What has caused her father's fall? Why do you think he sided with the Japanese? Finally, why do you think he gives Winnie some gold he has hidden away when she tells him that she is leaving Wen Fu? According to Winnie:

> I do not think my father was saying he loved me. I think he was telling me that if I left this terrible man, then maybe this terrible man would leave his house too. Maybe my father and his wives would no longer have to suffer. My leaving was their only chance. Of course, maybe he was telling me he loved me a little, too. (361)

Do you agree with Winnie's assessment? What does this action say about the kind of man her father was?

History and Context

Because a thorough understanding of Amy Tan's *The Kitchen God's Wife* depends on one's knowledge of certain historical events, including the Sino-Japanese War, the rape of Nanking, and the Communist Revolution, no matter what topic you choose to focus on in your essay, you will probably want to do some background reading. You might start with W. Scott Morton's *China: Its History and Culture* or J. A. G. Roberts's *A Concise History of China*. In addition to giving you a firm foundation for understanding and writing about any aspect of *The Kitchen God's Wife*, historical investigation might lead you to discover a topic or nuance you would like your essay to focus on. For instance, you might decide to analyze and evaluate the novel's presentation of the rape of Nanking or the Communist revolution, or you might elect to examine the way that the novel as a whole conceptualizes history.

Sample Topics:

1. **Japan's occupation of China and the rape of Nanking:** *The Kitchen God's Wife* deals with the Japanese occupation of China in the 1930s and 1940s and the 1937 rape of Nanking. According to literary critic Bella Adams, Tan took on the very difficult task of representing one of the most brutal and traumatic events in Chinese history. To be successful at representing this period in history, Tan has to describe and present the event in a way that leaves readers with no doubt that it actually happened while also using her entire novel as means of questioning and critiquing the way that history is constructed and passed on to succeeding generations. In your view, is Tan successful in these tasks?

   First of all, think about Bella Adams's comments. Why does she insist that Tan's work must meet both of these goals— making a historical event seem real and questioning the way we understand history—at the same time? How would the novel be flawed if it met one of these goals but not the other? You might want to read Adams's article "Representing History in Amy Tan's *The Kitchen God's Wife*" to get a better understanding of her argument, and you might want to do some historical research into the Sino-Japanese War as well, beginning with *A Concise History of China* or Paul Bailey's *China in the Twentieth Century*.

   Next, think about what the novel has to say about the nature of history. Whose version of events is usually taken as the truth? Take a look at Winnie's court case, for example. Whose story was validated by the courts and why? Is history an uncomplicated matter of recording a series of facts agreed on by everyone, or does it require interpretation, and if so, who gets to guide or control the interpretation that is set down as history for future citizens? Then, think about how Tan convinces the reader of the historical veracity of her descriptions of the war. Why, when the entire novel questions the way history is determined and emphasizes the way that memories and the past are changeable, do we believe Winnie when she describes the atrocities that happened to her in China, particularly when she speaks of the rape of Nanking? Is there something about Winnie, or her position in society, that makes us privilege her story? Is it the way she tells her story that makes it seem like truth? You will want to study passages in which she describes the war, passages like the following, to help you figure this out:

> Raped old women, married women, and little girls, taking turns with them, over and over again. Sliced them open with a sword when they were all used up. Cut off their fingers to take their rings. Shot all the little sons, no more generations. Raped ten thousand, chopped down twenty or thirty thousand, a number that is no longer a number, no longer people. (295)

Is there something about the way that she relates these atrocities that encourages us to believe her account?

2. **Communist revolution:** What does *The Kitchen's God's Wife* have to say about communist ideology and the revolution in China?

You may wish to begin with some research into the Communist revolution in China in *China in the Twentieth Century*. Then, you will want to locate and analyze any references to communism in the text. You might focus, in particular, on Winnie's cousin Peanut and her friends. What, for example, do you make of Winnie's explanation of how she recognized that the women Peanut lived with were revolutionaries?

> So nobody said to me, "I'm a Communist. How about you?" But you could tell by the things they said. When we all sat down to

> eat, for example, Little Yu's mother said to me, "I hope bitter melon doesn't disagree with you too much. I don't eat it very often myself. But when I do, I remind myself how grateful I am to have other things to eat." She laughed, and Peanut and the other women laughed with her. (355)

Why are Little Yu's mother, Peanut, and the other women laughing? What might the bitter melon represent? What is the larger significance of Little Yu's words? Consider also the fact that Peanut is the character most closely associated with the revolution; what light does this cast on the quoted passage? Is Peanut characterized as an intelligent and sincere person whose ideas should be valued?

Finally, you might wish to consider remarks that indirectly invoke China's political hierarchy and ideology, like this one from Winnie as she describes the village in which she was raised:

> A village that small could produce only one top-class house, maybe a few middle-class people. Almost everyone else who lived there was poor. I am not saying this was right, to have only one rich family, to have so many poor. That was the kind of life everyone had back then, no questions asked, the fate people were born with. That was China. . . . Of course, I did not think about these matters back then. (119)

Why does Winnie see things differently now? Did the Communist regime change things? If so, in what way?

Philosophy and Ideas

There are many philosophical and sociological ideas in Tan's *The Kitchen God's Wife* that will likely be unfamiliar to many Western readers. The moments in the novel in which the frame of reference or the worldview of one or more of the book's characters is at odds with a modern American psyche make excellent entry points for your investigation of the text. Take the idea of ownership of the female body as one example. In the contemporary United States, we take it for granted that a woman is in control of her own body and that she is responsible for making her own choices irrespective of her sexual behavior. Actually, we take it for granted that all people, even children, as Winnie points out to Pearl so poignantly, have sovereignty over their own physical bodies. It can be shocking for us to read about Winnie's experiences in mid-20th-century China and difficult for us to comprehend the fact that Winnie's own body did not belong exclusively to her and that she was, in large part, property to be used by her husband at his will. This different perspective should prompt us to think about the way that our relationships with our own bodies are culturally determined. You might do some research into the evolution of women's rights in the United States and compare what it was like for an American woman at the time that Winnie was married to Wen Fu, and what it was like for women in the United States and China in the 1990s when *The Kitchen God's Wife* was published. Once you begin to investigate an idea like this and do some background reading to gain additional perspective, you will find yourself with many angles from which you could approach writing an essay. You might, for example, decide to chronicle Winnie's evolving relationship with her own body: How and why do her beliefs about her rights to her own body change? You might also write about the effects on women's psyches and romantic relationships that the conceptualization of women as their husbands' property ultimately brings. Finally, you might compare and contrast Winnie's and Pearl's relationships with their bodies, exploring the significance of the fact that, in a sense, both women's biggest secrets have to do with some kind of shame or despair located in their bodies.

Sample Topics:

1. **Ownership of the body:** What does *The Kitchen God's Wife* ultimately have to say about ownership and control of the female body?

When Winnie explains to Pearl what life was like for her once Helen helped Wen Fu find her after she ran away from him the first time, she reveals that she aborted multiple pregnancies conceived through rape:

> That bad man was using my body. Every night he used it, as if I were—what—a machine! Today you teach your daughters

to say to a stranger, "My body is my body. Don't touch me." A
little child can say this. I was a grown woman, and I could not
say this. I could only stop those babies from coming. (312)

According to Winnie's explanation and the remainder of
the text as well, what is the difference between American and
Chinese ideas regarding ownership and control over the individual body? Consider this in terms of the rape as well as the
abortions. In each of these cultures, who has control over the
sexual use of the female body? Similarly, who has control over
the reproductive functions of that same body? How are these
issues of control decided? How does Winnie feel about these
differences? Does she come to believe that one framework,
either the American or Chinese, is the most fair, correct, or
good?

2. **Memory and changing the past:** What does the novel have to
   say about the nature of memory?

In her narrative, Winnie reflects on the unstable nature of
memory:

Helen always tells me, "Why do you think about those old
things? Useless to regret. You cannot change the past." She
doesn't remember. She and I have changed the past many
times, for many reasons. And sometimes she changes it for me
and does not even know what she has done." (62)

Do you agree with Helen that it is better not to think about
the past because it cannot be changed? Does not thinking about
bad things that have happened in the past make you immune
to them, or do these things have a way of haunting you if you
try to leave them behind? What does Winnie mean when she
says that she and Helen "have changed the past many times,
for many reasons"? And how has Helen changed the past for
Winnie without even realizing it? With so many changes and
redefinitions, does Winnie feel that she has gained some kind

of control of her past, or are these revisions ways to escape the truth? Consider just how much Winnie's comments may call into question the veracity of the story she is currently telling. Are we supposed to trust her memories as reliable?

3. **Fate, destiny, and free will:** What does the novel ultimately have to say about responsibility for the outcome of our lives?

Begin by identifying and analyzing those passages that seem to you to be most directly concerned with fate, destiny, and free will. You might start with the following passage in which Winnie describes to Pearl a conversation that she had with Pearl's father about their fortuitous second meeting:

> That's what I said to your father many years later, after we were married. How lucky we were that fate brought us together, but your father did not think it was fate, at least not the Chinese idea of *ming yuan.* "Fate," he told me, "is somebody else deciding your life for you. Our love was greater than that." And here he used the American world "destiny," something that could not be prevented. (341)

What is the difference between the ideas of "fate" and "destiny" as presented here? What are the connotations of each of these terms? What other events in her life does Winnie feel were determined by destiny or fate? How are these concepts related to luck? While Winnie often refers to fate as a guiding force, she speaks also about free will and the burden it imposes. Study the following passage in which she tells Pearl about her decision to leave Wen Fu despite the fact that she will have to leave her father behind as well:

> Isn't that how it is when you must decide with your heart? You are not just choosing one thing over another. You are choosing what you want. And you are also choosing what somebody else does not want, and all the consequences that follow. You can tell yourself, That's not my problem, but those words do not

wash the trouble away. Maybe it is no longer a problem in your life. But it is a problem in your heart. (360)

All told, in what ways does Winnie perceive of her life as governed by luck, fate, destiny, her own free will, or some combination thereof? Does the narrative as a whole seem to agree with Winnie's vision of the world, or does it suggest that she perceives events in a biased way?

Form and Genre

Thinking about how a book comes to be and how it fits in with other books can help us to better understand an author's goals and the work's meanings. You want to consider what story or stories are being told, who is telling them, and in what form they are being conveyed. You also want to think about where the stories in the book originated. Are these stories completely constructed in the author's imagination, or do they have a basis in reality, and if they do, then you might consider how the underlying facts affect your interpretation of the literary work crafted from them.

Sample Topics:

1. **Narration:** What conclusions can you draw about the themes and meanings of the novel from an analysis of the narrative technique Tan employs?

   Examine the narrative framework of this novel. Who is speaking when? How would you characterize Pearl's narrative voice? How about Winnie's? How does each of them treat the other in their narration? Do they include each other's dialogue? Do you think that one of the narratives, Pearl's or Winnie's, predominates over the other? What do you make of the fact that the secret that Winnie reveals takes up such a large part of the text as compared with Pearl's? Is Pearl's story important or does it serve as a mere frame for Winnie's history?

2. **Genre:** Winnie's story in *The Kitchen God's Wife* is based largely on the life of Daisy Tan, Amy Tan's mother. Is the book best considered a novel, memoir, or biography, and what are the ramifications of assigning it to one of these genres?

You will want to begin with some background reading into Amy Tan's life and the life of her mother. Then, return to the novel to evaluate how closely Daisy Tan and Winnie Louie are connected. How much did Tan fictionalize about her mother's life? What genre does Tan herself consider this work to belong to? How might we approach the text differently if we consider it as a memoir or a biography rather than as fiction?

Language, Symbols, and Imagery

The Kitchen God's Wife is rife with significant images and symbols, and focusing on one in particular could help you to arrive at a new interpretation of the text to present in your essay. You might, for example, focus on Lady Sorrowfree, the goddess created by Winnie for her daughter Pearl. An analysis of this symbol can tell you what it is that Winnie wants for her daughter and what she thinks her daughter needs. If you write about the box of secret treasures, you might discuss what the novel has to say about the nature of keeping secrets and what happens when those secrets are brought out into the open. If you choose to focus on the greenhouse and the painting of Winnie's mother stored inside, you might use your analysis of these two symbols to discuss Winnie's relationship with her mother and how she was nurtured into adulthood without a maternal presence. Whichever symbol you choose, you will want to be sure to do close readings of all of the passages that reference the symbol, and use your analyses of these passages to help determine what the symbol stands for. You will also want to determine whether the symbol has a static meaning or whether the meaning changes during the course of the story. And finally, you will want to use your observations to help you to arrive at a fresh and interesting interpretation on a certain aspect of or element in the novel.

1. **The Kitchen God's wife, Lady Sorrowfree:** What does the figure symbolize?

   Reread the final chapter of the novel in which Winnie buys and names the statue and gives it to Pearl. How did Winnie choose the figure? What does she find significant about it? How does she arrive at a name for the figure? What does this name signify? What do you make of Winnie's decision to create her own goddess figure instead of simply choosing one she liked better for Pearl to put in the altar bequeathed to her by Grand Auntie Du?

2. **Box of secret treasures:** What does this box symbolize, and what does it tell us about Winnie and Pearl?

Examine the passages in which the box is discussed and described. Why did Winnie give the box to Pearl? What does Pearl think of it initially? What does she ultimately do with it? What kind of message is Winnie sending to Pearl by giving her the gift of a box to hold her secret treasures? Why do you think Winnie decides to open the box? What does she find inside, and what do these discoveries tell her? Examine the passages near the end of chapter four that describe Winnie opening the box and detail what is inside.

3. **The greenhouse and the painting of Winnie's mother:** What does the greenhouse symbolize for Winnie? What about the painting of her mother stowed inside?

Think about what a greenhouse might represent. What is such a structure typically used for? What is this particular greenhouse used for? What does it contain? What happens to Winnie in this greenhouse? What kind of space is it for her? Next, think about what you know of Winnie and her mother. What was their early relationship like and how did Winnie lose her mother? Why do you think Tan locates the painting of Winnie's mother in the greenhouse? What exactly does this painting symbolize to Winnie? Examine the passages in which Winnie talks about the paining, and, in particular, this one in which she recounts inadvertently destroying it:

> I saw a little spot of mold growing on her pale painted check. I took a soft cloth and dipped it in water, washed her face. But her cheek grew darker. I washed harder and harder. And soon I saw what I had done: rubbed half her face off completely! I cried, as if I had killed her. And after that, I could not look at

that picture without feeling a terrible grief. So you see, I did not even have a painting anymore to call my mother. (89)

What is Winnie trying to do when she destroys the painting? Why does her care result in the painting's destruction? Why do you think Tan opted to have Winnie accidentally destroy the painting instead of having it ruined some other way?

Compare and Contrast Essays

Comparing and contrasting is one of the most fruitful tools of analysis you can bring to bear on a literary work or works, as it can throw into relief important details or significant patterns that you might not have perceived as meaningful if you were focusing on these same elements in isolation. You can compare and contrast elements within a single work, such as the two main male characters in *The Kitchen God's Wife*, Wen Fu and Jimmy Louie; elements common to two works by the same author, such as the character Pearl from *The Kitchen God's Wife* and Jing-mei from *The Joy Luck Club*; or elements in the works of two different authors, such as the presentation of China in works by Maxine Hong Kingston versus works by Amy Tan. Whatever type of comparison and contrast you decide to make, be sure to use your observations to make a larger, more complex point. You do not want your essay to be a mere catalog of similarities and differences. Instead, you want to use the observations to demonstrate a particular pattern or to help you interpret meaningful differences.

Sample Topics:

1. **Pearl of *The Kitchen God's Wife* with Jing-mei of *The Joy Luck Club*:** Compare and contrast Pearl and Jing-mei; use your observations to draw conclusions about the life experiences of second-generation Chinese-American women.

   Read or reread Tan's first two novels, *The Joy Luck Club* and *The Kitchen God's Wife*, paying particular attention to Jing-mei and Pearl. Compare and contrast their memories of their childhood, their adult careers and romantic lives, and their relationships with their mothers. What similarities can you identify? Based on your notes, what do you conclude Tan views as essential or fundamental characteristics of second-generation Chinese-American women?

2. **Wen Fu and Jimmy Louie:** Compare and contrast Winnie's two husbands, Wen Fu and Jimmy Louie.

Begin with an examination of the differences in these two mens' personalities. How does each treat Winnie and other people in general? What else do you know about each man and his background? What might account for the differences in their makeup? Do you think the fact that Wen Fu was born in China and Jimmy Louie in the United States has anything to do with it? Is Tan trying to say something about the nature of masculinity in China? To answer this question, think about some of the other men in the story. Would you say they are more like Wen Fu or Jimmy Louie? Finally, differences are easy to spot when comparing these two characters, but spend some time also looking for any similarities. Do Wen Fu and Jimmy Louie have anything at all in common?

3. **Tan's China versus Kingston's China:** Compare and contrast Maxine Hong Kingston's and Amy Tan's portrayals of China.

Literary critic Ruth Maxey makes the following argument about Kingston's and Tan's depictions of China:

> Their fiction represents China from an implicit position of insider knowledge which invites the reader's confidence; indeed, Kingston and Tan seem to present themselves as American-born custodians of the Chinese heritage. Yet their representations of China are not based on the lived experience which that insider status would presuppose, but rather on inherited memories and a China of the imagination. . . . Kingston and Tan could follow the option of satirizing orientalism on its own terms in this way. Instead, it has to be said, their attitude to the ancestral homeland remains depressingly

unquestioning and unproblematized, devoid alike of inventiveness (except at the most obvious level) and the spirit of parody. This self-orientalization also lays itself open to the charge of pandering to popularity and financial success. (13)

You might want to read Maxey's article "'The East Is Where Things Begin': Writing the Ancestral Homeland in Amy Tan and Maxine Hong Kingston" to get a fuller understanding of the argument she makes. Then, decide which of Kingston's and Tan's works you will focus on, and reread these, paying careful attention to each author's portrayal of China. Do you agree with Maxey's criticism of both of these authors? Do you think it applies to one more than the other? If so, which and why?

Bibliography for *The Kitchen God's Wife*

Adams, Bella. "Representing History in Amy Tan's *The Kitchen God's Wife*." MELUS 28.2 (2003): 9–30.

Bailey, Paul. *China in the Twentieth Century.* Malen, MA: Wiley-Blackwell, 2001.

Bloom, Harold, ed. *Amy Tan.* Modern Critical Views. Philadelphia: Chelsea House, 2000.

Huntley, E. D. *Amy Tan: A Critical Companion.* Critical Companions to Popular Contemporary Writers. Westport, CT: Greenwood, 1998.

Maxey, Ruth. "'The East Is Where Things Begin': Writing the Ancestral Homeland in Amy Tan and Maxine Hong Kingston." *Orbis Litterarum* 60 (2005): 1–15.

Morton, W. Scott. *China: Its History and Culture.* 3rd ed. New York: McGraw-Hill, 1995.

Roberts, J. A. G. *A Concise History of China.* Cambridge, MA: Harvard UP, 1999.

Shields, Charles J. *Amy Tan.* Women of Achievement. Philadelphia: Chelsea House, 2002.

Tan, Amy. *The Kitchen God's Wife.* New York: Putnam's, 1991.

THE HUNDRED SECRET SENSES

READING TO WRITE

L IKE HER first two novels, Tan's *The Hundred Secret Senses* centers on
family history, memories, and relationships between women, though
this time the women are two half sisters instead of mother and daughter.
Unlike the earlier novels, however, *The Hundred Secret Senses* takes up a
"precarious position somewhere between the real and the surreal, between
the prosaic and the magical" (Baker 121). This "precarious position" has gar-
nered the novel mixed reviews; many have criticized Tan for indicating a
belief in the supernatural, while others have praised the novel for its superior storytelling and character development. Reactions to the characters
are likewise mixed. Though Kwan is a favorite character of many readers, it
is Olivia's psychological journey that really drives the novel forward.

In the following passage, Olivia thinks about the end of her 17-year marriage to Simon and the way that she and Kwan convinced Simon to marry
her in the first place. Olivia asked Kwan to contact Simon's deceased ex-
girlfriend Elza so that she could tell him to move on with his life. Olivia
believes that Kwan will convince herself that she sees, or pretend that she
sees, Elza and that Elza will "say" exactly what Olivia has suggested that she
should say. Olivia is certainly not expecting to have the personal encounter with Elza that she does, in which she sees the dead woman clinging to
Simon and asking him to wait for her. This scene still haunts Olivia 17 years
later. She does not know what to believe:

> I never told Kwan what I saw or heard. For one thing, I didn't want to believe
> it was anything but a hallucination. Yet over these last seventeen years, I've

come to know that the heart has a will of its own, no matter what you wish, no matter how often you pull out the roots of your worst fears. Like ivy, they creep back, latching on to the chambers in your heart, leeching out the safety of your soul, then slithering through your veins and out your pores. On countless nights, I've awakened in the dark with a recurring fever, my mind whirling, scared about the truth. Did Kwan hear what I heard? Did she lie for my sake? If Simon found out we'd tricked him, what would he do? Would he realize he didn't love me? (107)

The first thing that might strike you about this passage is Olivia's painful and negative notion that the heart holds on to fear despite a person's wishes and attempts to stop it. She believes that it is the heart's "will" that "no matter how often you pull out the roots of your worst fears," they come back, "latching on to the chambers of your heart." We can understand why she feels this way upon further examination of the passage. When she wakens in the night, Olivia notes that she is "scared about the truth," suggesting that the fears she refers to earlier in the passage are inextricably linked to the "truths" she holds about her life.

Olivia provides some clues as to what those truths are in this passage as well. The first is the "hallucination" she refers to in which Simon's deceased ex-wife, Elza, tells him to wait for her, and the second hint or suggestion is that Simon does not love her. The final question in this passage—"Would he realize he didn't love me?"—indicates that Olivia does not just wonder whether or not Simon loves her, which he thinks he does, she truly believes that he does not. Thus, Olivia's fears are idle worries or "what-ifs": What she actually fears is the truth, or rather, that the lies on which, in her mind, she has built her life—Simon's love for her and Elza's blessing on that love—will be uncovered. We can understand, then, why Olivia imagines her fears "leeching out the safety of [her] soul." She feels constantly vulnerable and afraid that the life she has created on falsehoods will come crumbling down. Olivia's description of her fears "slithering through [her] veins and out [her] pores" indicates that she feels that these "fears" or "truths" she tries to keep hidden not only "[leech] out the safety of [her] soul," but somehow find ways to escape from her and find their way out. Perhaps she is referring here to her part in the deterioration in her relationship with Simon.

If you are interested in pursuing this line of inquiry, you might search for examples in which Olivia's fears cause her to behave in ways that sabotage her relationship with Simon and actually help make those fears come true.

Or you might decide to investigate the actual "truth" of Olivia's "truths." Does the novel suggest that her beliefs are correct or not? What are the ramifications for her life, Kwan's, and Simon's in either case? From this small example, you can see that paying attention to one passage in a work of literature can help you to see things from new angles and give you an array of questions to pursue that could ultimately lead to an essay topic and even a thesis for that essay.

TOPICS AND STRATEGIES

Amy Tan's novels are long and complex, often involving many different settings and a large cast of characters. There is often so much going on that it can be difficult to decide what to focus on when you are faced with the task of writing an essay on a book such as *The Hundred Secret Senses*. It is helpful to remember that your essay simply cannot cover everything of importance in the novel and that there are not "right" or "wrong" topic choices. Your goal is to find a topic that interests you and to develop something inventive or fresh to say about that topic, to provide an insightful argument for your readers so that they will have a fresh angle on the book to explore. So, inevitably, you will need to exclude some things that seem important in order to keep your focus on the topic you have selected. And even then, you will not include everything you could possibly say about your topic; you will want to stick to the points that support and develop your thesis. You should feel free to develop a topic all your own, using those below as examples, or to simply choose one of the topics provided to begin your brainstorming. No matter how many essays are written on each of these suggested topics, no two will be exactly alike, as your own analysis of the novel's language as well as your own thinking process and personal experiences will influence the way that you approach and develop the topic into an essay all your own.

Themes

While you could identify and analyze dozens of different themes in *The Hundred Secret Senses*, a few of the more prominent ones include love, the supernatural, and identity formation. Of course, these are very broad themes, so if you decide to write about any of them, you will definitely need to narrow your focus. For example, if you choose to write about love, you can guide your thinking process by identifying the many different kinds of love evident in the novel and comparing and contrasting various relationships. However, as you begin to formulate a thesis for your essay, you will need to exclude the ideas that are not central to your main argument. For instance, if you find yourself gravitating toward a discussion of Olivia and Kwan's relationship and the familial love and loyalty they share, you might discard any of the prewriting that you did involving Simon and Olivia's troubled marriage. Or if you decide to focus, for example, on more destructive kinds of love, you might look more closely at Miss Banner and the General or Simon's continued infatuation with Elza. In any case, you should not feel as though you have to cover all of the subtopics and additional questions posed in the section discussing the theme of love. These are designed to help you begin to generate ideas and arrive at a much more specific topic of your own. If you generate a lot of prewriting that you end up not using at all, as you turn your attention to developing and fleshing out the couple of ideas you find most interesting, then you are probably on your way to a successful essay.

Sample Topics:

1. **Love:** What does *The Hundred Secret Senses* ultimately have to say about the human need and capacity for love?

   What different kinds of love are represented in the novel? Are some kinds of love portrayed as greater, more authentic, or more powerful than others? How would you describe the love between Olivia and Kwan? How does each sister demonstrate her love for the other? Is their relationship beneficial to both of them, or does Kwan give more than she receives? If so, what are the consequences of such an imbalance? What about the relationship between Miss Banner and Nunumu? Is it similar to that of Olivia and Kwan? Kwan talks often of her loyalty to Miss Banner. In this novel, is loyalty the same thing as love? If not, what is the difference? Is loyalty always a virtue in the novel? Is love?

   What about Olivia and Simon's relationship? How would you characterize their love? What do they find to admire in each other? What are the obstacles to their love; what has driven them apart? Finally, focusing on these two relationships in particular, answer the following questions: Does the novel indicate that love is truly destined? Does the novel indicate that love can overcome even death? How then, does Elza fit into this equation?

2. **The hundred secret senses, or the supernatural:** What role does the supernatural play in the novel?

According to Charles Shields, "several critics said they had difficulty putting aside their skepticism about ghosts and the supernatural—the ghost, or 'yin' world in the novel—in order to appreciate *The Hundred Secret Senses*" (80). In an interview with *Salon* magazine, Tan answers this charge. She says, "I'm educated, I'm reasonably sane . . . and I know that this subject is fodder for ridicule. To write the book, I had to put that aside. As with any book, I go through the anxiety, 'What will people think of me for writing something like this?' But ultimately, I have to write what I have to write about, including the question of life continuing beyond our ordinary senses" (qtd. in Shields 80).

What does the novel conclude about the reality of the hundred secret senses and the spirit world? The novel, at least in part, is about Olivia trying to come to terms with Kwan's belief in the otherworldly, so in order to ascertain the novel's ultimate stance on the supernatural, you might examine Olivia's evolving relationship with it. What are her feelings about Kwan's "yin" eyes as a child? How do her feelings evolve as an adult? What happens when she travels to Changmian? Would you say that Olivia is a "believer" by the novel's end? If so, would you say that she is a happier or wiser person because of this belief? Why do you think that some critics have such a problem with Tan's treatment of the supernatural in this novel? Is this criticism justified? What do you make of Tan's response to this criticism?

3. **Identity:** The novel forces everyone, whether or not they believe that Olivia and Nelly Banner are the same person, to stop and think about how a person's identity is created and sustained. According to the novel, what makes a person distinguishable from all other people? What exactly comprises identity? Who constructs it? How does it evolve over time?

One of the main issues of the novel is Olivia's search for a meaningful identity. She does not feel fulfilled by her marriage, her work, or her familial relationships. What seems to be missing? Evaluate whether Olivia's sense of identity has grown stronger or weaker by the novel's end. What has prompted this change? You might want to consider other characters and their search for identity as well. How does Kwan, Simon, or Du Lili, for that matter, create and maintain a sense of identity? Based on your observations, what, according to *The Hundred Secret Senses*, is identity constructed of? Does it have to do with memories? With priorities or principles? With relationships?

Character

One especially interesting aspect of character in this novel is the theory it posits that several of the main characters, including Kwan, Olivia, and Simon, are reincarnations of other characters, namely Nunumu, Nelly Banner, and Yiban. As you prepare to write your essay, you will have to determine how you are going to treat these particular characters. Will you take the novel on its own terms and consider the supposed linked souls, Olivia and Nelly Banner, for instance, to be the same person? If so, then you will want to discuss Olivia's life in terms of Nelly's. Can some of Olivia's behavior and preoccupations be explained by events from her former life? Or you might decide to treat Olivia and Nelly as separate characters, considering Nelly's story a fiction made up by Kwan and believed by Olivia only in her desperation to find identity and meaning in her life. In this case, you might ask yourself why Kwan creates such a character as Nelly and why Olivia, in time, comes to identify with her.

Sample Topics:

1. **Olivia/Nelly Banner:** Analyze and evaluate the character of Olivia Bishop/Nelly Banner.

   Begin by recording everything you know about Olivia. You might start with her childhood. What are her childhood memories? What were her relationships like with her mother and father? What did she think of Kwan when she first met her? How did their relationship evolve? Think also about Olivia's relationship with Simon. Why does she fall in love with him so quickly? Why is Olivia so dissatisfied with her life after 17 years of marriage to Simon? What are her major complaints? What does she feel is missing?

According to Kwan, Olivia was Nelly Banner in her previous life. Based on Kwan's stories, what do you know about Nelly Banner? What would you say are her major characteristics? What were her primary motivations in life? What were her good qualities and her flaws? Compare and contrast Nelly Banner and Olivia Bishop. In the world of the novel, are we to believe they truly are the same person? If so, is Olivia continuing a journey that Nelly started in her life? Can you trace a journey of evolution from Nelly to Olivia? If you think that the novel does not indicate that these two truly are the same person, how do you see them as connected? Is Olivia simply supposed to begin to define herself, to learn lessons about loyalty and love, through hearing stories about another woman who faced problems in some ways similar to hers?

2. **Kwan/Nunumu:** According to literary critic Sheng-mei Ma, Kwan is "[a]t once a seer with 'yin eyes' (3) and a specimen of superstitious gibberish." What does she mean by this? How would you describe this enigmatic character?

Ma writes that "[b]y exploiting the thin line between the incomprehensible and the irrational, between the inspired and the insane, between the profound and the pathetic, between 'secret senses' and nonsense, Tan is able to hold in double vision the comic Chinese sidekick Kwan, Olivia's half-sister." Do you agree with Ma's assessment of Kwan's character? If so, how exactly does Tan manage to make Kwan wise and ridiculous at the same time? Does this double-sided presentation result in Kwan seeming like less of an authentic human being?

Finally, you will need to consider whether the novel indicates that readers should believe that Kwan was once really Nunumu. What were Nunumu's defining characteristics? Are they similar to Kwan's? What does Kwan believe she did in her previous life as Nunumu for which she is trying now to atone? Whether or not you conclude that, in the universe of the novel, Kwan and Nunumu are indeed one and the same, you will want to spend some time comparing and contrasting these two figures. Even if they are not literally the same, how do their stories complement and inform one another?

3. **Simon/Yiban:** Analyze and evaluate the character of Simon/ Yiban.

What do you know of Simon's youth? His relationship with Elza? With Olivia? What are his good qualities? His flaws? How does he feel about Olivia? Why do you think he agrees to go to China with Olivia and Kwan? Think also about what you know of Yiban. What kind of man was he? Does the novel convince you that Yiban and Simon are really one and the same person? What evidence convinces you? If you do view them as the same person, can you trace an arc of development or progress from Yiban's life to Simon? Or is Simon losing ground in terms of a larger journey of the soul to happiness?

4. **Elza:** What role does Elza play in the novel and in Olivia and Simon's relationship?

What do you know about Elza? What kind of person was she? What was her relationship with Simon like? Examine how her death affected Simon and how it became a part of his relationship with Olivia. You will want to examine the scene in which Kwan "speaks" to the dead Elza and Olivia sees her as well. What is truly going on in those passages? Although this staged scene gets Olivia what she wants—Simon as her husband—the ghost of Elza still complicates Simon and Olivia's marriage decades after her death. What do you think she represents to each of them?

5. **Big Ma:** Analyze and evaluate the character of Big Ma.

What kind of childhood does Kwan experience with Big Ma? What are the good and the bad things that she remembers? What does she want to say to Big Ma when she arrives in Changmian? Would you say that Big Ma is ultimately a sympathetic character? What were her motives for treating Kwan the way she did? Is Big Ma a complex human figure, or do you think Tan intends her to serve as a representative of a certain idea or way of life? Finally, in your opinion, does Kwan finally make her peace with Big Ma?

History and Context

For many, if not most novels, especially those set in other countries, some historical and social background research can be rewarding and expansive to your discussion. *The Hundred Secret Senses* has not one, but two, settings with which you might have limited familiarity. The portions of the novel that relate the story of Miss Banner and Nunumu are set in 19th-century China during the Taiping Rebellion. If you take the time to do a little reading on this time and place in history, you will certainly have a much better understanding of the text. Of course, you can figure out a great deal of the history through the context of the novel, but if you are aiming for a deeper understanding of the work, the kind of familiarity necessary to write a successful essay with historical context as its focus, then you will need to do more than simply rely on the historical details that you can decipher from the text. A broader framework, including the details of the rebellion, the vying ideologies, and the way that the revolt is viewed by modern historians, will help you put the characters that Tan has created and the plot events of the novel into sharper perspective. You will then be in a much better position to figure out what kind of commentary Tan is making on the causes and consequences of the Taiping Rebellion and, in particular, its effects on the lives of Chinese citizens. Some of the later scenes in the novel take place in another setting with which you may be unfamiliar, rural late 20th-century China, particularly the small village of Changmian. Researching what life is like in contemporary rural China would also be beneficial in your reading of the novel. Armed with some knowledge of Chinese village life, you would be better able to comment on and evaluate Tan's portrayal of it. Is her depiction accurate? What elements of this life does she emphasize? Which does she neglect? You can see that not only can historical research help you to better understand the basic elements of a complicated novel, it can also help you to arrive at a thesis for your essay.

Sample Topics:

1. **Taiping Rebellion and 19th-century China:** What kind of commentary does *The Hundred Secret Senses* make on the Taiping Rebellion?

    E. D. Huntley writes that the Taiping Rebellion, which occurred in China during the 1850s–60s, was the most important peasant-led revolt in Chinese history. The Taiping regime, led by the charismatic Hong Xiuquan, gained strength during the Qing Dynasty in the wake of the Opium wars, the opening of China's borders to foreign trade, and the loss of Hong Kong to the British crown. At its height, the rebellion involved over 600,000 men and 500,000 women. Borrowing their ideology and teachings from Christianity, the Taiping followers rebelled against what they considered to be corruption and obsolescence in the imperial court, demanding widespread changes that included equality for women, agricultural reform and the abolition of private property. Educated in part by Western missionaries whose teachings apparently resonated with his own naturally mystical leanings, Hong Xiuquan converted to Christianity, and thereafter claimed not only that he was Jesus Christ's younger brother, but also that his relationship to Jesus made him the Heavenly King on earth. (137)

Research the Taiping Rebellion to deepen your understanding of the philosophy and principles that the rebels adopted. Then, return to the novel, rereading the scenes that are set during the era of the rebellion. How does your new knowledge help you better understand the plot and the characters' motivations? What are the competing ideologies at work? How were ordinary citizens' lives impacted by this rebellion?

2. **Changmian, China:** We learn that Changmian, like many Chinese words, has two meanings. Kwan explains that it can mean either "something soft but go on forever like thread" or "long sleep," meaning death. Which of these best describes Changmian? How are these two meanings connected? What role does this ambiguous space ultimately play in the novel?

According to E. D. Huntley,

> Throughout the novel, Changmian displays two faces: one face presents the magical timeless village of Kwan's edited memories and Olivia's first impressions; the other face belongs to the poor but vibrant community that profoundly—and joyously—sends its

best and strongest citizens to fight for the cause of the Heavenly
King in the Taiping wars, and a century later participates with
equal enthusiasm in the frenzied rush to cash in on a significant
archaeological discovery—the luminous underground lake and
prehistoric village that come to light during the search for Kwan
in the mountain caves. (130)

How is the Changmian of the 20th century different from the
village that Nunumu experienced in the previous century? What
are its consistent characteristics? Does it surprise you that the citizens of Changmian are eager to take tourists' money even when it
results in the destruction of their underground lake?

What do Simon and Olivia find when they arrive in Changmian? How does the landscape and the way of life there affect
each of them and their relationship with each other? Look
closely at the way they behave and the things that they say in San
Francisco and compare that with their actions in Changmian.
How much of this difference is attributable to the new environment? You will also want to consider how Kwan responds to
Changmian. Does she find her village much the same, as it was
when she left it? What has changed and what remains the same?
What is the significance of Kwan getting lost in the caves?

Philosophy and Ideas

To write an essay about philosophy and ideas, you will want to think about
the larger issues at stake in *The Hundred Secret Senses.* You know that the
basic story is about two half sisters, one—Olivia—born and raised in the
United States to a white mother and Chinese father and the other—Kwan—
who was born to two Chinese parents and raised until the age of 18 in China.
When Kwan comes to join Olivia's family after the girls' shared father has
died, the story becomes one of a tense but loving relationship between the
sisters, with Kwan heaping on the unconditional love and Olivia feeling
affection for Kwan but also needing some time away from this sister who
claims she can see ghosts and tells stories of past lives. The sisters' story
is complicated by the slow revelation of another story, that of loyal friends
Nelly Banner and Nunumu, and ultimately it is revealed that these two figures that repeatedly show up in Kwan's stories are actually Olivia and Kwan
in their former lives; according to Kwan, she and Olivia are now actually ful-

filling destinies that were cut short due to the violence of the Taiping Rebellion. Based on just the basics of the story, a couple of topics dealing with philosophy and ideas come to mind. The first has to do with fate and free will. If the two sisters' lives are so governed by destiny and fate, then how much control does each sister really have over her own identity and life's journey? As we watch Olivia struggle to find meaning in her life and create a strong sense of self, we have to wonder how much of that struggle is based on Olivia's reorganization of her personal sense of priorities and deep self-reflection and how much is simply her refusal to accept her already planned out destiny. The second topic suggested by this basic outline of the novel springs from the vast difference between logical and pragmatic Olivia and her Chinese sister Kwan, who claims the power to communicate with ghosts and manages to convince her sister that the two of them were best friends in former lives. These differences might prompt you to devote some attention to analyzing Tan's treatment of Chinese characters, culture, beliefs, and settings. Is Tan's depiction of all things Chinese accurate? Is it ethical? In other words, exactly what associations does Tan make with Chinese culture, and what effect do these associations have on our interpretation of the novel?

Sample Topics:

1. **Fate versus free will:** Immersed in the world of *The Hundred Secret Senses*, we get the feeling that everything is progressing according to a grand master plan, that events are unfolding in the only way that they could ultimately unfold. Why is it, then, that we remain invested in the decisions that the characters, particularly Olivia, make as they progress on their journeys? Is Olivia simply making preordained choices, is she selecting one out of a few available paths that her life might take, or is she, despite indications to the contrary, completely in control of her destiny and shaping it with every decision she makes?

   Start by rereading the novel with this issue of fate and free will firmly in mind. What parts of the novel suggest that our lives are governed by fate or destiny? Are there other aspects of the story that indicate that free will plays a role as well? In what specific instances do the characters seem to be forced along preordained paths, and in what instances do they seem to make independent, spontaneous decisions? Can you spot a pattern or make a generalization about what seems to control the direction of these characters' lives? Write an essay in which you discuss just how much control each individual has over the course of his or her life in the universe of Tan's novel.

2. **Tan's treatment of Chinese culture and characters:** Amy Tan considers herself an American rather than an Asian-American, writer, yet she clearly has strong family ties to China, and much of her fiction deals with family stories and employs Chinese settings. How successful is this self-described American writer at creating believable and authentic Chinese scenes and characters?

Literary critic Sheng-mei Ma is very critical of Tan's treatment of Chinese culture and characters, suggesting that Tan creates a dichotomy between the complex, civilized, and utterly human West and a China associated with all things nonhuman, including both the divine and the animal. In Ma's words:

> "dog" spelled backwards becomes "god" (3). To Amy Tan, "Chinese dogs" and "Chinese gods" are one and the same, dogs deified, gods mongrelized. With both qualities instilled into "Chinese-ness," Tan's true motive is the construction of the American self which engineers and marionettes New Age ethnicity and primitivism. By rendering the Chinese simultaneously animalistic and divine, Tan in effect becomes an invisible creator, whose creatures reenact the Orientalist fantasies of her massive "mainstream" following. (4)

What do you think Ma means when she writes that Tan's focus is on the "construction of the American self which engineers and marionettes New Age ethnicity and primitivism"? How do Americans perceive themselves and their relationship with other peoples of the world? What are the "Orientalist fantasies" that Ma refers to? In other words, what do Americans expect or desire Chinese culture to be? Why do you think these expectations are such a problem to Ma? How does Amy Tan go about fulfilling these expectations with her fiction? After you digest and consider Ma's argument, you will also want to return to the novel to evaluate for yourself Tan's portrayal of Chinese culture. Do you feel that her depictions are accurate? Spend some time comparing and contrasting Tan's treatment of American characters and culture with Chinese. How would you describe her treatment of each?

As you think about these questions, you may want to read Ma's article "'Chinese and Dogs' in Amy Tan's *The Hundred Secret Senses*: Ethnicizing the Primitive à la New Age" to get a fuller sense of the argument she advances. Once you have considered Ma's evidence and conclusions and done some thinking of your own about Tan's portrayal of China in the novel, write an essay in which you either support, reject, or modify Ma's assessment of Tan's treatment of Chinese culture in *The Hundred Secret Senses*.

Form and Genre

When an author plans to write a story with as many characters and settings as Tan has incorporated into *The Hundred Secret Senses*, there are many decisions to make about how best to tell such a teeming story. In this case, Tan had to decide who would tell the various parts of the story and how to organize its telling—how much of each part of the story to reveal at each moment and in what order to present the various interlocking parts. One of the easiest ways to see how these decisions are crucial to the overall experience of reading a novel and its interpretations is to spend some time considering what the novel would be like had the author made different choices. Imagine, for example, that portions of *The Hundred Secret Senses* were told from Simon and Yiban's points of view. Or what if it were told entirely from Olivia's point of view, or Kwan's? What if the story of Nunumu and Miss Banner was told all in one piece, either in the middle of the book or at the end, as one big revelation from Kwan to Olivia after Simon is lost in the caves. How would these choices change the novel? Now think about the choices that Tan did make and consider why she made them. What is she trying to emphasize? What effects is she trying to achieve?

Sample Topics:

1. **Narrative strategy:** What narrative strategies does Tan employ in *The Hundred Secret Senses,* and what is the effect of those strategies on the overall themes and meanings of the novel?

To answer this question, return to the novel, chapter by chapter, and make a chart of narration. Who is narrating what parts of the story? Then, begin to make generalizations about each narrator. When Olivia is narrating, to whom is she speaking? What about Kwan? To whom are her stories told? What are each narrator's motives for telling the stories they tell? How would you characterize each voice? Is one more likable than the other? Stronger? More descriptive? More analytical? What effect do you think Tan was going for in having both sisters serve as narrators?

2. **Structure and chronology:** The events of *The Hundred Secret Senses* take place in multiple settings and in different time periods as well. Analyze, evaluate, and interpret Tan's strategy for the complicated narration that presenting such a multilayered story necessarily involves.

You will need to begin by returning to the novel and charting events as they occur or are revealed. What chapters are set in the present? Which ones are set in the past? How does Tan make the transition from present to past to present again? Are there "triggers" that prompt Kwan to reveal more of the story of Nunumu and Miss Banner? If so, what are these triggers? What determines how much of the past story is revealed at a time? Spend some time thinking about other possible ways Tan could have constructed this story. She might, for example, have used Olivia, Kwan, and Simon's story as a framework and included all of the Miss Banner, Nunumu, and Yiban story as a tale within a tale revealed all in one sitting. How would such an arrangement have altered your interpretation of the text? In what other ways might Tan have treated and managed this narrative, and how would they have changed your experience of the novel? Once you have spent some time considering alternatives, return to your notes on the actual organization of the novel and ask yourself again how this particular arrangement influences your perception of the novel's themes and meanings.

Language, Symbols, and Imagery

Tan creates many powerful and meaningful symbols and images in *The Hundred Secret Senses,* among them various kinds of cuisine, Miss Banner's music box, and the baby, Samantha Li. To write an essay on a particular symbol or image, you will want to first identify all of the passages in which the symbol you have chosen to analyze is featured or described. Then, analyze these passages, paying particular attention to the words and phrases used in the descriptions and the associations the author makes between the symbol and particular characters, events, or emotions. Often, focusing on discrete elements of a novel such as symbols can paradoxically help you to work toward more informed and nuanced interpretations of the text as a whole. For example, if you chose Samantha as your topic, you would analyze all of the passages in the novel that deal with Simon and Olivia's childbearing decisions, including why they have not had children in the past and what this new child, Samantha Li, signifies about their changing relationship. Once you have examined these passages and reflected on what Samantha means in the context of the entire novel, you will have a much greater understanding of the nature of Simon and Olivia's relationship, including their communication or lack thereof, their personal and joint life goals, and the nature of the future they are attempting to create together.

1. **Samantha Li:** What does Simon and Olivia's new baby come to represent?

Begin by thinking about what new babies traditionally symbolize. Then, return to the novel, rereading all of the portions that reference Simon and Olivia's struggles with childbearing, including the latter half of the novel in which Simon and Olivia reunite in Changmian, realize she is pregnant, and react to having a baby together. You will want to think about why Simon and Olivia do not have kids in their first 17 years of marriage. How is this decision arrived at? What does it mean to each of them? Then, think about the significance of the circumstances of Samantha's conception and how these circumstances affect what this new baby comes to symbolize. You will also want to consider how the baby's name is significant. How is she connected to Kwan? What does she mean for Simon and Olivia's relationship? Does Samantha Li represent what all babies typically represent, or is there something a little different about the symbolism of this particular infant?

2. **Miss Banner's music box:** What does Miss Banner's music box symbolize?

Begin by recording what you know about the music box. What is kept inside it? When does Miss Banner play it? What tune does it play, and what is the significance of this tune? Why does Nunumu bury the box when she thinks Miss Banner has eloped with General Cape? When and why does she return it to Miss Banner? Finally, what do Miss Banner and Nunumu put inside the box when they are forced to flee for their lives from the Ghost Merchant's house? You will want to consider also how the music box comes to figure in Olivia's personal journey. What happens when Kwan finds and opens the box for her?

3. **Food:** What does food symbolize for the various characters of *The Hundred Secret Senses*? How might an analysis of food and the characters' responses to it help you arrive at new insights about the novel's themes and meanings?

According to E. D. Huntley, "In the end, food for Olivia comes to represent Kwan's nurturing presence—and Olivia's own salvation" (132). Do you agree with this assessment? Can you locate some evidence in the text? On what occasions does Kwan feed Olivia? What emotions are associated with these events? Simon and Olivia arrange to travel to China in order to work on an article about the village cuisine of China. Do they find the kinds of foods and photo opportunities that they are expecting in China? What kinds of foods do they end up eating, and how do they react to them? Specifically, you might want to consider the duck eggs: What did they represent to Nunumu and ultimately to the other residents of the Ghost Merchant's house? What do they come to mean for Olivia?

Compare and Contrast Essays

As you begin to think about what sort of comparison and contrast essay you might like to write, you will want to consider the desired length and scope of your intended piece. You can compare and contrast elements within a novel, such as Kwan with Nunumu and Olivia with Nelly Banner, or elements from two or more novels, such as Jing-mei from *The Joy Luck Club* with Olivia from *The Hundred Secret Senses* and perhaps Pearl from *The Kitchen God's Wife*; or you might want to compare and contrast Tan's novels with the novels of other authors such as Louise Erdrich or Maxine Hong Kingston. Generally speaking, the more novels you include, the longer your essay will need to be, although the exact elements that you are comparing and contrasting have an influence as well. For example, an essay about the male characters in Tan's first three novels would likely be shorter than an essay about the female characters in these same novels simply because the female characters are more integral to the stories and therefore there is much more material about them to consider. Once you have decided on your topic and begun to take notes on similarities and differences, you will discover some interesting and surprising details that you might not otherwise have noticed. Remember that no matter how confident you are in discussing the likenesses you have discovered between the two characters or other elements you are studying, simply pointing them out will not result in a successful essay. You will need to analyze all the similarities and differences you have discovered, identifying both patterns and meaningful differences, and even then your task is not complete. Once you have identified these significant patterns and meaningful differences, you will need to press them into service, using your observations and analysis to help you make some useful and grounded generalizations about the works you have studied, generalizations that will help other readers of the novels to look at them in new ways.

Sample Topics:

1. **Kwan and Nunumu or Olivia and Nelly Banner:** Compare and contrast Kwan with Nunumu and/or Olivia with Nelly Banner.

   According to Kwan, and later in the novel, to Olivia as well, Kwan and Olivia are reincarnations of Nunumu and Nelly Banner. Whether you believe that the novel intends its readers to accept this as true or not, spend some time comparing and contrasting Kwan and Nunumu and Olivia with Nelly Banner; even if Kwan and Olivia are not reincarnations of these other women, their willingness to believe that they are reveals that there are connections strong enough for Kwan and Olivia to see themselves in these other women. What are these connections? What are the similarities between Kwan and Nunumu and Olivia and Nelly Banner? What might Kwan and Olivia learn about themselves by studying the stories of Nunumu and Nelly Banner?

2. **Jing-mei from *The Joy Luck Club* versus Olivia from *The Hundred Secret Senses:*** Compare and contrast these two characters.

Begin by reading or rereading both of these novels, taking notes on Jing-mei and Olivia. What are the main traits of each woman? What are her priorities and her obstacles in life? How did her childhood help to shape her identity? How would you describe the relationships of these American-born women with their Chinese family members? You will want to think also about each woman's trip to China. What is the trip meant to accomplish in each case? Is it successful? How does the trip affect the relationships between Jing-mei and her mother (or her understanding of her mother, as her mother is deceased when Jing-mei makes the trip to China) and Olivia and Kwan? Depending on the desired length and scope of your essay, you might bring in Pearl from *The Kitchen God's Wife* as well, asking the same questions of her that you have of Olivia and Jing-mei.

Once you have done some thinking about each of these characters, you will want to look for patterns. What do Jing-mei and Olivia (and Pearl) have in common? How is Olivia's relationship with her sister Kwan similar to and different from the relationship that Jing-mei shared with her mother (and the one that Pearl experienced with her mother Winnie)? Use the patterns you discover to help you make generalizations. What can you say about the way that culture influences family relationships in Tan's fictional worlds? What can you say about the way that growing up in a bicultural family affects a person's identity and self-perception?

3. **Tan's male characters:** Compare and contrast Simon in *The Hundred Secret Senses* with Wen Fu of *The Kitchen God's Wife* and any of the male characters in *The Joy Luck Club.*

Tan has been criticized for her tendency to create male characters who are one dimensional and often unlikable and even brutal. Revisit Tan's first three novels, and take notes on the male
characters who appear in each one. What are they like? What
would you consider their defining characteristics to be? How
would you describe their relationships with the women in their
lives and with other men? Are there differences between Tan's
portrayal of American men versus Chinese men? What are they?
You will also want to think about whether Tan's portrayal of
male characters remained consistent through these first three
novels, or whether you can chart some kind of evolution. Do
her male characters seem to be changing in a certain way as she
progresses through these novels? And if so, would you characterize this as a positive or negative development? Why?

Bibliography for *The Hundred Secret Senses*

Bailey, Paul. *China in the Twentieth Century.* Malen, MA: Wiley-Blackwell, 2001.

Huntley, E. D. *Amy Tan: A Critical Companion.* Critical Companions to Popular
Contemporary Writers. Westport, CT: Greenwood, 1998.

———. *"The Hundred Secret Senses" Amy Tan.* Modern Critical Views. Ed. Harold
Bloom. Philadelphia: Chelsea House, 2000.

Ma, Sheng-mei. "'Chinese and Dogs' in Amy Tan's *The Hundred Secret Senses:* Ethnicizing the Primitive à la New Age." *MELUS* (Spring, 2001).

Maxey, Ruth. "'The East Is Where Things Begin': Writing the Ancestral Homeland
in Amy Tan and Maxine Hong Kingston." *Orbis Litterarum* 60 (2005): 1–15.

Messud, Claire. "Ghost Story" (Review of *The Hundred Secret Senses*). *The New
York Times* 29 Oct. 1995.

Morton, W. Scott. *China: Its History and Culture.* 3rd ed. New York: McGraw-Hill,
1995.

Roberts, J. A. G. *A Concise History of China.* Cambridge, MA: Harvard UP, 1999.

Shields, Charles J. *Amy Tan.* Women of Achievement. Philadelphia: Chelsea House,
2002.

Tan, Amy. *The Hundred Secret Senses.* New York: Putnam's, 1995.

Yu, Su-Lin. "Sisterhood as Cultural Difference in Amy Tan's *The Hundred Secret
Senses* and Cristina Garcia's *The Aguero Sisters.*" *CRITIQUE: Studies in Contemporary Fiction* (June, 2006).

THE BONESETTER'S
DAUGHTER

READING TO WRITE

AMY TAN'S fourth novel, *The Bonesetter's Daughter* (2001), returns to one of the fundamental themes of her earlier work: the tension-fraught relationship that often exists between mothers and daughters, particularly when that relationship is complicated by cultural differences. In this novel, as in *The Joy Luck Club* and *The Kitchen God's Wife*, the mother figure had a traditional Chinese upbringing, while the daughter was raised in the United States; as such, the home becomes both an intergenerational and bicultural battleground. The mother in this novel, LuLing, is suffering from Alzheimer's. Luckily for her daughter, Ruth, LuLing took the time to write her life story while her memory was still functioning well enough to record it clearly. Much of the text of the novel is devoted to LuLing's story of her childhood in China and of her mother, whom she grew up knowing as her nursemaid and calling Precious Auntie. Becoming familiar with the nature of this relationship between her mother and her grandmother helps Ruth understand and make peace with her own troubled connection to LuLing.

LuLing's memoir reveals that she often asked her nursemaid, Precious Auntie, to tell her how she had gotten the burn scars on her face and how she had come to be her nursemaid. The stories that Precious Auntie would invent, such as the following, can perhaps tell us something about LuLing and Ruth's relationship and about the role of women in Chinese culture as well.

I was a fire-eater, she said with her hands and eyes. *Hundreds of people came to see me in the market square. Into the burning pot of my mouth I dropped raw pork, added chilis and bean paste, stirred this up, then offered the morsels to people to taste. If they said, "Delicious!" I opened my mouth as a purse to catch copper coins. One day, however, I ate the fire, and the fire came back, and it ate me. After that, I decided not to be a cook-pot anymore, so I became your nursemaid instead.* (3)

What might strike you first about this passage is the fact that Precious Auntie imagines herself using her mouth to prepare food for the masses. This image calls immediately to mind one of women's most traditional functions, the source of nourishment for society. Because in this particular image the sustenance is prepared not in a pot but in the woman's own body, it echoes woman's role as the creator of life as well, calling to mind the nourishment a woman's body provides a growing fetus. With this one powerful image, Precious Auntie evokes the role of woman as creator and sustainer of life, and by setting that image in the "market square" where she receives coins for her actions, she reminds us that this role functions within a particular economic context: After marriage, a woman becomes her husband's property and remains valuable to him only as long as she fulfills this obligation to create and sustain life, to have babies, to nourish these babies, and tend to her husband's needs as well.

Another aspect of this passage that might catch your attention is the fact that Precious Auntie is communicating with "her hands and eyes." She has no voice with which to speak. She has been badly scarred and so, physically, she cannot speak, but it is telling that in the story she informs LuLing, even before the burning takes place, when the "fire came back . . . and ate [her]," Precious Auntie could not speak. Her role as "cook-pot" prevents it. Metaphorically, this suggests that a woman's identity is wrapped up in her body and its social value instead of in her voice and the inner will and opinions it might express.

The novel, then, might be read as Precious Auntie's commentary on the role of women in Chinese society, particularly the role of married women. Precious Auntie, in this version of the story, trades in her life as a "cook-pot" for life as a nursemaid, and in real life, it is when Precious Auntie loses her chance at married life that she becomes LuLing's nursemaid. The suggestion, then, is that it is woman's role as wife that is most clearly connected to the image of the cook pot in the market square that Precious Auntie describes. In the story, Precious Auntie imagines herself giving up her job as "cook-pot," when in reality she was unable to marry after the tragedy of

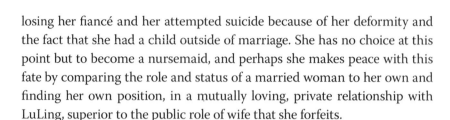

losing her fiancé and her attempted suicide because of her deformity and the fact that she had a child outside of marriage. She has no choice at this point but to become a nursemaid, and perhaps she makes peace with this fate by comparing the role and status of a married woman to her own and finding her own position, in a mutually loving, private relationship with LuLing, superior to the public role of wife that she forfeits.

At this point, you might decide to examine the other versions of her story that Precious Auntie tells LuLing to determine if they suggest some of these same ideas. Can you make a convincing case that Precious Auntie feels that her life is ultimately more satisfying than it would have been had she married, or can you make a case that she tries to convince herself that this is so? What, besides the fact that she is no longer of marriageable age, might have made her feel this way, as presumably she once thought otherwise and was planning to marry? You might also think about what message Precious Auntie is conveying to LuLing through these stories and whether she is doing so intentionally or not. Fire commonly signifies desire or passion. Do you think that Precious Auntie is warning LuLing that she will suffer terrible consequences if she gives into her own passions and desires? What else might she be conveying to LuLing with these stories? You might also consider why Precious Auntie devises these various tales. She cannot tell LuLing the truth, for LuLing is not supposed to know that Precious Auntie is her mother, but Precious Auntie could certainly have come up with an explanation for her burns and position as LuLing's nursemaid. Instead, she shrouds the events in mystery, making each explanation she offers fantastical. What purpose do you think this serves?

Whatever line of inquiry you decide to pursue, it is a good idea to identify several relevant passages and perform close readings on them, paying particular attention to the language and asking yourself why Tan wrote the words exactly as she did. After all, there are many ways to get the same idea across. You also may want to note what things Tan has chosen to leave out—is there something you would expect to see in a particular passage or chapter but do not? What might the significance of that authorial decision be? Once you have examined multiple passages, you will need to synthesize your findings, using them to help you arrive at a new insight into or interpretation of some aspect of the text. Then, as you craft your essay, you will use the most convincing evidence from your close readings to support this insight or interpretation, which will serve as your thesis, the grounding or focal point of your essay.

TOPICS AND STRATEGIES

In the following section, you will find many possible ways to approach writing an essay on Amy Tan's *The Bonesetter's Daughter.* Even this extensive list is nowhere near exhaustive, so you should feel free to develop a topic of your own if something about the book interests you that you do not see covered here. Reading through some of these topics might give you a sense of the kinds of questions you might ask regarding the topic you have devised. If you decide to use one of the topics listed here, remember that these are not test questions, and you are not expected to address each aspect proposed as part of a given topic. You should use the main questions and secondary questions to help you probe the topic more deeply and perhaps to lead you in directions you might not otherwise have thought about pursuing. The topics should aid you greatly as you prewrite, brainstorm, and select passages for close reading. Once you have generated enough ideas, you should synthesize your analysis and observations and use them to develop an argument or interpretation on which to base your essay.

Themes

The Bonesetter's Daughter is concerned with many universal themes, including the importance of memory to the human psyche and the relationships—both loving and fraught with tension—between mothers and daughters, among others. No matter what theme you choose to explore in your essay, it is helpful to remember that you will not be able to discuss everything related to that theme. You will need to develop an argument or interpretation connected to that theme and then construct your essay by laying out your strongest evidence in support of your argument. If you are writing about mother/daughter relationships, for example, you might focus on the rebellious acts of both LuLing and Ruth as teenagers and argue that their feelings and behavior are normal parts of growing up and asserting an identity independent from one's mother. Whereas Ruth gets the chance to move past that stage and to develop a relationship with her mother as an adult woman, LuLing never gets that chance, and thus she is perpetually stuck in the role of child, trying desperately to receive her mother's forgiveness and guidance from beyond the grave. If you were to build your essay around an argument such as this, you would need to focus strictly on the pertinent mother/daughter relationships. You would, therefore, not concern yourself with Dory and Fia and their relationship with Ruth as their stepmother or with GaoLing and her mother.

Alternatively, you might wish to write an essay that investigates what really constitutes a mother figure: How much does a blood relationship figure into it and what else enters into the equation? This kind of essay might entail an examination of Ruth's relationship with Dory and Fia as well as GaoLing and LuLing's relationship with GaoLing's mother and LuLing's relationship with Precious Auntie, who was in fact LuLing's biological mother although LuLing did not know this until after Precious Auntie's death. The particular material you include in your essay should be determined by the scope of your essay and by the particular argument that you, after much prewriting and brainstorming, have decided you want to put forward in your essay.

Sample Topics:

1. **Memory:** As LuLing is beginning to suffer from Alzheimer's disease, memory is certainly one of the fundamental concerns of *The Bonesetter's Daughter*. How would you summarize Tan's commentary on the nature of memory in this exploration of the intersection among identity, memory, and relationships?

   How are memories transmitted from one person to another in the novel? Why do you think that LuLing wrote down memories of her youth and passed them on to Ruth? What does Ruth learn about her mother through these memories? What does Mr. Tang, who translates the Chinese into English for Ruth, learn from them? What happens to Ruth's memory as the Alzheimer's progresses? How does her day-to-day life change, and how do her memories of her youth change? Do these changes in LuLing's memory make her into a different person? Why or not? In what ways do our memories make us who we are?

2. **Mother/daughter relationships and teenage rebellion:** Many of Tan's works have to do with the ambivalent relationships that can spring up between mothers and daughters. What does *The Bonesetter's Daughter* have to say about these relationships, and how is this different from Tan's previous novels?

   Describe the relationships between LuLing and Precious Auntie and between Ruth and LuLing. How would you characterize each?

As strong? Troubled? Both? Can you find any similarities in the way that LuLing and Ruth behave toward their mothers? What happens when each daughter struggles to assert her independence from her mother?

You might also compare the mother/daughter pairs in this novel to those in Tan's previous works, including Jing-mei and Suyuan or any of the other mother/daughter pairs in *The Joy Luck Club* or Winnie and Pearl in *The Kitchen God's Wife*. What is Tan saying about mothers and daughters in *The Bonesetter's Daughter* that she has not said before?

3. **Identity:** Ruth wonders at the fact that the man who translated her mother's account develops such affection for her that he comes to meet her and then begins to take her on weekly outings, even establishing a romantic relationship with her. Art suggests that Mr. Tang has truly gotten to know LuLing from her manuscript in a way that Art feels he has not gotten to know Ruth. What does he mean by this, and do you agree with him? What implications does such an idea have for our conception of identity?

Reread *The Bonesetter's Daughter,* paying particular attention to what makes Ruth and LuLing the women they are. What would you say are their defining characteristics? How do they define themselves? How do others define them? Why do you think Mr. Tang feels that he knows LuLing so well (and Art agrees that he does) after reading her version of her life story? Is it because he knows the events of her life? Is it because she revealed secrets that had previously been closely guarded? Or is it because some essential element of her personality comes through in the way she tells the story? What is it that makes LuLing unique? How much of that does she stand to lose as the Alzheimer's progresses?

4. **Romantic love:** Although this novel focuses a great deal on filial relationships among women, romantic love also plays a big part in the story of each of the main character's lives. What does Tan ultimately say about the nature of romantic love in *The Bonesetter's Daughter*?

How does Tan depict romantic love in *The Bonesetter's Daughter*? What do you know about the major romantic relationships of Precious Auntie and LuLing? What about Ruth's relationship with Art? This relationship definitely evolves during the course of the novel. How would you characterize the relationship at the start of the novel? What are its problems? What causes the changes that occur? What kind of a future do Ruth and Art have together? According to the novel, what makes a successful relationship? Are the benefits of love really worth the sacrifices one makes and the potential heartbreak it can lead to?

5. **Guilt:** Guilt seems to be a constant in all of Tan's mother/daughter relationships and those in *The Bonesetter's Daughter* are no exception. What does Tan ultimately have to say about guilt in this novel?

Why do LuLing and Ruth each harbor heavy feelings of guilt in regard to their mothers? Are their guilty feelings justified? How does this guilt shape their lives and affect their behavior? How does it affect their relationships with each other and with other people? What other characters take actions based on some type of guilty feelings? Is guilt, as it is presented in the novel, ultimately a productive emotion? Why or why not?

Character

The Bonesetter's Daughter is filled with characters you might decide to write about in an essay. Whether you elect to focus on Ruth, LuLing, Art, GaoLing, Precious Auntie, or another character not mentioned in the suggestions below, remember to consider the character's actions, speech, and any internal thoughts you are privy to. You will also want to be sure to consider how you are getting the information that will shape your interpretation and argument. For example, if you are writing about LuLing, you are getting information about her family history and her childhood in China from a written first-person account crafted before her memory failed to the point that Ruth recognized that her mother was ill. You will want to consider that these events are told from LuLing's own perspective and so are imbued with her own hopes, desires, and regrets. It is often helpful to stop and think about how the account might be different if it was presented by someone else, GaoLing perhaps, or simply a third-person narrator. When writing about a character, you will also want to determine whether that character remains static through the course of the work or whether he or she develops in some way, either negatively or positively. Determining the evolution of a character can often help you to gain perspective on the author's larger aims in constructing the novel. Perhaps, for example, you have observed that Ruth's willingness to listen to her mother ironically helps her to discover and begin to use her own voice. This is presented in the novel as unequivocally positive. Perhaps, then, you would want to look for other evidence that supports the theory that one of the novel's main messages is that listening well—being attentive and receptive to the stories of others—is a prerequisite for understanding and expressing ourselves.

Sample Topics:

1. **Ruth:** Analyze and evaluate the character of Ruth. What kind of person is she, and how does she evolve throughout the course of the novel?

   What do you know about Ruth? What was her childhood like? What were the major experiences and relationships that formed her character? What is the significance of Ruth's career choice? How would you describe her relationship with Art, his daughters, and with her mother, LuLing? How do these relationships evolve during the course of the novel? What is different about Ruth by the novel's end? Would you say that Ruth is a "better" person? If so, can you describe exactly how? What was it that sparked these changes in Ruth?

2. **LuLing:** Analyze and evaluate LuLing's character. Do you ultimately find her to be a likable, sympathetic character despite the harsh way that she mothers Ruth? Why or why not?

   How would you describe LuLing as a mother to Ruth? How would you describe her as a daughter to Precious Auntie? A sister to Gao-Ling? How does your opinion of LuLing change when you read the story of her childhood? How is LuLing changing because of the Alzheimer's disease? What things about her remain the same? Would you say that LuLing evolves as a person throughout the course of her life? At what point would you say she is at her strongest? Her wisest? Her most serene?

3. **Art:** Analyze and evaluate the character of Art, Ruth's long-term partner.

Record everything you know about Art. How would you describe him? How does Ruth perceive him? Is he a sympathetic character? Is he a fully realized fleshed-out character, or does he come across as one dimensional? What do you make of his relationship with Ruth? With his daughters Fia and Dory? What kind of partner is Art? What kind of father is he?

One way to help ascertain whether Art is a fully realized character is to investigate whether or not he evolves over the course of the novel. Would you argue that Art makes some fundamental changes in the course of the story? If so, what inspires him to do so? What realizations does he come to, and how does he arrive at them? Would you say that he is a "better" person by novel's end?

4. **GaoLing:** Analyze and evaluate the character of LuLing's "sister," GaoLing.

Record what you know about GaoLing. Is she a sympathetic character? How does she behave toward LuLing when they are children? How does her relationship with LuLing change when she finds out that the older girl is not really her sister? Would you say that their relationship with each other is a positive or negative force in each woman's life? Why?

You may want to compare and contrast the relationship between LuLing and GaoLing with the sisterly relationships of pairs in Tan's other novels, such as Winnie and Helen in *The Kitchen God's Wife*. Taken together, what can these two pairs of women—who, in both cases, are not full-blooded sisters but who decide to claim each other as such—tell us about Tan's vision of sisterhood and its potential influence in someone's life?

5. **Precious Auntie:** Analyze and evaluate the character of Precious Auntie, LuLing's nursemaid and biological mother.

What do you know about Precious Auntie? How would you describe her? Jot down what you know about her childhood. What hardships and privileges did she experience as a child, and how did these shape her personality? Did her character change after she poured the ink resin down her throat? In what ways? Would you say that this experience, along with the deaths of her father and her fiancé, embittered her?

What kind of a mother is she to LuLing? Think about the relationship that the two of them share. In what ways is it a typical mother/daughter relationship and in what ways is it something else, perhaps the relationship of a child to a nursemaid or servant? How do you think LuLing's role as Precious Auntie's sole translator affects their relationship? Did it give LuLing too much control? You might want to compare and contrast this aspect of their relationship with Ruth and LuLing's, as Ruth is forced to write on the sand tray to communicate with the spirit world for her mother.

History and Context

Because Tan's novels span continents and centuries, it is often helpful to do some background reading before writing an essay on any of her novels. In the case of *The Bonesetter's Daughter,* you will probably want to do some research on the history of China, particularly the latter part of the 19th century and early part of the 20th century, during which time Precious Auntie's and LuLing's stories take place. You may want to read about the opium trade and about opium addiction to understand fully the story of the Changs, and you also may want to learn more about the historical discovery of Peking Man. Finally, if you are not familiar with Alzheimer's, you might also want to do some research into the disease, particularly its progression and prognosis and the likely effects on those who are caring for sufferers. Some knowledge about all of these topics would help you to comprehend more fully the plot of the novel as well as its themes and meanings, but your research might also lead you to a paper topic and thesis as well. For example, if you are researching Christian missionary work in early 20th-century China, you might be so intrigued by what you find out that you decided to devote your entire essay to this topic. You might investigate how accurately Tan portrays a Christian orphanage and how typical LuLing's experiences in the school actually are. You might write about the potential ethical issues involved in the way that the girls are "encouraged" to believe in Jesus Christ and to eschew the traditional beliefs of their communities and their families. If you elect to write about any historical event or period, such as Christian missionary work in China or the discovery of Peking Man, you will want to make sure not to depend entirely on the novel or one outside source for your facts and perspective. Do thorough research, and make sure you have a sense of the general scholarly consensus on your subject before you rely on any information to help you make an argument or create a new interpretation of *The Bonesetter's Daughter.*

Sample Topics:

1. **Peking Man:** Tan's novel references the actual historical event of the discovery of Peking Man. W. Scott Morton writes, "In 1923 there were discovered in a limestone cave near Peking remains of a creature, *Sinanthropus pekinensis,* or Peking man, who certainly walked upright, who used fire, and who had a brain capacity about two thirds that of modern man" (11). In Tan's universe, it turns out that what the local people called "dragon bones" and used for healing were actually the remains of ancient human skeletons. How much of the story that Tan builds around this historical event is actually true? How are these "dragon bones" important, both literally and metaphorically, to the novel's plot?

   Do some research into the discovery of Peking Man and the significance of this historical find before returning to the novel. You might start with the article "The Search for Peking Man," which originally appeared in the March/April 2006 issue of *Archaeology* magazine or with Penny Van Oosterzee's *Dragon Bones: The Story of Peking Man.* Ask yourself why Tan decided to incorporate this particular historical event into *The Bonesetter's Daughter.* What happens to the meaning and value of the bones when the people begin to think of them as the bones of Peking Man rather than as dragon bones? What does this discovery mean to LuLing and her family in particular?

2. **Autobiographical elements:** How much of the events in *The Bonesetter's Daughter* are taken from the lives of people in Tan's family?

Tan's mother suffered from Alzheimer's, and Tan took some time off from writing to care for her as she declined. Tan has said that it was on the day her mother died that she learned her mother's and her grandmother's true names. Upon this discovery, she returned to *The Bonesetter's Daughter,* rewriting much of it until she arrived at the published version we have today. According to Tan, there are significant differences between her mother and LuLing and between Ruth and Tan herself. Do some research into Tan's life and her experiences with her mother and then return to *The Bonesetter's Daughter,* looking for similarities and differences. What parts of the novel have their foundations in Tan's own experiences, and how does knowledge of this connection affect your interpretation of the novel's themes and meanings? Think carefully about why Tan fictionalized the details she did and why she preserved the facts she did.

3. **Christian orphanage:** Analyze and evaluate Tan's portrayal of Christian missionary work in early 20th-century China.

What was life like in the orphanage that LuLing was sent to after Precious Auntie's suicide? What was the mission of the orphanage's leaders? How did they treat the question of religion? Of Chinese beliefs and customs? What do you make of the lines that the girls had to recite in English and Chinese every day:

> We can study, we can learn,
> We can marry whom we choose.
> We can work, we can earn,
> And bad fate is all we lose. (262)

What were the school's leaders trying to instill in the girls? Do you think this is an ethical thing to do? Why or why not?

Do some research into missionary work in China. You might start with Kenneth Scott Latourette's *A History of Christian Missions in China.* Use your knowledge to evaluate Tan's portrayal of the orphanage. Is it, in your view, an accurate representation of such an institution? Why or why not? How does living in the orphanage change LuLing? Would you argue that these changes made things better or worse? Would you say that they are because of or in spite of the orphanage's dogma?

4. **Opium addiction:** GaoLing's husband, Fu Nan, is an opium addict. What does the novel have to say about this powerful addiction and its consequences?

Do some research into the opium trade. You might start with Peter Lee's *Opium Culture: The Art and Ritual of Chinese Tradition.* How widespread was this problem in China? What are the physical and psychological effects of such an addiction? How does Fu Nan and his family's problem with opium ultimately impact LuLing's family?

Philosophy and Ideas

Tan's novel tackles some interesting and thorny ideas. As one example, there is the question of a parent who has been diagnosed with Alzheimer's disease. Art and Ruth manipulate LuLing into choosing to live in the assisted-care facility. The facility seems nice; it appears that LuLing would be very well taken of, and it is clear that she will soon need a level of care greater than Ruth could provide alone or even with the assistance of Art and LuLing's sister, GaoLing. Art and Ruth's decision to place LuLing in the facility seems based on genuine concern for her well-being. But what about the way in which they get her to the facility, first telling her that there is a radon leak at her home and then lying to her about the cost of the accommodations, among other things? Would it have been more ethical to tell LuLing the truth about her illness, to try and convince her to move to the facility by using logic and reasoning, and then force her hand if she failed to agree? Or was Ruth and Art's chosen course of action best, because it allowed LuLing to preserve her happiness and to believe that she is still in control and making choices about her life?

Sample Topics:

1. **Treatment of the elderly:** *The Bonesetter's Daughter* has a lot to do with the evolving relationship between Ruth and her mother LuLing as LuLing's Alzheimer's gets progressively worse. What does the novel ultimately have to say about the aging process and

the ethics of caring for a loved one who is becoming increasingly unable to care for him- or herself?

How are the patients at the assisted-care facility convinced to live there? How do Ruth and Art convince LuLing that moving into the facility is not only a good idea but her own free choice? Do you think that Ruth and Art's manipulation of LuLing—and the manipulation of the other patients as well—is ethical? Why or why not? What obligations does Ruth have to provide for her mother? Specifically, does Ruth have a stronger imperative to provide for her mother's physical well-being than to be honest with her? Does this balance replicate that of a parent's obligations to a small child? How does it differ? Is this fair?

2. **Romantic commitment and marriage:** What kind of commentary does the novel ultimately make about marriage?

Why have Ruth and Art never married? Do you think they each have the same reasons for this choice? Do these reasons seem logical? What would getting married mean to each of them? How has their decision not to marry affected each of them individually, and how has it affected them as a couple? Why do they eventually decide to marry? Do you think that this is a good move for them, or will they only end up facing the problems they initially feared would develop with marriage?

You might compare Ruth and Art's relationship to Lena and Harold's in *The Joy Luck Club*. Are their reasons for not getting married similar? Which relationship would you argue is healthier, and why? When viewed through the lens of these two couples, what would you say is Tan's stance about romantic commitment and marriage?

Form and Genre

Some of the most interesting and insightful essays can spring from a careful focus on the writer's choices regarding form and genre. Think about the number of decisions a writer faces when she crafts a piece of literature. She has to decide what story to tell and what characters will allow her to do so. These main elements are the particular decisions we tend to focus on, but she also has to decide who will tell the story and what information each teller is privy to. She has to decide how to structure the telling of the story, as well as determine the scope and form of the telling. Should the story of Ruth and LuLing be told in poetry? In short stories? In a novel? In what order should events be revealed? Who should tell the story? What should the parts of the novel, the sections and chapters, be titled? What should the entire work be called? Tan's answers to each of these questions profoundly affect the final result that we experience when we read *The Bonesetter's Daughter*. Examining her choices can help us better understand what she was aiming for.

Sample Topics:

1. **Structure:** The novel is divided into three parts, the first telling part of Ruth's story, the second telling her mother's, and the third picking up with Ruth's again. Why do you think Tan opted to structure the story this way, and how does this decision affect your interpretation of the novel?

   Return to the novel, paying particular attention to the way it is structured. What is revealed in sections one, two, and three? In what order do events unfold? Why do you think Tan chooses to relate the story in precisely this way? Why do you think she enfolds LuLing's story inside Ruth's? What does this say about their relationship? Spend some time imagining what the novel would be like if Tan had organized it another way, perhaps in strict chronological order with no section divisions. How would this change your experience of the book?

2. **Point of view:** Tan uses a third-person point of view to tell Ruth's portion of the story and first person to tell LuLing's. What effects do these choices have on your interpretation of the novel?

   Whom do you think we come to know better, Ruth or LuLing? How would the novel have been different if we were given Ruth's story in her own voice? How about LuLing—do you think she reveals her authentic self in the memoir she writes for her daughter, or does she invent a persona for herself, crafting the account in certain ways to convey a particular impression of herself to Ruth?

3. **Ending:** In the closing pages of *The Bonesetter's Daughter,* many problems are resolved neatly. Reviewer Nancy Willard notes in her *New York Times* review: "Some readers will not agree with Tan's decision to tie up all the loose ends of the novel's plot as neatly as if Glinda the Good had waved her wand over everybody's problems." Do you think the ending successfully resolves or cheapens the difficult issues that the novel presents? Why or why not?

Make a list of all of the problems that the novel sets up. What are its central issues and concerns? Next, record how each of these problems is resolved. How do you feel about the way Tan handles the problem of LuLing's Alzheimer's? How likely is the scenario she creates? Is the assisted-care facility she describes too good to be true? How about LuLing's new relationship with Mr. Tang? How likely is a situation such as this? What about the resolution to Ruth and Art's relationship problems? How are they resolved? Are Art's epiphany and his significant efforts to make things right with Ruth believable? What about the relationships between Ruth and Art's daughters, Fia and Dory? How do these rocky relationships turn out? As you think about these questions, you might want to spend some time imagining other possible endings for each of these situations. How would a situation like LuLing's most likely end in your community, for example?

Do you think that the happy endings that Tan creates for these stories in any way detract from the enormity and severity of the issues she wants to highlight, Alzheimer's in particular? Write an essay in which you critique or defend the ending of *The Bonesetter's Daughter,* arguing either that resolutions to the novel's fundamental problems contribute to or detract from its power.

4. **Title:** Discuss the significance of Tan's decision to title the book *The Bonesetter's Daughter.*

Why do you think that Tan would choose to name this book not after LuLing or Ruth but after Precious Auntie? Do you think that Precious Auntie is the central character of this story? Why or why not? And further, why do you suppose that Tan would call the book *The Bonesetter's Daughter* instead of simply *Precious Aun-*

tie? Is there a reason that Tan would refer to Precious Auntie as someone's daughter? Does this suggest that the characters in the novel are defined by their families, particularly their fathers, or does Tan perhaps want to highlight the tradition of bonesetting in Precious Auntie's family?

Language, Symbols, and Imagery

Symbols and images abound in *The Bonesetter's Daughter.* You might write about the yearly laryngitis that Ruth suffers, the many appearances of bones in the novel, or the various types of writing represented in its pages. Or after reading about the suggested topics below, you might think of another symbol or image you would like to investigate. Irrespective of the particular image or symbol you want to write about, you will want to begin by identifying several key passages that feature that image or symbol. Then, analyze those passages to see what deeper meanings the symbol or image is carrying and how those meanings resonate with the overall themes of the novel. Ideally, you want your essay to be not simply an analysis of your particular image but to express fresh insight about the novel supported by your analysis of that image or symbol.

1. **Ruth's annual laryngitis:** Discuss the symbolic meaning of Ruth's problem with her voice and the way that she copes with this annual affliction.

   When is the first time that Ruth loses her voice? What are the circumstances surrounding this loss? When does she lose it again, and when does this loss become an annual event for Ruth? What does this physical inability to speak say about Ruth's psychological and emotional state? What do you conclude about Ruth's decision to stop using her voice of her own free will during the week that she knows the laryngitis will return? What is her purpose for doing this? Is she successful? How has Ruth's relationship with her voice changed by the end of the novel? In your opinion, is Ruth's voice and her evolving relationship with it connected to her sense of agency and ability to communicate?

2. **Bones:** Discuss the symbolism of bones throughout the novel.

According to Carol Cujec:

> Images of bones haunt the manuscript. They are instruments of healing, such as the dragon bones used as medicine. They are also vehicles for communication, such as the oracle bones used to speak with the gods. Then when scientists begin excavating fossils from the mountain, they become keys to understanding the past. . . . Precious Auntie worries about safeguarding her family's bones in a secret cave, and after Precious Auntie's death, LuLing becomes obsessed with her bones, which were never properly buried. (par. 15)

And then, of course, there is Ruth's broken bone, which initiates complex developments in her relationship with her mother. Identify what you feel are the most meaningful scenes and passages involving bones. Analyze each of these carefully to determine what bones represent in the novel. Do they mean the same thing in America that they do in China? Do they mean different things to different characters? What do you think is the central role or roles played by bones in the novel?

3. **Writing:** *The Bonesetter's Daughter* is filled with depictions of writing: diaries, memoirs, sand writing. How is writing characterized in the novel? What characteristics and qualities is it associated with?

Begin by jotting down the various instances of writing integrated into the novel. There are the written stories of Precious Auntie and LuLing, who each record their stories for their daughters. What is the significance of their choices to record these memories in writing rather than to present them orally? What are the consequences of their choice to express themselves in the written word? How is Ruth's diary writing similar to and different from Precious Auntie and LuLing's missives? Additionally, you will want to think about the beggar girl's sand writing as well as Ruth's. How are these forms of writing different from the ones mentioned above? What, if anything, do they have in common?

4. **The beggar girl's communication from Precious Auntie:** When LuLing and GaoLing come across a blind beggar girl who says she can communicate with the dead, the temptation is too much for LuLing. She must know what Precious Auntie, who has just committed suicide, has to say to her. What do you make of the lines she reveals to LuLing?

The beggar girl writes these four lines in limestone silt with a slender stick:

> A dog howls, the moon rises.
> In darkness, the stars pierce forever.
> A rooster crows, the sun rises.
> In daylight, it's as if the stars never existed. (258)

Do you think these words are truly a message from Precious Auntie, or do you think the beggar girl repeats these same lines to everyone? How does LuLing interpret these lines? When LuLing explains her interpretation to GaoLing, her sister insists that "That is one meaning. There are others" (251). How else might these lines be interpreted as a communication from Precious Auntie? How might they be interpreted as a commentary on the novel as a whole?

Compare and Contrast Essays

Comparing and contrasting two elements of a literary work, whether they are within the same novel or factor into several novels by the same author, can be illuminating. In the case of *The Bonesetter's Daughter,* you might want to compare and contrast the two main characters of the work, LuLing and Ruth, in order to understand their relationship better, or you might compare the mother/daughter relationship described in *The Bonesetter's Daughter* to those depicted in *The Joy Luck Club.* One of the most important things to remember when you are choosing a topic of this sort is not to let the essay become a list of similarities and differences, no matter how interesting they are or may seem. It might actually be more helpful to think of your comparison and contrast selection not as a topic, per se, but as a tool. For example, if you have decided to compare and contrast LuLing and Ruth, you would of course begin by figuring out the most significant similarities and differences between these two characters. You would not, however, conclude your analysis at this point and start writing your essay. Instead, you would begin to examine these similarities and differences and use them to help you to come to some strong, tightly defined observation or interpretation of the text. This insight would then become your topic, and some of your comparison/contrast notes would become the support and evidence you cite in the course of your essay. For example, you notice in your reading of the novel that LuLing clearly thinks that young people should obey their elders, while Ruth thinks that adults should respect the growing individuality and independence of their children. You note as well that LuLing and Ruth are both proud, strong-willed, emotional, and a bit self-absorbed. Instead of simply listing all of these observations in your essay, you will want to synthesize them and use them to help you make some sense of the novel, thinking about the implications of the patterns you have observed. You might, for example, ultimately write an essay that argues that Ruth and LuLing are two very similar people raised in cultures that value different things, Ruth's American culture valuing youth and rebellion, while LuLing's Chinese upbringing stresses obedience and respect of elders and tradition. While this difference certainly makes the mother/daughter relationship a difficult one, it is actually the traits the two women share—willfulness, pride, and a high degree of emotion and sensitivity—that get in the way of their attempts to bridge these cultural differences.

Sample Topics:

1. ***The Bonesetter's Daughter* and *The Joy Luck Club*:** A starred review of *The Bonesetter's Daughter* in *Publishers Weekly* reads: "In its rich character portrayals and sensitivity to the nuances of mother-daughter relationships, Amy Tan's new novel is the real successor to, and equal of, *The Joy Luck Club*. This luminous and gripping book demonstrates enhanced tenderness and wisdom, however; it carries the texture of real life and reflects the paradoxes historical events can produce." Would you agree that *The Bonesetter's Daughter* is the "real successor" to *The Joy Luck Club*? In what way or ways? Compare and contrast these two novels. Taken together, what do they have to say about mother/daughter

relationships, particularly those colored by cultural as well as generational differences?

Reread both novels, and make a list of what they have in common. How are the mothers and daughters in these novels similar? How are they different? What common threads do you see running through both novels? If we think of *The Bonesetter's Daughter* as the "successor" to *The Joy Luck Club*, this implies that the latter novel surpasses the first or extends its message in some way. Would you argue that this is the case with these two novels? Does *The Bonesetter's Daughter* reveal more accurate or sophisticated insights into the complex relationships between mothers and daughters that it presents? What new ground does it break when compared to Tan's previous novel?

2. **LuLing and Ruth:** Compare and contrast this mother and daughter. Would you argue that it is their similarities or their differences that most complicate their relationship?

Begin by recording what you know about LuLing and Ruth. What would you say are the best qualities of each? What are each woman's strengths? What are her flaws? What kind of relationship does she have with other members of her family? How does she perceive herself and her position in larger society? What are her priorities? Looking at this list, what do the mother and daughter have in common? What are their most striking differences? How do these similarities and differences influence their relationship with each other?

3. *The Bonesetter's Daughter* **and Maxine Hong Kingston's "No Name Woman":** Compare and contrast these two works. Taken together, what do they have to say about violating social mores and, more importantly, about telling the stories of those society wishes to forget?

Compare and contrast the stories that the narrator in "No Name Woman" creates to explain how her aunt got pregnant out of wedlock to the stories that Precious Auntie creates and tells to LuLing to explain her scarred face and how she became LuLing's nursemaid. Why does each woman create many stories instead of only one? What, if anything, do the stories have in common? For whom are the stories meant? What messages are they meant to convey? What can they tell us about women's roles in traditional Chinese society?

Bibliography and Online Resources for *The Bonesetter's Daughter*

Bailey, Paul. *China in the Twentieth Century.* Malen, MA: Wiley-Blackwell, 2001.

Bloom, Harold, ed. *Amy Tan.* Modern Critical Views. Philadelphia: Chelsea House, 2000.

Cujec, Carol. "Excavating Memory, Reconstructing Legacy." *The World & I.* Retrieved 10 Sept. 2008. <http://www.worldandi.com/specialreport/bonecut/bonecut.html>.

Hooker, Jake. "The Search for Peking Man." *Archaeology* 59.2 (2006): 59–66.

Huntley, E. D. *Amy Tan: A Critical Companion.* Critical Companions to Popular Contemporary Writers. Westport, CT: Greenwood, 1998.

Latourette, Kenneth Scott. *A History of Christian Missions in China.* New York: Macmillan, 1929.

Lee, Peter. *Opium Culture: The Art and Ritual of Chinese Tradition.* Rochester, VT: Park Street, 2005.

Maxey, Ruth. "'The East Is Where Things Begin': Writing the Ancestral Homeland in Amy Tan and Maxine Hong Kingston." *Orbis Litterarum* 60 (2005): 1–15.

Morton, W. Scott. *China: Its History and Culture.* 3rd ed. New York: McGraw-Hill, 1995.

Roberts, J. A. G. *A Concise History of China.* Cambridge, MA: Harvard UP, 1999.

Shields, Charles J. *Amy Tan.* Women of Achievement. Philadelphia: Chelsea House, 2002.

Tan, Amy. *The Bonesetter's Daughter.* New York: Penguin, 1991.

Van Oosterzee, Penny. *Dragon Bones: The Story of Peking Man.* Perseus, 2002.

Willard, Nancy. "Talking to Ghosts" (Review of *The Bonesetter's Daughter*). *The New York Times.* 18 Feb. 2001.

SAVING FISH
FROM DROWNING

READING TO WRITE

A MY TAN's fifth novel, *Saving Fish from Drowning,* represents a significant departure from her previous books. This one has a large cast of contemporary American characters and deals with moral responsibility and politics more than it does with history and familial relationships. In this story, 12 Americans take a tour of China accompanied by the spirit of their initial tour guide who died under mysterious circumstances shortly before the tour commenced. When they reach Myanmar, they are abducted by a tribe of people who believe that one of the tourists, a teenager named Rupert, is the fabled "Younger White Brother" who will help them to stay safe from the Burmese soldiers who are always hunting them down.

Saving Fish from Drowning does, though, have one significant theme in common with Tan's earlier work and that is an explanation of what exactly it means to be an American. Examine the following passage in which the American tour guide Bennie and the Burmese tour guide Walter discuss just that:

> "What I can't get over," Bennie now said, "is how Walter here can switch back and forth between perfect Burmese and excellent English. Have you noticed his English is better than mine? He's more American than I am." Bennie meant that Walter had a British accent, which in his mind sounded more high-class than his American mid-western one.

> Walter was pleased by the flattery. "Oh, but being American has less to do with one's proficiency in English and more to do with the assumptions you hold dear and true—your inalienable rights, your pursuit of happiness. I, sad to say, don't possess those assumptions. I cannot undertake the pursuit. (161)

Look at the two opinions offered here on what identifies one as an American. For Bennie, it has to do with how well one can speak English. At first glance, Benny's idea of how to identify a fellow American seems to be sound. After all, doesn't the way we express ourselves and interact with other people say a great deal about our innermost values and beliefs? It is not, however, self-expression or the quality or character of social interaction that Benny is evaluating: It is a person's accent and perhaps grammatical correctness, arguably the least significant features of linguistic interaction. Bennie's suggestion that it is external markers, not internal qualities, that make us Americans confers on "Americanness" a problematic superficiality. Further, in Bennie's view, the only way that a person's English can confer Americanness upon him is for others to hear his language and assert their approval. In this way, not only does he portray Americanness as superficial, but as impermanent and completely outside of one's control. One's claim to Americanness is always tenuous as it depends on the validation of others.

Walter seems to understand the problem with Bennie's statement right away. Walter insists that being American has "more to do with the assumptions you hold dear and true—your inalienable rights, your pursuit of happiness." Those qualities that Walter identifies as defining American characteristics do not depend on the validation, approval, or even existence of others. In fact, it is impossible to tell from a cursory glance or casual conversation whether a person possesses these qualities. It is also interesting to note that the particular internal qualities that Walter associates with Americans are a fundamental concern with the rights of the individual and one's ability to pursue his or her own goals. Walter does not mention other classic American assumptions and ideals—freedom and justice for all, for example. What might be the reason that Walter's definition of Americanness has to do with individual self-fulfillment? Is the novel suggesting that other cultures perceive Americans to be fixated on the success of the individual and neglectful of the more communal aspects of life? According to the novel, would such a perception be accurate? When Walter presents the definition of Americanness that he does, is he speaking about the particular group he has in front of him or about Americans in general? For that matter, are the tourists a good representative cross section of America? Might they be giving Walter and others a skewed vision of the American psyche?

Think, too, about the narrator's contribution to this passage. Bibi explains that Walter has an English accent which to Bennie "sounded more high-class than his American mid-western one." Why do you think Bibi stops to explain this? What do you make of the irony of Bennie's association of a British accent with Americanness? As an immigrant from China, what are Bibi's own assumptions about Americanness and linguistic aptitude? How do these assumptions figure in the way she narrates the story? Finally, you will also want to think about the elitist implications of the thought process explained by Bibi. According to Bennie, the more upscale a person's English, the more "American" he can be. And if one can be "more" American based on these factors, it follows that one can also be less American based on these same factors. A hierarchy of Americanness based on accent seems to be a decidedly un-American idea. How does this notion fit in with Bennie's belief that a British accent is actually more "American" than his Midwestern one? You might want to spend some time thinking about whether the other tourists share Bennie's associations. If they do not, you might investigate what it is about Bennie that attracts him to these ideas.

As we have seen, close attention to one particular passage can result in many interesting observations and possible directions for continued investigations. If you are struggling to select a topic for your essay, you might begin by identifying a particular passage that seems especially interesting or meaningful to you. Read the passage many times, focusing on words or phrases and considering the significance of each. It is more likely than not that a possible topic or two will evolve from this process. Alternatively, if you select one of the topics from the suggestions below, you might begin your prewriting by locating and analyzing the passages that seem to have the most connection to the theme you have chosen. Your analysis of these passages will help you to arrive at an argument or thesis for your essay.

TOPICS AND STRATEGIES

Because Amy Tan's *Saving Fish from Drowning* is such a rich and complicated work, there are many, many ways to approach writing an essay about it. Below you will find some topics and strategies to help get you started. After reading through them, you might be inspired to create one of your own, or you might want to combine a couple of related topics or modify them to suit your own interests. Remember that the topics and strategies are designed to get you thinking. Use them to help you figure out how to approach the novel and figure out what kinds of questions to ask about the text. As these are not exam questions, do not feel that you have to address each point discussed in the topic or restrict yourself to the aspects of the novel mentioned there. Simply use them as a jumping off point. Once you have completed your analysis of the aspect of the novel you decided to focus on, you can abandon the topic questions entirely. At this point, you should synthesize your observations and analysis and use them to develop the thesis, or major focal point, of your essay.

Themes

Saving Fish from Drowning covers a lot of ground, both figuratively and literally. This novel about a group of Americans on an ill-fated trip to Myanmar deals with themes including moral responsibility, the importance of intentionality, what it means to be an American, the nature of group interactions, and much more. If you decide to write about theme in *Saving Fish from Drowning,* you first need to select which of the many possible themes you would like to focus on; you can choose one of the themes suggested below or identify another significant theme running through the novel that interests you more. Then, you will want to select several passages that relate to your theme and close read them, carefully analyzing the language Tan employs. Once you have analyzed several passages and spent some time thinking about the implications of your analysis, you will need to synthesize your findings and your thoughts into a thesis for your essay. If you are writing on group dynamics, for example, you would not want your thesis to merely say that one of the most important themes in *Saving Fish from Drowning* is the interaction of a group when there is no clear method of making decisions. This is obvious and not something you would need to prove in your essay. Instead, your thesis might say: Tan's novel illustrates that in strained group situations, the title of leader means little as those with the most aggressive and forceful personalities wind up seizing control of the group and making all the decisions, which are not always the right ones for group as a whole. Or you might argue that the novel actually illustrates group behavior at its most evolved, that even though there is some personality conflict, the tour group members consistently put aside their differences and their personal preferences for the greater good of the group, and that this is what enables them to survive. You will use your own analysis and observations to arrive at a statement that encapsulates your view on what the novel has to say about group interactions. Then, you will use the notes you have generated as support for your thesis as you craft your essay.

Sample Topics:

1. **Moral responsibility:** According to the novel, what responsibility do we as human beings have to other human beings?

According to Bibi, people tend to avoid knowledge of the pain of others. She admits to this tendency in herself:

> Memoirs of sacrilege, torture, and abuse, one after another—they are so difficult to read, without a speck of hope to lift you, no redeeming denouements, only the inevitable descent into the bottomless pits of humanity . . . But tell me honestly, who does read political books on horror-ridden regimes except scholars of history and those studying that particular part of the world? Others may claim they have, but more likely they skim the descriptions in the *New York Times Review of Books,* and then say that they are informed, qualified to make judgments. How do I know? I've done it. I just never saw the point in spending days and days reading stories only to disturb myself with problems I was powerless to fix. (146)

She also remarks on the fact that even when tourists set out to explore and learn about the world, they don't really expect to see the reality of how people in other parts of the world live;

rather, they want to have their fantastic ideas confirmed. She explains,

> That's what we visitors love, a rustic romanticism and anti-quated prettiness, no electric power lines, telephone poles, or satellite television dishes to mar the view. Seek and you shall find your illusions through the magic of tourism. (147)

Does Bibi's estimation seem accurate? The tourists are intelligent and sophisticated people: Are they intentionally seeking an illusion on their trip to Myanmar? Do you find this behavior to be ethical? How do the tourists rationalize their decision to travel to Myanmar despite its oppressive regime? How do they feel when confronted with the violence suffered by the Karen people? What do they try to do to help? What kind of responsibility do they feel toward the Karen people? Does this sense of responsibility last, or does it melt away as the tourists resume their American lives. All told, what does *Saving Fish from Drowning* have to say about the moral responsibility of human beings to find out about and/or do something about the suffering of other human beings?

2. **Americanness:** When a group of American characters travel to a place in which they are unfamiliar with local customs and beliefs, it can be easier to define what it is about them that one would identify as "American." Based on the group's behavior in China and Myanmar and their interactions with the local people, what kind of commentary would you say that Tan makes on American values and identity?

The members of the tour group are certainly very different, but considering that they, together, make up the picture of Americanness developed in this novel, spend some time thinking about what they have in common. What values or opinions do they all share? What makes them different from the Chinese and Burmese people that they meet? How do they interact with these people? Would you say that the Americans' core values are challenged or changed by their experience in Myanmar? In what way(s)?

3. **Good intentions:** According to Tan's *Saving Fish from Drowning*, how much do our intentions matter? How exactly do they influence our actions and their consequences?

In an interview, Tan has mentioned that this novel is primarily about intentions and whether good intentions are enough. Tan asks, "When the outcomes are bad, who actually suffers the consequences?" Do we take credit and blame equally for those things that happen as a result of our intentions? Think about these questions in terms of the novel. What were the tourists' intentions in traveling to Myanmar? What were their intentions toward the Karen people? What happens as a result of their intentions, and do they accept responsibility for these consequences? Do a person's intentions seem to have direct bearing on how things play out? How so?

Think about this question in terms of the novel's two epigraphs, both having to do with intentions. In the first, Camus writes that "The evil that is in the world almost always comes of ignorance, and good intentions may do as much harm as malevolence if they lack understanding." In the second, a fisherman claims that when he pulls fish out of the water, he is "saving them from drowning." Of course, he is always too late, so he sells the fish so as not to be wasteful and buys more nets in which to save more fish. In this passage, the fisherman assumes that the fish need what he needs, oxygen, to survive. By misunderstanding their needs, he kills them when they were doing perfectly well left to their own devices. This interpretation of the story assumes that the fisherman is being sincere with his explanation. The more likely scenario is that he knows full well what will happen to the fish, especially after the first time he pulls them up in his net and sees them die, but is able to mask his destructive behavior by framing it as actions based on "good intentions." How do these epigraphs help you to interpret the story that follows? Which characters do you think have good intentions but "lack understanding"? Who might Tan be comparing to the fisherman? The tourists? The Burmese government? The Karen people?

4. **The group dynamic:** What does *Saving Fish from Drowning* have to say about the nature of groups and how they make decisions?

When, after Bibi's death, the group takes on a less experienced and prepared tour guide, the Americans find themselves in China and Myanmar without a strong or clear leader. How does the group make decisions and govern itself? What happens as a result of this lack of leadership? What happens when the tourists are abducted by the Karen people? Does the increase in their stress levels change the way the group interacts? Does someone emerge as the leader of the group? Would you say that their interactions are productive and healthy? Why or why not? How did the group describe their interactions for Harry, who was including their discussion of their trip in his new book? Why do you think they described it the way they did?

5. **Art:** What kind of commentary does *Saving Fish from Drowning* ultimately make about the nature of art, particularly writing and fiction?

To begin, you will want to think about the way that Tan sets up this novel, with the largely fictitious opening note to the reader and the "news article" she invents about the tourists missing in Myanmar. Why do you think that Tan makes herself into a character in this story by including this fictional account of the origin of the novel? What themes does this strategy introduce? What kind of relationship does it create with the reader? Once you have considered Tan's choice to include these seemingly true yet fictional elements, you will want to analyze what they have to say about the nature of art and fiction writing in particular.

You will also want to look at the passages in which Bibi talks about the myth of Shangri-La and how the stories that have come to define it were developed. And finally, you will want to think about Bibi's narration and how it might function as a work of art, as a created and fashioned story. Once you have considered all these elements, as well as any others you have identified, write an essay in which you articulate for your readers just what this novel wants to say about the origin and power of art in its many forms.

Character

Saving Fish from Drowning is populated by a diverse and interesting cast of characters, any one of whom would make an interesting character study. You might focus on just one of the characters—Bibi and Harry would make particularly good choices—or you might focus on a group, such as the Karen people, or a certain segment of the tour group, parents and children, for example. No matter which character(s) you decide to focus on, you will want to study their behavior and their dialogue. You will also want to consider their motivations and any information about their pasts that helps to explain their idiosyncrasies. Remember, too, that all of the information you are getting is being filtered through Bibi, so you will have to factor her personality and biases into your analysis as well. Finally, be sure to evaluate any changes that occur in your character as the novel progresses. What inspires these changes? Are they positive or negative? What might Tan be trying to say through the development of this particular character? If your character does not change in the course of the story, then think about why not. Does your character represent an opinion or idea that needs to remain consistent or stable? What is his or her function in the novel?

Sample Topics:

1. **Bibi Chen:** Bibi is perhaps the most three dimensional and interesting of the many characters populating *Saving Fish from Drowning.* She becomes perhaps even more interesting when we

consider the fact that Bibi's voice is based on Tan's own mother's. Take a close look at Bibi Chen, and write an essay in which you evaluate her character, paying particular attention to whether or not she evolves at all in the course of the novel.

Begin by recording what you know about Bibi's childhood. How does she feel about her family life, particularly the ill treatment she received at the hands of her stepmother, Sweet Ma? How did Bibi's relationship with Sweet Ma help to define her character? Now record what you know about Bibi as an adult. What has she accomplished in her life? What was she most proud of? What did she regret? What do her friends think of her?

Finally, consider Bibi as a "ghost." What does she accomplish after her death? Is she different as a ghost than she was in life? How so? How does she come across as a narrator? Is she likeable and sympathetic? Why or why not? Does Bibi learn anything or change in any way by accompanying her friends on their trip to Myanmar? What do you make of the way that Bibi dies? Why does Tan have Bibi die the first time she truly allows herself to feel love and joy, as she cradles her mother's jade hair comb?

2. **Harry Bailey:** Analyze and evaluate the character of Harry Bailey.

Why does Harry go on the trip to China and Myanmar? What has his life been like up until this point? What kind of person is he? What kind of relationships has he sought out? How does he feel about his work? Now think about what Harry goes through on the trip and during the weeks that his friends are missing. Does Harry seem to feel guilty for being the only member of the party who did not wind up on the ill-fated expedition?

You will want to spend some time thinking about Harry's relationship with Marlena. What does he like about her? Is there something about Harry that is fundamentally changing, particularly in his feelings about romance? If this is so, then why does he seem so enamored of his ex-girlfriend who arrives in Myanmar with the search and rescue dogs? Do you think it's likely that Harry and Marlena's relationship will be a lasting one? Why or why not?

3. **Treatment of the Karen culture:** In his *New York Times* book review, Andrew Solomon criticizes *Saving Fish from Drowning*, saying that "the book is patronizing to the Karen people." Analyze and evaluate Tan's portrayal of the Karen culture.

What are the Karen people like? Are they sympathetic, despite the fact that they abduct the tour group? What do you make of their religion and beliefs, particularly that of the Younger White Brother. According to the novel, how did their beliefs and their lifestyle develop?

Do some research into the Karen people. You might start with the Friends of the Karen Web site: http://www.friendsofthekaren.org/index.htm. Once you have established some background knowledge, consider Amy Tan's treatment of this group. Would you describe it as realistic? Flattering? Satirical? Would you agree with Andrew Solomon that the book is patronizing to the Karen people? Why or why not?

4. **Bennie:** Analyze and evaluate the character of Bennie.

What do you know about Bennie? What is his life in America like? What are his motivations for going on the tour? How does he cope with the challenges the group faces in China and Myanmar? Does he change at all during the course of the trip? In what way? How is Bennie different when he returns to America? Several of the other group members would serve as interesting subjects for character analysis as well. For instance, you might choose to write about Wyatt, Wendy, Vera, Roxanne, Dwight, or Heidi, asking the same sorts of questions you would ask of Bennie's character.

5. **Parents and children:** Analyze and evaluate the relationships between Marlena and her daughter Esme, and Moff and his son Rupert.

What were the relationships between Marlena and Esme and Moff and Rupert like at the start of the trip? How did they treat each other? Why did Marlena and Moff decide to bring their children on this trip? Why did Esme and Rupert want to go? What significant events happen in the lives of these four in China and Myanmar, and how do they affect the dynamics of the parent/child relationship?

History and Context

Your understanding of *Saving Fish from Drowning* can be greatly enhanced if you take the time to do some background reading, particularly on the political history of Burma/Myanmar and its current cultural and political climate. Once you have studied this issue, you might decide not simply to use it for background knowledge but to fashion your essay into a discussion of Tan's treatment of the political situation in Myanmar. Does Tan, via Bibi, present an accurate picture of contemporary Myanmar? Where do her sympathies seem to lie? Alternatively, you might think about United States foreign policy and the influence of television on society's behavior and values as contextual elements. What kinds of cultural conversations were going on in 2005 regarding these issues? How about now? What does the novel have to say about the United States' behavior as an international citizen? How does it perceive its place in the world and its relationship with other countries? What does the novel have to say about the power of television? How has it shaped our modern world? In what ways does it change our behavior and beliefs?

Sample Topics:

1. **The political situation in Myanmar/Burma:** What, if anything, does *Saving Fish from Drowning* ultimately have to say about the political situation in Myanmar/Burma?

Do some research into the history of Burma/Myanmar. You might begin with the documents related to Myanmar available

in the World History Archives at http://www.hartford-hwp.
com/archives/54/index-b.html. After you have obtained some
solid background knowledge, return to the novel and ask yourself how accurately Tan has described the political situation in
Myanmar. What aspects of it does she emphasize? Which does
she neglect? Why do you think she chose to set this story in
Myanmar? Is there a political point she wants to make? If so,
is it to condemn the State Law and Order Restoration Council
(SLORC) and military rule? To bring to light the plight of indigenous peoples in Myanmar? How successful is Tan at getting
this point across?

2. **U.S. foreign policy:** *Saving Fish from Drowning* certainly comments a great deal about the politics of Myanmar/Burma. What
does it say, both implicitly and explicitly, about America's foreign policy?

You will want to have a close look at the following passage in
which the tour group, having seen a bunch of freshly caught
fish dying, discusses the old Burmese saying that suggests that
the fisherman is really "saving fish from drowning." At this
explanation, Heidi exclaims:

> "It's worse than if they just killed them outright rather than
> justifying it as an act of kindness."
> "No worse than what we do in other countries," Dwight
> said.
> "What are you talking about?" Moff said.
> "Saving people for their own good," he replied. "Invading
> countries, having them suffer collateral damage, as we call it.
> Killing them as an unfortunate consequence of helping them.
> You know, like Vietnam, Bosnia."
> "Those aren't the same thing," Bennie said. "And what are
> you suggesting, that we just stand around and do nothing when
> ethnic cleansing goes on?"
> "Just saying we should be aware of the consequences. You
> can't have intentions without consequences. The question is,

who pays for the consequences? Saving fish from drowning. Same thing. Who's saved? Who's not?" (162–63)

Examine this conversation. Do you agree with Dwight's claim that America's foreign policy in the last half of 20th century and the early part of the 21st century can be summed up as an attempt at "saving fish from drowning"? What do you make of the fact that Tan makes these ideas come out of Dwight's mouth instead of, say, Heidi's or Vera's? Can you identify other passages or scenes in the novel that might be making a subtler commentary on America's foreign policy?

3. **The influence of television:** According to *Saving Fish from Drowning,* how much of an effect do the television news media and other television staples such as reality shows have on society's perceptions and behaviors? Is the effect generally positive or negative?

Think about the role that Harry Bailey's television appearances have on the outcome of the story. How were the actions and opinions of the missing tourists, the Burmese government, and the American population in general shaped by his performances? Think about the reporter who posed as a schoolteacher and the deception she used to get her story as well. Was the way she tricked Harry into getting a copy of the videotape and recording his story ethical? What were the consequences of her handing Roxanne's tape over to the Global News Network? You will want to spend some time thinking about the reality shows *Darwin's Fittest* and *Junglemaniacs!* as well. How did these television shows influence the ultimate fate of the Lord's Army?

Philosophy and Ideas

Saving Fish from Drowning engages in many philosophical and ideological conversations. One of the most overt is the idea of ethical tourism, which the American group discusses at Bibi's funeral. What answer does the novel as a whole make to the questions that the group brings up? Does the group ultimately do more harm or good by visiting Myanmar? The novel also makes direct references to karma and transcendental experiences. You might investigate what Tan ultimately has to say about either of these topics when the novel as a whole is taken into consideration. Ultimately, is the notion of karma spiritually or practically beneficial to the individual? To society? What about the reality and authenticity of transcendental experiences? What conditions are necessary for humans to experience such moments and how does it change them? Finally, you might take on the challenge of discerning what the novel ultimately has to say about the power and the value of religion and spiritual belief systems.

Sample Topics:

1. **Ethics in tourism:** According to *Saving Fish from Drowning*, what kind of ethical responsibility do tourists have in regard to the regions they visit?

At Bibi's funeral, the group gathers to discuss whether or not they should cancel the trip to Myanmar. One of the possible reasons for canceling the trip has to do with the ethics of touring a country with a corrupt regime:

> "It's the ethics that bother me," Roxanne now said. "If you go to Burma, it's in some ways a financial collusion with a corrupt regime."
>
> Marlena stepped in: "Roxanne makes a very good point. When we signed up, it seemed that the regime was improving matters. They were on the verge of some kind of rapprochement with that woman, the Nobel Peace Prize winner—"
>
> "Aung San Suu Kyi," said Dwight.
>
> "—and to go," Marlena continued, "when many are honoring the boycott, well, it's similar to crossing a picket line, I think—"
>
> Dwight cut her off again. "You know what kind of people blindly follow boycotts? Same ones who say that eating hamburgers means you approve of torturing cows. It's a form of

liberal fascism. Boycotts don't help anyone, not real people. It just makes the do-gooders feel good. . . ."

"What is the point of *not* doing something?" he went on arguing.

"Don't eat beef, feel good about saving cows. Boycott Burma, feel good about not going. But what good have you really done? Whom have you saved?" (35–36)

What do you make of Dwight's argument? Do boycotts have the potential to instigate change? Can "not" doing something make a real difference in the world? Why do you think the group decides to go on the trip despite Roxanne and Marlena's argument that they should not support Myanmar's corrupt regime? What is their rationalization?

You will also want to spend some time thinking about what happens during and after the trip. How does the group's visit ultimately affect the people of Myanmar? Are the people worse off because of the group's willingness to travel to Myanmar despite the boycott? Is the group able to do any good for the people they come into contact with? All told, does the novel portray the tourists' decision to visit Myanmar as an ethical failing, or does it suggest, to the contrary, that more good than harm comes from the trip, as the plight of some indigenous peoples is brought to light and the tourists' minds are opened by their exposure to the reality of life in Myanmar?

2. **Karma:** How does *Saving Fish from Drowning* portray the notion of karma?

When the group of American tourists sees a blindfolded water buffalo being forced to walk in circles to smash mud for building houses, they are distressed at what they see as its mistreatment. The group's tour guide tries to explain: "Past life this buffalo must be doing bad things. Now suffer so next life get better. . . ." Bibi Chen continues:

> What she was trying to say was this: Your situation and form in life are already determined before you are born. If you are a buffalo suffering in mud, you must have committed wrongs upon others in a previous existence, and thus, you deserve this particular reincarnation. . . . It's an accepted way of thinking in China, a pragmatic way of viewing all the misfortunes of the world. You cannot change a buffalo into a man. And if a buffalo does not mash the mud, who else would do this job? (77)

Does Bibi's explanation of karma seem to be truly "pragmatic"? In what ways? What effect does this philosophy have on the way that people behave in the world? According to the novel, does the karmic philosophy encourage people to do good so that they might be rewarded in the next life, or does it provide them with an excuse to treat less fortunate people and animals badly, allowing people to rationalize that those in low stations must deserve such treatment?

3. **Transcendent moments:** What stance does the novel take on miracles and transcendent experiences?

Examine in particular the experience that the tourists undergo upon hearing the drumming of the Lord's Army:

> They felt bigger and lighter. They seemed to see themselves, not their physical bodies, but their own thoughts and truths, as if there were a mind mirror that could reflect such things. They all had those mirrors. Now that they were outside of their bodies, they could hear without the distortions of ears, speak without the tangle of tongues, see without the blinders of experience. They were open portals to many minds, and the minds flew into the soul, and the soul was constrained in the minds of everyone . . . They struggled for words to describe what they felt, that they were every thought they had ever had and those of others . . . the greatest knowledge now

effortlessly known, and the greatest knowledge was love. Just
love. (417)

What precisely is happening here? What brings about this
feeling? What happens once it is over? How do the Americans explain it to themselves? Does the experience change
them in a profound way? Are there any other experiences of
this nature represented in the novel? Would you argue that
the novel takes this transcendent experience seriously, or is
it presented more like an exotic illusion? What are the consequences for the overall meaning of the novel if the moment is
read as an authentic experience or a delusion?

4. **Religion:** What does the novel ultimately have to say about
religion?

Think in particular about the Lord's Army. How did they
arrive at their belief system? How did the myth of the Younger
White Brother develop? What sustains them in their beliefs?
Would you say that the Lord's Army's religious values improve
their quality of life? What do the American tourists make of
these religious beliefs?

Locate other references to religion in the novel. Think
about the references to Chinese versus American Buddhism,
for instance, and Bibi's commentary on the way that Chinese
beliefs have tended to mingle with those of the peoples they
have conquered. What does the novel as a whole have to say
about the role of religion in contemporary society and in the
lives of individual human beings? Is it presented as something
necessary and empowering, or superfluous and problematic?

Form and Genre

Tan's interesting choices in regard to form and genre provide some good
opportunities for essays. You might consider, for example, her decision
to include a fictitious "Note to the Reader" and newspaper article pref-
acing chapter 1 of *Saving Fish from Drowning*. Many readers believed

that these elements were true and that the fiction created by Tan began with chapter 1 of the novel. You might investigate whether creating fictional preface material is a well-established literary convention that Tan employs or one she invented. Should readers have understood that the material was invented, or are they right to feel duped? You might consider as well the impact of such a "Note" and newspaper article on the readers' experience of the text as a whole as well as Tan's motives for including them. You might also choose to write about Tan's unusual decision to employ a spirit narrator. Why do you think she employed this device? What can Tan do with Bibi that she could not do with another narrator? How does Bibi's presence affect the telling of the tale and its overall meaning?

Sample Topics:

1. **Narration:** What do you make of Tan's choice to have Bibi narrate the story?

You might begin by thinking about how the novel would be different if it were narrated by a member of the tour group or by an unnamed omniscient narrator. Why do you think Tan opts to have the ghost of the dead tour leader narrate this tale? What does it add to the story? How do Bibi's own perceptions, prejudices, and hopes influence the way she presents events? Do you find Bibi to be a likable and sympathetic narrator overall? Why or why not? How does Bibi's narration likely differ from the narration that would be offered by a living narrator?

2. **"Note to the Reader" and newspaper article:** Analyze Tan's "Note to the Reader" and the newspaper article she includes before the beginning of chapter 1.

In an interview, Amy Tan speaks about how surprised she was that readers took the "Note to the Reader" to be true when she clearly intended it, as well as the newspaper article that precedes chapter 1, to serve as part of the fiction. How did you perceive these elements when you first encountered *Saving Fish from Drowning*? How do you think most readers perceive them? Why do you think Tan elected to include this "Note to the Reader" and the newspaper article? Return to the note and consider it carefully. How is Tan setting up the story with this note? Why does she inject herself as author into the fiction of the story? How does the note affect your interpretation of the novel? Why do you think Tan includes the fictional newspaper article? How does it influence your response to the text that follows. Is the article supposed to function as some kind of commentary on the nature or the power of the news media?

Language, Symbols, and Imagery

1. **Shangri-La:** According to Tan's *Saving Fish from Drowning,* what does Shangri-La stand for?

Bibi talks at length about the mythical Shangri-La:

> Shangri-La: ethereally beautiful, hard to reach, and expensive once you get there. It conjures words delightful to tourists' ears: "rare, remote, and strange." . . . I would have brought up the link to geography as well, the descriptions of the botanist Joseph Rock, whose various expeditions for *National Geographic* in the 1920s and 1930s led to his discovery of a lush green valley tucked in the heart of a Himalayan mountain topped by a "cone" of snow. . . . But the most interesting aspect to me is the *other* Shangri-La alluded to in *Lost Horizon,* and that is a state of mind, one of moderation and acceptance. Those who practice restraint might in turn be rewarded with a prolonged life, even immortality, whereas those who don't will surely die as a result of their uncontrolled impulses. In that world, *blasé* is bliss, and passion is *sans raison.* Passionate people create too many problems. They are reckless. They endanger others in their pursuit of fetishes and infatuations. . . . [O]ne might bottle [Shangri-La] as Sublime Indifference, a potion that induces people to follow the safest route, which is, of course, the status quo, anesthesia for the soul. Throughout the world you can find many Shangri-Las. I have lived in my share of them. Plenty of

dictators have used them as a means to quell the populace—be quiet or be killed. It is so in Burma. (43–44)

Analyze Bibi's remarks here. What are tourists really looking for when they search for Shangri-La? According to Bibi, the original descriptions of Shangri-La had much to do with moderation and following the status quo that she equates with "anesthesia for the soul." Do you think that the meaning of "moderation" is still associated with the myth of Shangri-La? Why might such an association have fallen away? What associations does Shangri-La carry now, and how might these still be connected to Bibi's idea of "anesthesia for the soul"?

2. **Visual art:** According to the novel, what is the role of art in society and the life of the individual?

Art plays an integral role in Bibi Chen's life. She explains that the harsh treatment she received at the hands of her step-mother caused her to disconnect from her feelings at a very young age. The only way that she could find her way back to them was through the world of art, and she devoted herself to collecting and studying art as an adult. Talking about the oppressive regime in Burma, Bibi again remarks on the power of art to enable expression when other avenues are cut off: "in art, lovely subversive art you see what breaks through in spite of restraint, or even because of it. Art despises placidity and smooth surfaces. Without art, I would have drowned under still waters" (44).

Would you say that art enables Bibi to live an emotionally healthy life, or does it function not as emotional stimulation but as an emotional substitute? What do you think Bibi's life would have been like had she not discovered art? In what way is Bibi's use of art in her personal life similar to the "subversive art" that turns up in oppressive political climates? Do the other tourists who signed up for Bibi's tour share her devotion to art? What does art mean to each of them? All told, are Bibi's views of the power of art confirmed or challenged by the novel as a whole?

Compare and Contrast Essays

Comparing and contrasting multiple elements, whether within a single work or across novels, can help you to see patterns and to identify meaningful details that might otherwise escape your notice. Comparing and contrasting Bibi's relationship with Sweet Ma with Kwan's relationship with Big Ma, for instance, would enable you to write an essay that discusses Tan's portrayal of stepmothers in Chinese families. You might take this idea even further by comparing both of these relationships to the relationships of daughters with their biological mothers, such as the pairs introduced in *The Joy Luck Club*. Or you might remain focused on just one novel. If you decide to focus on the theme of life after death in *Saving Fish from Drowning*, for example, a comparison and contrast of Vera's and Bibi's ideas on this subject would make a nice focal point. The key to writing a successful compare and contrast essay is to remember to use your observations and analysis in the service of a larger argument. Do not simply explain how the elements you have isolated are alike and different; tell your audience why these observations matter.

Sample Topics:

1. **Bibi's relationship with Sweet Ma versus the relationship between Kwan and Big Ma in *The Hundred Secret Senses*.**

   Examine *Saving Fish from Drowning*, paying particular attention to any information about Bibi's relationship with her stepmother, whom she called Sweet Ma. How would you characterize this relationship? How did the dynamics of the relationship affect Bibi's personality? Now, think about the mother/daughter relationships in another of Tan's books, such as Kwan's relationship with Big Ma in *The Hundred Secret Senses*, for instance. How would you characterize this relationship? How did it shape Kwan's personality and influence her decisions, such as the one to move to America to live with her father's family? Now, think about both of these relationships. What do they have in common? How are they different? Taken together, what do these two novels have to say about the nature of relationships between stepmothers and daughters. Do the novels suggest that these relationships are profoundly and fundamentally different from relationships between daughters and their biological mothers? If so, how and why are they different?

2. **Vera's attitude about "life" after death versus Bibi's:** With a ghost narrating the story, *Saving Fish From Drowning* definitely poses questions about the nature of "life after death." Compare and contrast Bibi's notion of life after death with Vera's. What can these ideas tell us about these two characters?

According to Vera: "Death was not a loss of life, but the culmination of a series of releases. It was devolving into less and less. You had to release yourself from vanity, desire, ambition, suffering, and frustration—all the accoutrements of the I, the ego. And if you did, you would disappear, leave no trace, like the mist at dawn over the lake, evaporating into nothingness, into nibbana" (229). Bibi is "appalled at [this] idea. Evaporate?" She "wanted to expand, to fill the void, to reclaim all that [she] had wasted, . . . to fill the silence with all the words [she] had not yet spoken" (229).

Why do you think these two women have such different ideas about death? Look back at what you know about their lives and their personalities. How happy is each woman with what she has accomplished in life? What are each woman's ultimate goals; what does she see as the purpose of a life? What would she consider a life well lived? What do you know about each woman's spiritual beliefs? Do you think Bibi's view might have been closer to Vera's had she been asked about life after death while she was still alive? Does Bibi's viewpoint change as the novel progresses? If so, would you say it becomes closer to or further from Vera's perception, and is that change presented as positive or negative?

Bibliography and Online Resources for *Saving Fish from Drowning*

Aung San Suu Kyi. *The Voice of Hope: Aung San Suu Kyi; Conversations with Alan Clements.* Rev. ed. New York: Seven Stories Press, 2008.

Bailey, Paul. *China in the Twentieth Century.* Malen, MA: Wiley-Blackwell, 2001.

Bloom, Harold, ed. *Amy Tan.* Modern Critical Views. Philadelphia: Chelsea House, 2000.

Friends of the Karen: People of Burma. 30 Mar. 2009. <http://www.friendsofthekaren.org/index.htm>.

Huntley, E. D. *Amy Tan: A Critical Companion.* Critical Companions to Popular Contemporary Writers. Westport, CT: Greenwood, 1988.

Roberts, J. A. G. *A Concise History of China.* Cambridge, MA: Harvard UP, 1999.

Shields, Charles J. *Amy Tan.* Women of Achievement. Philadelphia: Chelsea House, 2002.

Solomon, Andrew. "*Saving Fish from Drowning*: A Bus of Fools" (Review of *Saving Fish from Drowning*). *The New York Times* 16 Oct. 1995.

Tan, Amy. *Saving Fish from Drowning.* New York: Putnam's, 2005.

Wintle, Justin. *Perfect Hostage: A Life of Aung San Suu Kyi: Burma's Prisoner of Conscience.* New York: Skyhorse, 2008.

World History Archives: The History of the Union of Myanmar (Burma). <http://www.hartford-hwp.com/archives/54/index-b.html>.

THE OPPOSITE OF FATE: A BOOK OF MUSINGS

READING TO WRITE

IN THE collection of essays entitled *The Opposite of Fate,* Tan reveals a great deal about her family and personal history and offers her thoughts on her writing and its reception. This collection occupies a unique position in Tan's canon. Whereas her novels are often interpreted as being thinly veiled biography and autobiography, this work, purported to be nonfiction, clearly displays some elements of carefully constructed fiction, particularly when Tan comments upon her own writing. The following passage, in which Tan analyzes her fiction, contrasting it to other types of works that feature literary devices at regular intervals, gets to the heart of many of the book's themes:

> The truth is, if I do include symbols in my work, they are carefully nudged out of hiding places by others. I don't consciously place symbols in such clever fashion as some students have given me credit for. I'm not that smart. I can't plot where I will use literary devices, posting them like freeway signs that regularly announce rest stops, scenic outlooks, and the last exit before the denouement. I'm not that methodical. If I write of "an orange moon rising on a dark night," I would more likely ask myself whether the image is clichéd than whether it is a symbol of the feminine force rising in anger, as one academic suggested. . . . I'm not suggesting that I write my stories without any consideration of the words and images

I include. I choose my words carefully, and with much anguish. They are, each and every one, significant to me, by virtue of their meaning, their tone, their place in the sentence, their sound and rhythm in dialog or narrative, their specific associations with something deeply personal and often secretly ironic in my life. (302–03)

In this passage, Tan attempts to set herself apart from writers with a clear literary bent; she describes these literary writers as creating frameworks or systems of symbols that, like a system of freeway signs, guide the reader through the text and its meanings. She characterizes writers who produce this type of text as "clever," "smart," and methodical. Ironically, then, she implies that the more "literary" a piece of writing is the more analytical and plodding—not creative and insightful—its author. According to Tan, one will not find a system of symbols to decode in her work—indeed, she gently mocks the students and academics who claim to have identified such symbols—because her fiction stems from her own psychological and emotional needs and is not driven by a desire to impress or confound readers. She notes, for example, that she chooses her words with "anguish" and that those words often have associations with things that are "deeply personal and often secretly ironic in [her] own life." Thus, Tan sets up the idea in this passage that a "literary" text is a performance or even a puzzle designed for the reader while her own works are something more akin to personal meditations.

While examining this passage, you would certainly want to ask yourself why a writer like Tan, a writer who creates literary works obviously replete with symbolism and who repeatedly puts herself and her work through the rigorous editing and publication process so that her novels can find their way to readers, would downplay the craftsmanship and symbolic power of her fiction. But perhaps the question to ask first is whether we can take what Tan is saying here at face value. A close reading reveals that Tan does, in fact, own up to the symbolism clearly present in her work. Take the first sentence, for instance. Tan writes that "if I do include symbols in my work, they are carefully nudged out of hiding places by others." She suggests here that there are, in fact, symbols in her novels that can be identified by careful readers, contradicting her suggestion later in the passage that critics who find and discuss symbols in her work are investing empty images with their own meaning. Additionally, when Tan writes that she doesn't "consciously place symbols in such clever fashion as some students have given [her] credit for," she leaves wide open the possibility that she includes symbols on an unconscious level and even suggests that their inclusion is part of a natural, organic writing process rather than a planned, strategic implementation. This seems genuine enough. In fact, it makes so much sense that it leads one to question Tan's characterization of "literary" writers and their texts. Do these writers really insert symbols in an academic and analytical fashion or do most symbols and sets of symbols in fact grow organically from a rich, nuanced text?

If you decide that Tan is setting up a false dichotomy here, you will want to ask yourself why she might do so. Why might she insist that she does not use symbols, and that if she does, they grow naturally from the intensely personal and emotional nature of her own writing? What does such an argument accomplish? Interestingly enough, it seems to be designed to make it impossible for students to analyze and interpret her writing. Much better, and fairer, according to Tan, is to investigate the writing of one of those "methodical" authors who "posts [symbols] like freeway signs." Any interpretation given to her prose will likely be wrong, as there is no way readers can know the "deeply personal and often secretly ironic" meanings her words and images carry, if they carry any at all. Tan's ultimate goal here seems to be to exert control over her body of work, protecting it from all manner of dissection, criticism, and analysis. In fact, a desire to exert and maintain control of her writing might be the very reason she would create a collection like *The Opposite of Fate* in the first place. This would be an interesting line of thought to pursue in an essay. You might investigate how this collection as a whole tries to influence readers' perception of Tan's previous work.

Of course, it is entirely possible that Tan is being "secretly ironic" with this whole passage, knowing that readers will analyze it even as she says her work should not be scrutinized in that way. How do the implications of the passage change if you read it this way? Can you locate other passages in *The Opposite of Fate* that would support such a reading?

TOPICS AND STRATEGIES

The following topics and strategies are designed to get you thinking about what kind of essay you might write on Amy Tan's *The Opposite of Fate: A Book of Musings*. There are many ways to approach writing an essay on a collection of essays, and there are many topics you might focus on. Use the following suggestions as a guide only. If, through reading them, you develop your own way to approach this volume, then by all means pursue your idea and your vision. If you choose to use one of the sample topics listed below, be sure to treat it as a thinking prompt and not as an essay question. In other words, use the sample topic to help you generate ideas and formulate additional questions. Don't feel compelled to answer all of the questions in the prompt or restrict your thinking to these particular questions. Once you have studied the topic thoroughly and used the sub-questions to generate observations and analysis, you are ready to construct your essay, and at this stage, you can and should leave the sample topic behind. Turn to the notes you have compiled and synthesize them to create an argument or interpretation that you want to present to your readers. This will become your essay's thesis. The remainder of the essay should present the best evidence you have amassed to support that thesis.

Themes

There are many themes that run through this collection of essays, but perhaps the most consistent and the most powerful are these: motives for writing, speech and language, the authorial persona, and the intersection of American and Chinese cultures. You might select any one of these topics to investigate. If you select motives for writing as your topic, you will want to peruse the entire collection of essays looking for any references, both direct and indirect, to Tan's impetus for writing fiction. Then, you will want to analyze each of these references and compare and contrast them. You will want to know—is Tan's portrayal of her motivations for writing consistent across the essays in this volume or does her sense of her inspiration and driving force change from time to time? Does she describe her motivation for writing as the desire to create art, to entertain readers, or as a personal exploration of her family history? Once you have a sense of the answers to these questions, you will also want to consider whether it seems as though Tan is presenting an accurate, authentic image of herself and her motivations or whether she is casting them in a certain way to achieve a particular goal, such as deflecting criticism, perhaps.

Sample Topics:

1. **Motives for writing:** Titled *The Opposite of Fate: A Book of Musings,* this collection obviously has much to say about Tan's relationship with and attitude toward writing. According to all of the essays collected here, what would you say are Tan's major reasons for writing? What drives her to keep creating works of literature?

Locate and analyze the passages in which Tan describes her motives for writing. You might begin with "The CliffsNotes Version of My Life" in which Tan explains that moving around so much and having to constantly adapt to new situations made for "excellent training for a budding writer. It sharpened my skills of observation. It deepened my sense of alienation, which, while not a prerequisite for a writer, is certainly useful as an impetus for writing" (22). You will also want to look at "My Grandmother's Choice," in which Tan writes:

> A relative once told my mother, "Why do you tell your daughter these useless stories? She can't change the past." And my mother replied, "It *can* be changed. I tell her, so she can tell everyone, tell the whole world so they know what my mother suffered. That's how it *can* be changed." (103)

So far, Tan has given two major reasons for writing, a sense of alienation and a desire to change the past. She indicates yet a third in the following passage in which she describes her feelings when fans offer to tell her their life stories, always filled with many tragedies and interesting events, so that she can write them in a novel:

I'd never be able to borrow from a stranger's life to create my stories. What's *my* reason for writing the story in the first place, if not to masochistically examine my own life's confusion, my own hopes and unanswered prayers? The metaphors, the sensory truths, the questions must be my own progeny—conceived, nurtured, and fussed over by me. (109)

Analyze these three passages along with others in the collection that discuss Tan's motivations for creating fiction. Do all of the reasons she lists have something in common? You might spend a little time here thinking about all the possible reasons that a writer might feel compelled to write, including everything from a desire for fame and/or fortune to a desire to explore one's psychology to the desire to educate readers about a particular culture or group of people. Now think about Tan's motives as they are presented in *The Opposite of Fate* in comparison to this list of possibilities. Would you say that Tan's motives for writing are based more on her own needs or the perceived needs of her readers? What is she looking to achieve with her writing? How do her motives for writing affect the types of stories she creates?

2. **Communication:** What does *The Opposite of Fate* ultimately have to say about the cultural meanings carried by one's fluency in the English language?

In "Arrival Banquet," Tan tells of her mother correcting her grandson's English. She writes:

I know my mother is not trying to intimidate Xiao-dong. She is only doing for her grandson what no one did for her: teaching him correct English so that he does not have to suffer the same pain she has had to endure—being misunderstood at banks, misdiagnosed by doctors, ignored by her teenage children. Poor service, bad treatment, no respect—that's the penalty for not speaking English well in America. (165)

How does this theme play out in Tan's novels? Pick any of Tan's books and look closely at the Chinese characters and their English-language skills. Do the characters who speak proper English command more respect? What happens to those whose English is not so good?

Read the essay "Mother Tongue." How does Tan herself feel about her mother's "broken" language? How would you describe the way Tan perceives and evaluates a person's speech, and how does this compare to the way that she feels the rest of the world judges it?

3. **Authorial persona:** How does Tan define her role as author/writer in this collection?

Look in particular at "The CliffsNotes Version of My Life" and "Persona Errata." Why does Tan call herself a writer instead of an author? How does she feel about having her work covered in Cliffs Notes? How does she deal with reviews of her books and scholarship that discusses the meaning and symbolism in her work? Reread "The Ghosts of My Imagination"; how does Tan present her creative process? Return to "Required Reading and Other Dangerous Subjects" to investigate why Tan identifies herself as an American writer rather than an Asian-American writer.

In "Persona Errata," Tan lists many myths about herself and corrects them in a humorous and sometimes self-deprecating way. Why do you think she felt the need to write such a piece— does she feel, perhaps, that the image of "Amy Tan" being created by these rumors threatens to obliterate the real Amy Tan or the authorial persona she wants to convey—and why do you think she writes this piece in the style that she does? Based on all of the details of her writerly life that Tan gives us in this collection, what kind of an image is she trying to create of herself as an author? What does she see as the writer's role in society?

4. **"American Circumstances and Chinese Character":** What does *The Opposite of Fate* have to say about the intersection of Chinese and American cultures?

Reread the section of *The Opposite of Fate* called "American Circumstances and Chinese Character." Keep the italicized opening passage, taken from *The Joy Luck Club*, in mind as you read, particularly the first two sentences: *"I wanted my children to have the best combination: American circumstances and Chinese character. How could I know these two things do not mix?"* (123). As you read through "Fish Cheeks," "Dangerous Advice," "Midlife Confidential," "Arrival Banquet," and "Joy Luck and Hollywood" focus on the intersections of American and Chinese culture and character. How would you describe each? What makes them different? What common ground do they share? How do people like Tan and her mother who are to varying degrees bicultural survive and flourish in both worlds? Do the essays in this section bear out or challenge the notion that American circumstances and Chinese character do not mix?

Character

The people who populate this collection are not characters in a pure literary sense. They are not fictional creations of Tan's. As the collection's subtitle—*A Book of Musings*—indicates, these essays are Tan's reflections on her life and the people in it. Therefore, the people, such as Tan herself, her mother Daisy, and her friend Pete are figures who exist, or existed, in the real world. Because, however, a writer cannot transfer the essence of a person, not even his or her own person, directly onto the page, even the figures in this text can be written about as characters. Take Tan's mother, for instance. Tan could not possibly have included every detail she remembers about her mother. How did she decide what to include? What to leave out? Obviously, Tan and her mother had some rough patches in their relationship. How does Tan present these situations? As her mother's fault? Her own? Tan has to make important decisions about her own presentation as well. What will she reveal; what will she keep private? How does she want her readers to view her and what does she want them to understand about her? All of these factors play a role in how Tan presents herself and her mother, and these presentations, or representations, become the characters that populate *The Opposite of Fate*.

Sample Topics:

1. **Amy Tan:** Analyze and evaluate the way that the author Amy Tan functions as a character in this collection of essays about herself and her experiences.

In a way, Amy Tan herself becomes a character in this volume of essays. How does she present herself? What does she choose to divulge about her life? What elements of her life does she neglect to talk about? Do you take everything she says at face value? What kind of image is she constructing by writing, gathering, and publishing this collection? Consider in particular "Persona Errata" and "What the Library Means to Me." Why do you think that Tan included these essays in this collection? In what light do they present her?

Reread the essays in the section "Strong Winds, Strong Influences." How do these essays, and others in the collection as well, present Tan's relationship with her mother? Specifically, how do generational and cultural factors play into their complicated and constantly evolving relationship? How does Daisy's Alzheimer's affect their relationship? Trace the evolution of this relationship: What kind of a daughter was Tan as a child? A teenager? An adult? How important would you say that this relationship was to Tan's personal psychological development?

2. **Daisy Tan:** How does Amy Tan's mother Daisy function as a character in this volume?

Daisy Tan is, of course, a real person, who served as inspiration for several characters in Amy Tan's fiction, particularly Winnie in *The Kitchen God's Wife*. In *The Opposite of Fate*, Amy Tan writes about her mother directly and discusses the relationship they shared in Amy's youth and adulthood, yet Daisy can still be considered a character of sorts as the careful way that Amy Tan crafts these essays results in a particular representation of her mother. How does Tan want us to perceive her mother in *The Opposite of Fate*? Is she a sympathetic character? Why or why not? How is the Daisy Tan who appears in *The Opposite of Fate* different from and similar to the one appearing in *The Kitchen God's Wife*? What do you think accounts for these differences?

3. **Pete:** Analyze Tan's portrayal of her roommate Pete in "A Question of Fate" and describe Pete's role in the evolution of Tan's perception of the world and goals for herself.

Tan tells Pete's story in "A Question of Fate." What kind of a person was Pete? What role did he play in Tan's life? What role do supernatural elements play in Pete's life and in Tan's relationship with him? What life lessons does Tan attribute to her relationship with Pete and the dreams she experiences after his death? How does Pete's death change the direction of Tan's life? Would you say that this essay is primarily about Pete or about Tan herself? Why? What point(s) do you think Tan is trying to make by including this essay on Pete in this collection?

History and Context

There are several historical and contextual issues, such as Tan's biography, Alzheimer's disease, and World War II, that you might decide to investigate as you prepare to write about *The Opposite of Fate.* Any background reading you do into these topics will help you to better understand *The Opposite of Fate* as well as Tan's other works and therefore help you to write a more thoughtful, nuanced essay on whatever topic you choose to study. It's worth noting, however, that your research and investigation into these topics can do more than provide you with useful context. They can actually become the focal point of your essay. You might, for instance, decide to devote your essay to a discussion of what Tan reveals about her family's stories in *The Opposite of Fate* and the way that she uses them in her fiction. Or your research into Alzheimer's disease might lead you to investigate the psychological struggles of both Alzheimer's patients and their caregivers as represented in *The Opposite of Fate* and *The Bonesetter's Daughter.* Finally, your studies into the Chinese arena of World War II might inspire you to examine what Tan has to say about the Chinese experience in World War II in *The Opposite of Fate* as well as in her novel *The Kitchen God's Wife.*

Sample Topics:

1. **Use of biographical material:** How much of Tan's work is based on biographical details and how does this affect her work?

In her essay "Thinly Disguised Memoir," Tan discusses the manner in which she uses biographical material in her fiction writing:

> This is not to say I've been writing autobiographically, at least not in the sense that most people assume. If I write about a little girl who lives in Chinatown and plays chess, this does not mean that I did those same things.
>
> But within that story is an emotional truth. It has to do with a mother who has helped her daughter see the world in a special way. It is a world in which the mother possessed rare magic. She can make the girl see yin when it is yang. The girl sees that her mother, who is her ally, is also her adversary. And that is an emotional memory that I *do* have, this sense of double jeopardy, realizing that my mother could both help me and hurt me, in the best and worst ways possible. (109)

Read the remainder of "Thinly Disguised Memoir," as well as "What She Meant," "Last Week," and "My Grandmother's Choice." Then, return to Tan's novels in which she incorporates the stories of her family, including *The Kitchen God's Wife* and *The Bonesetter's Daughter.* Based on what you know about the real story of Tan's family, how closely do her novels parallel the stories of her mother and grandmother? How has Tan changed some facts and details yet still captured the "emotional truth" of these powerful stories? Would you argue that the stories would be stronger had Tan stuck to the facts and labeled the books as biographies? Or do you think they are more successful the way they are presented, and why?

2. **Alzheimer's disease:** What kind of commentary does *The Opposite of Fate* ultimately make about Alzheimer's disease and its effects on families?

In "Last Week," Tan discusses her mother's Alzheimer's and the way that their relationship evolved during this ordeal. Do some background reading on Alzheimer's disease before taking another look at "Last Week." How common are Daisy Tan's experiences and symptoms? What makes her particular experience unique? Think about Tan's response to her mother's illness as well. How do family members typically cope with losing a loved one in this way? How did Tan handle the situation, and how did her approach affect her relationship with her mother? What would you say is the most important thing that Tan's experience with her mother's Alzheimer's disease taught her? What might readers who are going through a similar experience learn from Tan's personal revelations?

You might also choose to examine Tan's novel *The Bonesetter's Daughter* in which she describes the experiences of a woman, LuLing, who is becoming increasingly debilitated due to Alzheimer's and her daughter Ruth's efforts to care for her. How closely do LuLing and Ruth resemble Daisy and Amy? What is Tan trying to say about Alzheimer's disease and its effects on the psychology of the patient and his or her family as well as their relationships with each other?

3. **World War II:** Many Western students grow up like Tan herself did, with "no idea that China had ever been involved in World War II—let alone that the war in China had started in 1937" (208). Through her mother's stories, Tan finally learns what life was like for Chinese citizens during World War II. What does she convey about those experiences in *The Opposite of Fate?*

Do some background reading into World War II in China. You might begin with an investigation into the Sino-Japanese War, starting with *A Concise History of China* or *China in the Twentieth Century*. Then, locate and analyze any mention of the war in *The Opposite of Fate*, in particular the following extended passage in which Tan asks her mother about the war in China:

> "Hey, Ma, what was it like during the war?"
>
> My mother considered the question, paused to cast back to her life in China. "War? Oh, I was not affected."
>
> I assumed by her answer that she had been tucked away in free China, that her experiences with World War II were similar to mine with Vietnam: observed from a safe distance. Ah well, some parents have interesting war stories to tell. My mother did not.
>
> So it was not until later in our conversation that I learned what my mother really meant by her answer. She was telling me about her first marriage, to a pilot to whom she could never refer by name, only by the words "that bad man." And now, she told me, somebody had sponsored that bad man to come visit the United States as a former Kuomintang hero.
>
> "Hnh! He was no hero!" my mother exclaimed. "He was dismissed from air force for bad morals." And she began to tell me details of their life in China—of bombs falling, of running to escape, of pilot friends who showed up for dinner one week and were dead the next.
>
> I interrupted her. "Wait a minute, I thought you said you weren't affected by the war."
>
> "I wasn't" insisted my mother. "I wasn't killed." (207–08)

What image does this passage give of the life of Chinese citizens during World War II? What does it suggest about their daily lives? What does the misunderstanding caused by Daisy saying "I wasn't affected"—by which she meant she wasn't killed in the war while her daughter assumes this meant the war had not touched her—signify about these two women's perspectives? Why do you think China is not typically discussed in Western lessons about World War II?

Tan states that she eventually wrote a book about this period of her mother's life. To do so, she "read scholarly texts and revisionist versions of the various roles on the Kuomintang, the Communists, the Japanese, the Americans. [She] read wartime accounts published in popular periodicals—with different perspectives on these same groups" (211). You might want to expand your discussion to include the novel Tan refers to here, *The Kitchen God's Wife*, which includes a great deal of information concerning the occupation in the 1930s and 40s of China by Japan and the 1937 Rape of Nanking as these events provide important context for Tan's mother's story. You might want to read Bella Adams's article "Representing History in Amy Tan's *The Kitchen God's Wife*" for an interesting perspective on Tan's use of history in this novel. Why do you think Tan chooses to write about this period of history? Why did she do such careful research before doing so, and why does she then write about that research in another essay? What is Tan trying to say about the Chinese experience of World War II and the Western response, or lack of response, to that experience?

Philosophy and Ideas

It wouldn't be exaggerating to say that two of the most fundamental concerns of *The Opposite of Fate* are hope/fate and the supernatural. You might choose to focus your essay on either of these topics, or any other philosophical or ideological issue you identify in the collection. No matter what topic you decide to focus on, you will want to begin by identifying all of the relevant passages in the text and analyzing them carefully. Allow your analyses to spark additional questions and pursue the answers to those as well. You do not, however, want to stop there, presenting your analyses of each passage in your essay in sequence, explaining that this particular passage says one thing about hope and faith, while the next one says something else, and the third something altogether different from the first two. While this may in fact be true, your job as a writer has not been completely finished. You have to synthesize your findings and interpret them. What does it mean that those three paragraphs say different things about the nature of hope and faith? Are Tan's definitions evolving? Does each paragraph present a slightly different nuance? Do her discussions of hope and fate contradict themselves in a way that seem to suggest that Tan herself is unsure of the way in which she views each of these concepts? Ultimately, you are trying to work toward a thesis, some significant claim you can make about the topic that will help your readers to understand the collection better or to appreciate it in a new way. Once you have discovered your thesis, you will then decide which parts of your analyses work best to support that thesis, and it is these parts that you will present in the essay, omitting those that do not serve your argument.

Sample Topics:

1. **Hope and fate:** What does *The Opposite of Fate: A Book of Musings* ultimately have to say about the nature of hope and fate and their functions in our lives?

In "A Note to the Reader," Tan writes that the pieces in this collection "explain [her] fiction" by revealing that all of her writing deals in some form or fashion with the concept of hope. She writes:

> Thus, although each of these writings came about for its own reasons, collectively they hold much in common, and at times they overlap in my mention of ideas, people, and pivotal moments. They are musings linked by my fascination with fate, both blind and blessed, and its many alternatives: choice, chance, luck, faith, forgiveness, forgetting, freedom of expression, the pursuit of happiness, the balm of love, a sturdy attitude, a strong will, a bevy of good-luck charms, adherence to rituals, appeasement through prayer, trolling for miracles, a plea to others to throw a lifeline, and the generous provision of that by strangers and loved ones. I see

that these permutations of changing fate are really one all-encompassing thing: hope. (3)

In your mind, does the concept of "hope" encompass all the elements Tan lists in the above passage? Are choice, luck, and a strong will actually manifestations of hope? How so? Can you come up with another term or concept that links all of the elements Tan refers to? Taking Tan at her word that all of her work has to do in some way or another with hope, what would you say is her main message about hope? What exactly does it mean? How does it function in the world?

In her note to the reader, Tan frames hope and all of its constituent parts, including faith, as alternatives to the concept of fate. Yet, in "The CliffsNotes Version of My Life," she writes about their similarities:

> These days I realize that faith and fate have similar effects on the believer. They suggest that a higher power knows the next move and that we are at the mercy of that force. They differ, among other things, in how you try to cull beneficence and what you do to avoid disaster. Come to think of it, those very notions are the plotlines of many novels. (23)

What exactly is it that makes faith and all of the other manifestations of hope different from fate? How does one "cull beneficence" and try "to avoid disaster" if operating with a sense of faith versus fate? How might one behave differently and how would one's perception of the power of personal choice and action be affected?

2. **The supernatural:** What kind of commentary is Tan making in this collection about the role of the supernatural in her own life and in our contemporary culture at large?

In "The CliffsNotes Version of My Life" Tan recalls that her mother thought she was sensitive to spirits and would ask her to communicate with them through a Ouija board. She writes:

> In my memory, which I admit can be subjectively poor and riddled with a wild imagination, I recall that our sessions with the Ouija board were often accompanied by eerie signs that ghosts were indeed in the room. It would suddenly become not just cold but windy. A flower would snap from its stem as if in answer to an important question. A sound would be heard in the distance—first by my mother, then by me—seemingly the voice of a crying woman. And once the board rose in the air several inches, then crashed to the floor. That is what I remember, although logic tells me it was the result of either hysteria or peanut butter stuck to my fingertips. (27)

What can you tell about Tan and her beliefs from this passage? Does she believe that she witnessed supernatural phenomena, or does she lean more toward the belief that her imagination conjured up any ghosts she thought she sensed? What happens when memory and logic do not agree? In another piece in this collection, called "A Question of Fate," Tan tells the story of her friend Pete's murder and of the dreams she had after his death in which Pete visited her and revealed important life lessons. She writes:

> Today I am neither a believer nor a skeptic. I am a puzzler. I still puzzle over what Pete's story presents: what I fear, what I dream, what I believe. I ask myself: What's real? What's important? What do I gain in believing one reality over another? What do I lose? And if we understand the mysteries of the universe, if they end up being explained entirely by mathematics, as Pete said they could be, will they still bless us with the same amazing joy? (59–60)

Does Tan position herself in this passage the same way she does in the first? If she is neither a "believer nor a skeptic," then how does she process and understand the supernatural elements she has experienced in her life? What do they mean to her? How does she present them to other people? Locate other instances in the collection in which Tan refers to the supernatural and its role in her life and her writing. If you had to summarize Tan's views on the existence and significance of supernatural phenomena, how would you do so? How do these impact her writing? How are supernatural elements treated in her fiction?

Form and Genre

The Opposite of Fate is a collection of personal pieces, written in many different styles and for many different occasions, which come together to function as a memoir. It would make for a very interesting essay to study the organization and structure of this unusual collection. You might think about why Tan chose the pieces she did as well as the reason she grouped and sequenced them in this particular way. You would also need to study the titles Tan gave to each set of essays and to the significance of the quotes from her novels that preface each section. Or you might decide to write an essay that focuses solely on the significance of the volume's title: *The Opposite of Fate: A Book of Musings*. You might investigate any references to the title that appear throughout the text, as well as all references made to "fate" and what its opposite might be. Additionally, you will want to discuss the significance of the fact that the final essay, about Tan's experience with Lyme disease, carries the same title as the entire collection.

Sample Topics:

1. **Structure:** Analyze and evaluate the structure of *The Opposite of Fate: A Book of Musings*.

   Reread *The Opposite of Fate*, focusing specifically on its structure and organization. What do you make of the way she groups the essays and the titles she gives each group? Analyze the passages that preface each section. How do they relate to the essays that follow, and what do they add to your interpretation of each section and of the book as a whole? To help you analyze the structure and its significance you could spend some time thinking about what other thematic groups Tan might have arranged the essays into. How would the book be different if she had done so? How would it be different if Tan had arranged the essays chronologically according to the time period in which they were written? Write an essay in which you articulate for your reader the thematic significance of Tan's arrangement.

2. **Title:** Analyze and evaluate the significance of the title *The Opposite of Fate: A Book of Musings.*

Before you read the text for the first time, what did the title suggest to you? What might Tan mean by "the opposite of fate"? What is fate's opposite? How does the initial section, "A Note to the Reader," help to explain the title? How does the title and the note that contextualizes it affect your perception of the text as a whole? Why do you think the final essay, which discusses in detail Tan's experience with Lyme disease, shares the same title as the collection as a whole? What does this mean about the significance of that final piece and its relationship to the other essays in the collection?

Language, Symbols, and Imagery

Tan offers practically irresistible opportunities to discuss symbols and images in *The Opposite of Fate.* First, there is the short piece entitled "Scent" in which Tan traces the evolving symbolic meaning of the gardenia plant and its fragrance in her own life. If you write about this piece, you can not only study this interesting evolution, but you can treat the essay as a study of the way symbols function as well. Or you might turn to the photographic images contained in this volume, examining them for what they have to add to the written text. You might also think about how these images work differently from images crafted in prose and then speculate on the reasons Tan opted to include photographs in this collection.

Sample Topics:

1. **Gardenias:** Analyze and evaluate the symbolic meaning of gardenias in the short piece entitled "Scent." Discuss also what the piece has to say about the nature of symbolism itself.

In "Scent," Tan discusses what the scent of gardenias has meant to her during various periods of her life. She tells of longing for a gardenia corsage until she is oppressed by their scent during the funerals for her father and her brother. Afterwards, she is reminded of that grief whenever she encounters the scent of gardenias. Then, finally, she buys a gardenia plant of her own and finds that it reminds her of happy expectations, linking back to her earlier associations of a gardenia corsage. Despite her neglect, the gardenia plant survives, and Tan ends the piece with the wish that the flowers will soon bloom again. How does the symbolic meaning of the gardenia change during Tan's life? What prompts the changes? What might the changes tell us about Tan's psyche? What does this piece tell us about the nature of symbolism?

2. **Photographs:** Analyze and evaluate the photographs included in *The Opposite of Fate.* What do these images add to the themes and meanings of the individual essays and the collection as whole?

The Opposite of Fate includes pictures of Tan's editor Faith Sale posing with Tan's mother Daisy, Tan's grandmother, and an unnamed relative; the Tan family a day after Amy's birth; and Daisy Tan in China in 1945. It also includes several pictures of the author, with her husband, with the Rock Bottom Remainders, and receiving an award for an essay at the age of eight. Why do you think these particular photos were selected for inclusion? Why do you think they were placed where they are in the text? Study the images carefully. Are they posed or candid shots? What do the backgrounds contain? Are the people in the pictures smiling? Is there a particular occasion being commemorated by the picture?

You might want to look in particular at the two photos of Tan and her mother, each taken when the women, respectively, were eight years old. Tan's mother is pictured with many other family members (98) and Tan herself is shown receiving an award (270). What do these two images say about the two women and the environment in which they were raised? You will also want to study the opening of Tan's "My Grandmother's Choice," in which she provides commentary on the picture which includes her eight-year-old mother. What does this picture mean for Tan? How does it help her to put her own life in perspective? What does it mean for readers of *The Opposite of Fate*?

Compare and Contrast Essays

Comparing and contrasting elements across works can provide you with insights that you simply could not get from studying one work in isolation. Using *The Opposite of Fate* as one of your points of comparison is especially interesting since this work reveals much of Tan's biography and offers her personal reflections on many issues that crop up in her novels. For example, comparing the mother/daughter relationship in Tan's *The Opposite of Fate* with her presentation of that same relationship in another, or several other, of her works can allow you to really investigate the personal impetus for the exploration of these kinds of relationships and to study the models on which many of Tan's fictional characters are in some manner based. Likewise, you might compare and contrast Tan's reflections on the life of her own grandmother in *The Opposite of Fate* with the character resembling her grandmother who appears in *The Joy Luck Club*, namely, An-mei Hsu's mother. Yet another interesting angle would be to compare and contrast Tan's memoirs with a similar work, such as Joyce Carol Oates's *The Journal of Joyce Carol Oates: 1973–1982*, to develop a sharper, more nuanced analysis of Tan's perception of her role as writer and her response to the tremendous success her writing has brought her.

Sample Topics:

1. **Tan's own grandmother and An-mei's mother in *The Joy Luck Club*:** Compare and contrast Tan's real grandmother and the

fictional woman she created for *The Joy Luck Club* who shares many of the same experiences.

You will want to begin by reading "My Grandmother's Choice," in which Tan tells the story of her grandmother who, after becoming a widow, was raped by "a rich man who liked to collect pretty women." She revealed that her grandmother became a concubine of that man and that she killed herself after she bore the man's son. Her daughter, Tan's mother, "could never talk about the shame of being a concubine's daughter, even with her closest friends." Then you will want to reread *The Joy Luck Club*, particularly the sections focusing on An-mei Hsu. Like Tan's mother Daisy, An-mei sees her mother become the concubine of a rich man and kill herself after giving birth to the man's son. How are these women's circumstances similar and different? What elements of her grandmother's story does Tan alter in *The Joy Luck Club*? Which does she emphasize or omit? You may also want to compare and contrast An-mei with Daisy Tan. How do the two daughters react and respond to their mothers' fates?

2. **Mother/daughter relationships in *The Opposite of Fate* and in Tan's works of fiction:** Compare and contrast the mother/daughter relationship between Tan and her own mother presented in this collection of essays with the mother daughter relationships presented in her fictional works, including *The Joy Luck Club*, *The Kitchen God's Wife*, and *The Bonesetter's Daughter.*

Many of the essays in *The Opposite of Fate* address the relationship between Amy Tan and her mother, Daisy. Begin by analyzing these essays and generating some notes on the nature of this relationship, the major factors that affected it, and its evolution as Tan and her mother age. Mother/daughter relationships are central to Tan's fiction, and since much of her fiction draws from her own family history, it is not surprising to find echoes of the Daisy and Amy relationship in works such as *The Joy Luck Club, The Kitchen God's Wife,* and *The Bonesetter's Daughter.* You might choose to focus on one, two, or all three of these texts depending on the scope of your intended project. No matter which text you decide to study, you will need to begin by performing the same kind of analysis you did on the characters in *The Opposite of Fate.* How would you describe the mother and daughter figures individually? What drives them? What are their priorities? What are their fears? Then, think about the way they interact with each other. How do they treat each other? What would you say are the positive and negative elements of the relationship?

Your final task will be to compare and contrast the relationships you have studied individually. How is the relationship between Amy Tan and her own mother similar to and different from the relationships you have studied in her novel(s)? What elements of her relationship with her mother did Tan transfer directly to her fiction? What did she alter? Does it seem to you that Tan is trying to work out her own relationship with her mother through her fiction? Or is she offering a lesson in mother/daughter relationships to other families based on her own hard-won knowledge? In short, what do you think Tan is trying to say in her fiction about the nature of mother/daughter relationships?

3. ***The Opposite of Fate* with Joyce Carol Oates's *The Journal of Joyce Carol Oates: 1973–1982*:** Compare and contrast these two memoirs. What do they have to say about the nature of creativity and writing fiction?

You will want to start by reading Oates's memoir, which contains excerpts from the journal she kept during the first 10 years of her writing career. Then, begin to compare and contrast Oates's work with Tan's. How does each woman describe her writing process? Where does inspiration come from? How do her family history and family relationships come into play? How does each writer respond to book reviews, good and bad, and to critics and academics who study and comment on her work? How have the two writers responded to their enormous success? Why did each of them feel motivated to create a commentary on their writerly lives? Once you have answered these questions, you can begin to ascertain what these writers have in common and what distinguishes them from each other. What generalizations about the life of a contemporary female writer can you make by studying these two works? You will also want to consider the fact that Tan's memoirs were written in the 1990s and early 2000s while Oates's volume was written in the 1970s and '80s. How might this approximately 20-year time difference have affected these authors' accounts? What other factors set these writers apart?

Bibliography for *The Opposite of Fate: A Book of Musings*

Adams, Bella. "Representing History in Amy Tan's *The Kitchen God's Wife.*" MELUS 28.2 (2003): 9–30.

Bailey, Paul. *China in the Twentieth Century.* Malen, MA: Wiley-Blackwell, 2001.

Bloom, Harold, ed. *Amy Tan.* Modern Critical Views. Philadelphia: Chelsea House, 2000.

Huntley, E. D. *Amy Tan: A Critical Companion.* Critical Companions to Popular Contemporary Writers. Westport, CT: Greenwood, 1998.

Morton, W. Scott. *China: Its History and Culture.* 3rd ed. New York: McGraw-Hill, 1995.

Roberts, J. A. G. *A Concise History of China.* Cambridge, MA: Harvard UP, 1999.

Shields, Charles J. *Amy Tan.* Women of Achievement. Philadelphia: Chelsea House, 2002.

Tan, Amy. *The Opposite of Fate: A Book of Musings.* New York: Putnam's, 2003.

WORKS FOR
CHILDREN:

The Moon Lady and
The Chinese Siamese Cat

READING TO WRITE

IN ADDITION to her novels and essays, Amy Tan has also published two successful children's books, *The Moon Lady* (1992) and *The Chinese Siamese Cat* (1994), both of which were illustrated by Gretchen Schields and published as picture books. The two books were generally well received, and *The Chinese Siamese Cat* became the basis of the PBS animated Emmy-winning series "Sagwa." These works of Tan's have received less critical attention than her adult novels, but they can be analyzed and critiqued in much the same way. Thinking about *The Joy Luck Club*, for instance, we might ask ourselves how the characters move from innocence to experience—what are their primary "growing up" moments—and how are they shaped by these moments? We might also ask how being female informs their particular journeys to adulthood. In the context of *The Joy Luck Club*, we understand that these types of questions are difficult to answer and are the starting points for meaningful essays on the novel. The same can be said for Tan's literature for children. For instance, we can bring the same kinds of questions we ask of *The Joy Luck Club* to *The Moon Lady*.

Look, for example, at the following passage in which Ying-ying stands too close to the woman cleaning fish and winds up ruining her elaborate festival costume:

> It was not until then that I noticed my new clothes were covered with spots of eel blood, flecks of fish scales, bits of feather and mud. And then I heard Amah's voice, "Ying-ying, where are you?" What a strange mind I had! I quickly dipped my hands into the bucket of eels. I smeared the mess on my sleeves, on the front of my pants, and the rest of my jacket. This is what I truly thought: I could cover the dirty spots by painting all my clothes crimson red, and if I stood perfectly still no one would notice this change.

Ying-ying leads a protected life; her Amah takes care of her and shelters her from all of the unpleasant aspects of life. In keeping with this routine, Ying-ying is supposed to be sleeping when she witnesses the fishermen and women hard at work. Her curiosity, however, puts an end to the naïveté that her family has cultivated in her. No longer protected, Ying-ying is now fully aware of tough, dirty work that must be done by people like the old woman gutting the eels and the animals that must be slaughtered in preparation for her family's feasting. After she witnesses this scene, Ying-ying is no longer the innocent girl she once was. The spots of "eel blood, flecks of fish scales, bits of feather and mud" that ruin her new clothes also mark her as changed, as sullied even, and can be seen as a mark of passage into adulthood.

This experience also seems to be connected to Ying-ying's transformation not just into general adulthood but into womanhood specifically, for she decides to smear herself with eel blood and then to remain perfectly still to disguise her transformation. This notion that if she "stood perfectly still no one would notice [the] change" recalls the advice that her mother gives her earlier in the story: "A boy can run and chase dragonflies, but a girl should stand still. If you are still for a very long time, a dragonfly will no longer see you. Then it will come and hide in your shadow." The notion of remaining perfectly still to escape notice, essentially to become invisible, is definitely connected to the female.

According to Ying-ying's mother, to be a proper girl meant that Ying-ying had to cease moving until she completely blended in with the natural landscape, until even a dragonfly would no longer distinguish her from the rest of its environment. She has to disappear into the realm of nature, relinquishing her human agency. When Ying-ying assumes the identity of a woman, she finds herself again trying to lose herself in the natural work, but this time by cloaking herself in its darker elements, in the death and violence that is represented by the eel blood.

After a close look at this passage, you might want to continue along this line of thinking. What are the consequences of teaching girls and women to give up agency and individuality? How is this different from what boys are taught? What does this say about the relative position of women to men in Chinese culture? You might examine the rest of the book for references to gender identity issues—what are the characteristics and qualities associated with men and with women—and for clues as to what it means for a girl to become a woman. Or you might focus on Ying-ying's entrance into the adult world and compare and contrast the Ying-ying of the early part of the story with the Ying-ying who has covered herself in eel blood. Finally, you might decide to study how Ying-ying's "double" fits into the equation. Does she represent an eternally innocent version of Ying-ying? What are the ramifications of this?

In any case, you will want to closely examine any passages related to the theme you are interested in studying in the text, looking closely at the language and decoding the symbolism. Your job is then to synthesize your findings into some coherent argument or interpretation of the text that you can present in your essay.

TOPICS AND STRATEGIES

The following topics are suggestions for writing an essay about Amy Tan's works of literature for children, *The Moon Lady*, *The Chinese Siamese Cat*, or both. Feel free to use any of these topics as they are or to use them to create a topic of your own, to modify a topic, or to combine two or more topics. These are designed to spur your thinking, not to restrict it. While the sub-questions included under each topic can be very helpful in the prewriting stage, when you are ready to craft your essay, you want to be careful not to wind up with what amounts to a series of answers to these questions. Instead, you will want to use the thesis you have arrived at to help you determine what points to include and in what order to arrange them in your essay.

Themes

When you are asked to write about theme in a work of literature, it is important to remember that there are multiple themes and that these themes can be viewed from many different angles. In the case of Amy Tan's children's stories, you might elect to restrict your discussion to one of the texts, writing, for example, about desire in *The Moon Lady*. Or you might write about a theme common to both texts, such as the passing of cultural knowledge from one generation to the next or the child's role in society. Whatever topic you decide to pursue, be sure to ask yourself exactly what the text has to say about your chosen theme. It's not enough, for example, to argue that desire is a fundamental theme in *The Moon Lady*. You might argue instead that the text suggests to children that the only virtuous wishes are actually personal goals that we ourselves have the power to realize or, alternatively, that the text suggests to readers that while we may harbor desires in our hearts, we should not express those desires to others lest we seem weak and discontent.

Sample Topics:

1. **Wishes and desires in *The Moon Lady*:** What does *The Moon Lady* ultimately have to say about the nature of desire? What different wishes are expressed throughout the book? What does the story that the girls' grandmother tells them teach about wishes?

   You will want to consider what Ying-ying's Amah tells her about the definition of a secret wish—"If you ask then it is no longer a wish but a selfish desire." Why do you think it is that the expression of a desire is what makes it selfish? What does this say about the nature of wishes and desires in Chinese culture?

   When Ying-ying sees the Moon Lady on stage, she hears her reveal that her husband was given a magic peach for saving the world, and that she, wanting to live forever, ate that peach when her husband was away. For this, the Moon Lady's husband "banished [her] from this earth, and sent [her] to live on the moon. . . . An eternity had passed, for this was her fate: to stay lost on the moon, forever regretting her own selfish wishes." What lesson does Ying-ying take from this story? How are her own wishes changed by it? Many years later as she recounts this memory to her granddaughters, Ying-ying sums up what she learned this way:

> I now knew that there were many kinds of wishes, some that came from my stomach, some that were selfish, some that came from my heart. And I knew what the best wishes were: those I could make come true by myself.

What do her granddaughters learn from this story? How might their future wishes be shaped by it?

2. **Passing on wisdom and cultural knowledge:** Both *The Chinese Siamese Cat* and *The Moon Lady* deal with the passing down of family stories from one generation to the next. What kind of knowledge is being transferred and how will it affect the lives of the younger generation?

In *The Chinese Siamese Cat*, Ming Miao calls her kittens to her to tell them the story of their ancestors before they are sent out to new homes. In *The Moon Lady*, the grandmother tells her three granddaughters about her earliest memory from when she was a little girl in China. What prompts the telling of each of these stories? Why are these particular stories told? What are they designed to teach the young people? How do the young people respond to these stories?

3. **Children:** Most of the main characters in each of these stories are children. How does Tan characterize children and their relationships with adults?

Think about the young characters in each of Tan's children's books, the kittens in *The Chinese Siamese Cat* and the three little girls—as well as the grandmother who is a child in the story she tells—in *The Moon Lady*. How would you describe them? What do they have in common? Would you say that Tan presents children as essentially innocent and good or as flawed creatures right from the start? What are their relationships with the adult characters like?

Character

When analyzing character, you want to make sure to take into account your character's behavior and dialogue as well as the way that your character is perceived by other characters. You also want to consider whether the author portrays your character as essentially sympathetic and likable, as someone readers might want to emulate. Are your character's views ones the author him- or herself likely holds? Also evaluate whether or not your character experiences some kind of change throughout the course of the text. If so, ask yourself whether this change is for better or worse and what prompts it. Finally, do not forget to examine the illustrations for more details about your character and his or her relationship to others in the story. Is your character drawn in a particular style? How is he or she positioned on the page in relationship to the other characters? Are there any details you can observe about your character in the illustrations that do not show up in the text?

Sample Topics:

1. **The Moon Lady:** What is the significance of the Moon Lady to the story as a whole?

   What do you know about the Moon Lady? What does she look like? What story does she tell? How does her story affect Ying-ying? What does Ying-ying plan to wish for when she rushes up to the Moon Lady after the show is complete? You will want to examine the passage in which Ying-ying approaches the Moon Lady, eager to make her wish, and is surprised by what she sees:

   > shrunken cheeks, a broad oily nose, large glaring teeth, and red-stained eyes. And then her silk gown slipped off her

shoulders as she wearily pulled off her long hair. Before the secret wish could fall from my lips, the Moon Lady looked at me and became a man.

How does Ying-ying react to this discovery? How does this experience change the way that she thinks about wishes and desires? What effect do you think it might have on her notion of gender roles?

2. **The Foolish Magistrate:** Analyze and evaluate the character of the Foolish Magistrate in *The Chinese Siamese Cat.*

Begin by recording everything you know about the Magistrate. Remember to examine the illustrations for information as well as the text. What is the Magistrate motivated by? What changes his behavior? Is the change in his character believable? Why or why not?

3. **Sagwa:** Analyze and evaluate the character of Sagwa in *The Chinese Siamese Cat.*

What kind of kitten is Sagwa? How is she different from the rest of her family? How does she end up changing the rules of the land? How is she remembered by her descendents? What does this story, and Sagwa's character in particular, imply are the best characteristics for a child to have? Is Sagwa a positive example of an extraordinary child? A negative example to be used as a warning to mischievous children? A combination of both?

History and Context

Researching the history and context of a piece of literature is not only beneficial in helping you to develop a deeper understanding of a book's themes and meanings; it can often help you to arrive at an argument to make in your essay as well. You might research the mid-autumn festival, for example, and use your knowledge of this element of Chinese culture to help you come to a new interpretation of *The Moon Lady* by asking yourself why Tan chose to set the story during this special time of year. Or you might investigate how Amy Tan's two books fit into the general context of picture books portraying Chinese culture. Are they pretty standard fare, or did they offer something new to the world of picture books, especially as they relate to Chinese culture?

Sample Topics:

1. **Mid-autumn, or Harvest Moon Festival:** Explore the significance of the setting on the overall themes and meanings of *The Moon Lady*.

You will want to do some research into the Chinese mid-autumn festival. What is being celebrated? What do people usually do to celebrate? How do men and women celebrate the festival differently? Is the celebration that Ying-ying remembers a fairly standard one? Why do you think Tan sets Ying-ying's story during the Moon Festival? Does this setting invest the story with some special significance? In what way?

2. **Children's books about Chinese culture:** How have Amy Tan's children's books, *The Chinese Siamese Cat* and *The Moon Lady*, affected or contributed to the image of China offered in picture books set in China?

You will want to begin by placing Amy Tan's children's books in the context of other picture books published during the same time period that deal with Chinese culture. You might look at *Lon Po Po* by Ed Young and various titles by Demi, such as *The Magic Tapestry* and *The Magic Boat*. How are Tan's books similar to and different from these other titles? Remember to think about the texts as well as the illustrations. Imagine not only how Western children might read these books but also how Chinese, or Chinese-American, children might perceive them. Do Tan's books seem to be aimed more at one audience than another?

Philosophy and Ideas

Although you might be tempted to think that literature written for children does not engage philosophy or ideas in a meaningful or sophisticated manner, if you take a good look at Amy Tan's *The Chinese Siamese Cat* and *The Moon Lady*, you will see that it most certainly does. *The Chinese Siamese Cat* is concerned with government's relationship with the people and the issue of free will versus fate, and you might write about either of these issues in an essay. Or if you elect to focus on *The Moon Lady*, you might write about gender roles or social hierarchy. Whatever philosophical or ideological topic you choose, your job will be to determine and then articulate for your readers precisely what message the story is conveying about your topic. For example, if you elect to write about government in *The Chinese Siamese Cat*, you will want to investigate what it presents as the flaws and benefits of being governed by a single magistrate. What makes a poor ruler? What makes a good one? How do ostensibly powerless citizens make changes in their government?

Sample Topics:

1. **Government in *The Chinese Siamese Cat*:** What does *The Chinese Siamese Cat* ultimately have to say about the nature of governance and power? What lessons does it teach?

   Analyze and evaluate the passages that talk about the type of ruler the Magistrate is. You might focus particularly on paragraphs like the following:

   > He made up rules that helped only himself. Because he wanted to command respect, he ordered people and animals to bow down to him. Because he was afraid people laughed at him behind his back, he made up a rule that people could no longer laugh. Because he wanted more money, he charged people fines for breaking his rules.

   What kind of a ruler is the Magistrate? How does he make decisions? What are his priorities? How do the people react to a ruler of this type? You will want to look at what prompts the change in the Magistrate's behavior as well. What does he learn about government and how does he learn it? What kind of relationship does the Magistrate have with the people by the end of the tale?

2. **Gender roles in *The Moon Lady*:** What does *The Moon Lady* ultimately have to say about gender roles in Chinese and American cultures?

You will want to analyze the explicit references to gender roles throughout the text, including the following passage in which Ying-ying's mother scolds her for running around the courtyard chasing dragonflies:

> A boy can run and chase dragonflies, because that is his nature, she explained in a gentle voice. But a girl should stand still. If you are still for a very long time, a dragonfly will no longer see you. Then it will come and hide in the comfort of your shadow. The other ladies clucked in agreement and then they all left me alone in the middle of the hot courtyard.

What does Ying-ying make of this advice? Does she heed it? What does this passage tell us about the way that Chinese culture expected boys and girls to behave and to engage with the world around them? Later that same night, after she has been separated from her family, Ying-ying hears the story of the Moon Lady, including the following lines:

> For woman is yin. . . . The darkness within, where passions lie.
> And man is yang, bright truth lighting our minds.

How is Ying-ying affected by this pronouncement? Does she display any understanding of it? How do you think young readers will process this portion of the story? And finally, you will want to think about whether the contemporary American culture reflected in the story's frame envisions gender roles in the same way as the culture of Ying-ying's childhood as you evaluate what Tan intends for young readers, particularly girls, to take away from the book about the position of women in history and in the modern world. Why do you think, for instance, that the girls are inside with their grandmother while "a boy ride[s] his bicycle through rain puddles"? Is there any evidence that this disparity is a gender issue? What about the final scene of the story when the girls are dancing, "shouting, and laughing by the light of the full moon." Is this behavior that Ying-ying's mother would have engaged in with her?

3. **Free will versus luck in *The Chinese Siamese Cat*:** Does this children's story imply that improvements to society come from concerned and courageous citizens or largely by accident? Is our fate determined by our own intentions or by luck? What are the ramifications of this implication?

Sagwa hears her parents complain about the Magistrate's new rule that prohibits singing until the sun goes down. Sagwa's father laments: "Yes, many things in life are not fair. . . . But we're only cats. We're helpless. We have no power to change the world." Overhearing their conversation from a perch high up on a shelf, Sagwa "wanted to cry out to them, 'We're not helpless. We can change the world.' But then she saw how high up she was, how helpless she was herself. Far down below was the Magistrate's desk, with the scroll of the Rules lying next to the ink pot. Finally she realized: Leap she must. There was no other choice." Sagwa lands in the ink pot, changing the rule by obscuring the word "not" with ink. Sagwa then continues to make other changes to the scroll by dancing around on it. Does this passage suggest that Sagwa really is powerless? What is her intent as she jumps from the shelf? Does her intent matter? What ultimate message does this scene convey about power and change?

4. **Class issues in *The Moon Lady*:** What can you tell about the position in society which Ying-ying's family occupies? What

does the story ultimately have to say about class in Chinese society?

Because Ying-ying does not take a nap as she is supposed to, she sees much of the work going on to prepare her family's evening meal. Do you think she normally witnesses such work? Why or why not? As Ying-ying watches two boys using a bird to catch fish, she thinks to herself, "How I wished I could be one of those boys!" Why do you think she cannot? Is it a gender or class consideration? Ying-ying then sees a "toothless woman . . . dipping her hands into a bucket filled with eels. . . . The woman picked up a long, wiggly one, and with a sharp, thin knife, sliced it from end to end and threw it back into the bucket." When Ying-ying gets closer still, she sees that the "water had turned red. The old woman laughed and said, 'tasty soup for your dinner tonight!'" What do you make of this exchange? What do you think the woman thinks of Ying-ying?

Look also at the scene in which the lost and disheveled Ying-ying is discovered by people in another boat:

> "Maybe she is a beggar girl," said the man. "Look at her clothes. She is one of these children who ride the flimsy rafts to beg for money." [Ying-ying] was filled with terror. Maybe this was true: [she] had turned into a poor beggar girl, lost without [her] family. "Anh! Don't you have eyes?" the woman said crossly. "Look at her skin, too pale. And her feet, the bottoms are soft. This is the kind of girl who's worn shoes all her life."

How does Ying-ying as a child, and as an adult telling this story, understand her own social position and the social hierarchy as a whole? Would you argue that the story uses the class structure as plot and detail support only, or that Tan is making some kind of commentary on it?

Form and Genre

When you write about form and genre, you are focusing on the foundational elements of a piece of literature, elements often overlooked in favor of symbolism or characterization, but no less important or revealing when properly examined. When you set your sights on form and genre, you are examining the basic choices a writer makes as he or she creates the work. Who is going to tell this story? How will it be told? How will it be structured? Who will be the audience? In what format will the work be printed? In the case of Amy Tan's children's books, you might decide to focus on the storytelling framework she employs in both *The Chinese Siamese Cat* and *The Moon Lady*. Why do you think Tan chooses to tell these stories in this way? What is the impact of this choice on the work(s) as a whole? Alternatively, as both of these works were published in picture book format, with illustrations by Gretchen Schields, you might want to use your essay to investigate the relationship between the text and the illustrations. Why do you think Tan opted to use the picture book format for these particular stories? How do Schields's illustrations contribute to the meaning of the texts?

Sample Topics:

1. **Storytelling framework:** In both of her stories for children, Tan creates a narrative frame in which we learn that a mother cat and a grandmother are telling stories to their kittens and grandchildren, respectively. Why do you think she employs this type of framework and what effect does it have on your interpretation of these stories?

   Reread both texts, paying careful attention to the opening and closing scenes. Why are the storytellers telling their stories at this particular moment? What is the significance of the particular stories they decide to tell? How do their listeners respond to their stories?

2. **Illustrations:** *The Moon Lady* and *The Chinese Siamese Cat* were both published in picture book format, and both were illustrated by Gretchen Schields. How do the illustrations work together with the text to create the overall effect of each book?

   Reviewer John Philbrook writes, "The illustrations are an integral part of this version [of *The Moon Lady*] and can best be described as phantasmagorical or Chinese baroque. They are extremely detailed, providing both the accurate cultural detail of the period . . . and a child's imaginings" (255). Examine the illustrations in each of the books. How would you describe them? Look carefully at the detail work in each spread and take notes about what each illustration conveys. Then, read each story again and imagine what it would be like without the illustrations? How about with illustrations done in a different style?

Language, Symbols, and Imagery

Every literary work is filled with language, symbols, and imagery. If you choose to focus on one of these elements in your essay, your first task is to identify a particular pattern of language, a symbol, or a set of images that you find integral to your interpretation of the text. You might investigate several possibilities before finding the one you would like to focus on in your essay. Once you have decided on your topic, you will want to locate all references to it in the text and to analyze carefully the most interesting passages you have located. Then, your task is to synthesize all of your observations into a coherent argument or interpretation of the text that you can present in your essay. For example, if you analyze Ying-ying's double, you will want your essay to offer an interpretation of the story based on your analysis of this figure. You might conclude, for instance, that Ying-ying's double serves as an alter ego for Ying-ying, representing the girl that her parents wish for, one who remains well behaved and well dressed and does not wind up smeared in eel blood and in the boat of strangers. By creating this alternate Ying-ying, you could argue, Tan emphasizes the life-altering nature of this particular experience; after this night, Ying-ying will literally be a new person.

1. **Ying-ying's shadow:** What does Ying-ying's shadow symbolize and what message is Tan trying to convey through the use of this symbol?

   When Ying-ying's mother scolds her for running around chasing dragonflies, Ying-ying does just what her mother advises and stands still for a few moments:

> Standing perfectly still like that, I discovered my shadow. It had short legs and long arms, two dark coiled braids just like mine. It had the same mind! When I shook my head, it shook its head. We flapped our arms. We raised one leg. I turned to walk away and it disappeared!! I shrieked with delight at my shadow's own cleverness. How I loved my shadow, this dark side of me that loved all the things no one else could see.

Why do you think Ying-ying is so enamored of her shadow? What does it mean to her? What do you think she means when she calls it "the dark side of [herself] that loved all the things no one else could see"?

2. **Ying-ying's double:** What does Ying-ying's double symbolize? How does Tan using it to convey meaning in *The Moon Lady*?

When Ying-ying's rescuers take her to her family's boat, Ying-ying sees another version of herself standing on the deck:

> "That's not me!" she cried. "I'm here. I didn't fall in the water." The people on the boat roared with more laughter, then turned away. "Little miss," said the fisherwoman sadly as we glided away, "you were mistaken."

What does the girl standing on the deck look like in the illustrations? How is she similar to and different from the Ying-ying in the fishermen's boat? Why does Tan have Ying-ying see this other version of herself? What do you think happens to this version of Ying-ying when the "real" Ying-ying returns to family at the end of story?

3. **Moon Cake:** What is the significance of the moon cake in Tan's *The Moon Lady*?

Do some research into the traditional meaning of the moon cake. What are these cakes meant to symbolize? Why does Ying-ying's Amah give her a moon cake? In what shape is her cake? What does she do with it? What can you gather about Ying-ying from the illustration of her with the moon cake?

Compare and Contrast Essays

Comparing and contrasting two works or elements within works can help you to focus on meaningful elements of those works that you may otherwise have overlooked. You might, for instance, think about the differences between Tan's presentation of the Moon Lady saga in her novel for adults, *The Joy Luck Club,* and in her version of the tale for children, *The Moon Lady.* Is she driving home the same point in both versions, or do the stories serve different functions in these two separate contexts? Alternatively, you might decide to compare and contrast Amy Tan's two works designed for children, *The Moon Lady* and *The Chinese Siamese Cat.* Setting these two next to one another, what generalizations can you make about Tan's writing for children? You might want to think about how both of these works differ from Tan's writing for adults to help you discover some patterns. In any case, remember that your initial notes on similarities and differences, made in the prewriting and brainstorming stages, will serve only as a starting point. You will want to examine these lists for meaningful patterns and use these patterns to help you to arrive at an interpretation of the work(s). This interpretation will serve as the foundation of your essay, and you will then use the details regarding similarities and differences as evidence to support that interpretation.

Sample Topics:

1. **The story of the Moon Lady as presented in** *The Joy Luck Club* **with the version presented in Tan's children's book** *The Moon Lady:* Compare and contrast these two versions of the same story. What can setting them side by side tell you about the nuances and meanings of this story in each context?

   Review the story of the Moon Lady as told in *The Joy Luck Club* and then reread *The Moon Lady* in picture book format. What similarities and differences are apparent? Who is telling the story in each case? Who is the audience? For what purpose is the story told? How did Tan adapt the story for younger readers? How do these adaptations affect your interpretation of the story? Look closely at the illustrations in the picture book version of the tale. How does the addition of these impact the children's version of *The Moon Lady*? Would you say that one version of the story is superior? Why or why not?

2. **The Moon Lady and The Chinese Siamese Cat:** Compare and contrast Amy Tan's two works of literature for children.

What similarities can you find in these two works? Are they concerned with the same themes? Do they send similar messages? What distinguishing differences can you find? What can you tell about Tan's conceptualization of the child as reader and the picture book as genre through an examination of both these books?

Bibliography for *The Moon Lady* and *The Chinese Siamese Cat*

Bailey, Paul. *China in the Twentieth Century.* Malen, MA: Wiley-Blackwell, 2001.

Bloom, Harold, ed. *Amy Tan.* Modern Critical Views. Philadelphia: Chelsea House, 2000.

Demi. *Liang and the Magic Paintbrush.* New York: Holt, 1980.

———. *The Magic Tapestry: A Chinese Folktale.* New York: Holt, 1994.

Huntley, E. D. *Amy Tan: A Critical Companion.* Critical Companions to Popular Contemporary Writers. Westport, CT: Greenwood, 1998.

Ma, Sheng-mei. "Amy Tan's The Chinese Siamese Cat: Chinoiserie and Ethnic Stereotypes." *The Lion and the Unicorn* 23.2 (1999): 202–18.

Morton, W. Scott. *China: Its History and Culture.* 3rd ed. New York: McGraw-Hill, 1995.

Philbrook, John. "Review of *The Moon Lady*." *School Library Journal* (1992): 255.

Roberts, J. A. G. *A Concise History of China.* Cambridge, MA: Harvard UP, 1999.

Shields, Charles J. *Amy Tan.* Women of Achievement. Philadelphia: Chelsea House, 2002.

Tan, Amy. *The Chinese Siamese Cat.* New York: Macmillan, 1994.

———. *The Moon Lady.* New York: Macmillan, 1992.

Young, Ed. *Lon Po Po.* New York: Philomel, 1989.

INDEX